250-54

D0718963

# The Colleges and the Courts

## FACULTY AND STAFF
## BEFORE THE BENCH

143964

# The Colleges and the Courts

## FACULTY AND STAFF
## BEFORE THE BENCH

by

M. M. CHAMBERS

Department of Educational Administration
Illinois State University

KF4240
C43

THE INTERSTATE
Printers & Publishers, Inc.

Danville, Illinois

Copyright © 1973 by

M. M. CHAMBERS

All Rights Reserved

Library of Congress
Catalog Card Number: 72-96730

Printed and Published by

THE INTERSTATE PRINTERS & PUBLISHERS, INC.

Danville, Illinois

Printed in U.S.A.

# FACULTY AND STAFF BEFORE THE BENCH

Eighth Volume in the Series on
*The Colleges and the Courts*

"[There is] an acceptance of the revolutionary principle that everyone is entitled to civilization's benefits. . . . It is an economic, social and cultural revolution, affecting politics, business, the arts, social behavior, and the totality of our existence. The forum of revolution includes all of our social institutions: factories, stores, schools, theaters, political parties, public institutions, churches. But central to all its phases is the Court's rediscovery of the human values which our Constitution states; and the Court's vindication of the individual's power to secure his human rights through litigation and the judicial mechanism. . . . It is a revolution founded on the principle of entitlement, not grace or charity. It is a revolution based on the principle of human rights."—Abe Fortas, former associate justice of the United States Supreme Court, in the *New York Times*, November 26, 1972.

# PREFACE

*Faculty and Staff Before the Bench* is the eighth volume in the series under the general title of *The Colleges and the Courts.*

It is also the second in a trilogy, of which the first was subtitled *The Developing Law of the Student and the College,* which appeared in June 1972.

The third in this cycle of three is to be entitled *The Colleges and the Courts: Entity, Property, and Finance.* It is intended to be published in 1974.

This present volume is largely the story of a beneficent revolution in the attitudes of the federal judiciary, involving the extension of the civil rights guaranteed in the United States Constitution into the realm of relations between institutions of higher education and the members of their faculties.

As such, it is a companion volume to its immediate predecessor, in which a somewhat similar story of the rights and obligations of students was recounted. Together, the two bring up to date the unfolding story of the law of university and college *personnel* in a broad sense: students, faculty, staff, and administration.

Assistance comes to me from too many sources to acknowledge them all; but let me mention the work of Joan Marie (Mrs. Peter F.) Schuetz, assigned as my secretary and general assistant, whose intelligent and industrious help merits repeated commendation.

M. M. Chambers

Illinois State University
Normal, Illinois
March 2, 1973

# ANALYTICAL TABLE OF CONTENTS

No contract exists except as voted by governing board, 1

An allegation that appointment is denied on unconstitutional grounds must be tried on the merits, holds the Fifth Circuit U.S. Court of Appeals, 4

An instance wherein a university Board of Regents rejects an applicant for a position after he had been preliminarily appointed and had moved to the vicinity, 6

In practice, the Board's "letter of appointment" is an offer; and no contract exists until the recipient accepts, 8

If the board's offer is not transmitted to the offeree, no contract comes into being, 9

Minimum fairness for the professor who is to be dropped, 12

When is "reasonable expectation of renewal" a "protectible interest"?, 14

The burden of proof of violation of civil rights is upon him who alleges it, 16

Minimal requirements of procedural due process in non-renewal

# INTRODUCTION: TRENDS OF THE TIME

A preview of the sequence of chapters in this volume will be helpful.

## 1

In a class by itself, focused exclusively on the beginning of the contract of the faculty member, is Chapter 1. The cases recounted as illustrative also deal with a wide variety of other points of law. Both the facts and the law of the cases are treated here in one place, and will serve to provide an initial taste of the breadth and diversity of college law, without confusing the reader, who will remember the central focus.

## 2, 3, 4

The rights of the non-tenured short-term faculty member who is dropped at the expiration of the contract constitute the major issue in this series of chapters. Is such a teacher entitled to a written statement of reasons, or an administrative hearing, or both? What are the rights of the faculty member who alleges that the real reason for the non-renewal of the contract was solely because of exercise of a constitutional right belonging to all citizens?

Recently it has come to be settled that such an allegation entitles the aggrieved teacher to a trial of the facts in a federal court. As to cases in which it is not alleged that any First Amendment right of the faculty member has been violated, the U.S. Supreme Court, on June 29, 1972, declared that unless state law gives the short-term teacher some clear basis on which to claim reappointment, and no derogatory charges are made against the teacher by the governing board, nor any action taken that would plainly hinder the teacher from obtaining other similar employment elsewhere, then no cause of action exists.

Prior to June 1972, a majority of the 11 U.S. Courts of Appeals had held, under varying sets of facts, that in such cases the faculty member may plead in federal court and ask for an appropriate remedy. Some U.S. District Courts were in accord; others were to the contrary. State Court decisions were generally adverse. The lack of consensus is shown in chapters 2 and 3.

Chapter 4 deals only with the two companion cases decided by the U.S. Supreme Court on June 29, 1972. Each was sent back to the U.S. District Court in the state in which it originated (Wisconsin and Texas respectively) for further proceedings. In neither instance had there been a District Court trial of all the allegations. Hence, though the Supreme Court declared the law on the issues before it, the high tribunal did not decide regarding all the alleged facts and left the appropriate remedies, if any, for further decision by the respective U.S. District Courts. Thus, for the time being, the cases continued pending, and neither plaintiff knew the ultimate outcome of his suit.[1]

The new applications of the Bill of Rights and the Fourteenth Amendment to college teachers indicate incipient trends that mean much to the openness, candor, and integrity of future relations between college and university faculty members and their governing boards. The significance of this change is cogently discussed in the opinions of the three Justices who dissented in the two Supreme Court cases, both of which were decided by a divided vote of five to three of the Justices.

## 5, 6

Continuing with the faculty member's contract of employment, and concerned with the acquisition of tenure, promotion, salaries, leaves of absence, and other conditions of employment, is Chapter 5. Chapter 6 goes on with the termination of service by discharge for cause, prior to the expiration of the contract, and by resignation and retirement.

---

1. The press of December 5, 1972, briefly reported that the case arising in Texas had been settled out of court by payment to the plaintiff (Professor Robert P. Sindermann) of $48,000 for back pay and attorneys' fees, by the defendant (Odessa Junior College). The college also offered Sindermann reinstatement, which he declined.

## 7, 8, 9, 10

Next is a group of four chapters dealing with the expanding entitlements of faculty members under the Fourteenth Amendment, the Bill of Rights, and the Civil Rights Acts.

Discrimination on grounds of race, religion, sex, and ideology is the subject of Chapter 7. Sex bias prevails widely, though prohibited by Civil Rights legislation and by presidential executive orders of some years' standing, with which a degree of compliance is currently being obtained by federal administrative persuasion. Few cases have yet come to judgment in federal courts. Often the complainant, alleging sex discrimination, is faced by a phalanx of colleagues and administrators who testify to the contrary.

The First Amendment guarantees of free speech, expression, assembly, and petition are receiving new and progressive interpretations, as is shown in Chapter 8. The related matter of ridding the states of the rash of statutes, largely the product of post-war and cold-war hysteria, prescribing disclaimer oaths of loyalty as a condition of the employment of faculty members and other public employees, has proceeded apace within a decade. The story is in Chapter 9.

Then there is the right of association, which to faculty members means freedom to form and join organizations of their own choice, including the election of such organizations as bargaining agents for the purpose of collective negotiation with their governing boards. The rapid recent progress in this field is sketchily recited in Chapter 10.

## 11, 12

Finally, two chapters are concerned, not with faculty members, but respectively with members of the non-academic staff and with administrative officers, whose rights and obligations are in some features quite different from those of members of the teaching faculties. Chapter 12 also discusses a few recent decisions regarding the appointment and election of members of the governing board.

## A FEW OF THE QUESTIONS AND THEIR CURRENT ANSWERS

Q. Can a faculty member's contract begin before being voted by the governing board and accepted by the faculty member?

A. Only rarely, in instances where the chief executive officer has been authorized by the board to make appointments to the lowest rank.

Q. Is a faculty member on a short-term appointment entitled to a statement of reasons and an administrative hearing if dropped at the expiration of the contract?

A. Some federal courts have said yes, some no. The fact that many federal courts have heard such cases is itself an important forward step. The U.S. Supreme Court, by a divided vote of 5 to 3, has declared the answer is no, in a case where *state law provides no recourse, and where no charges are made against the teacher that might damage professional reputation, and where the pleadings do not allege any violation of the teacher's substantive rights of free speech, expression, assembly, or petition, as guaranteed by the First Amendment, as interpolated into the Fourteenth Amendment.*

Q. When a faculty member alleges that the real reason for the termination of his service was in retaliation for his exercise of free expression as protected by the First Amendment, is he entitled to a trial of the facts in a federal court?

A. Yes. This is now firmly established, and is a significant advance.

Q. May a public university, college, or school deny tenure to a faculty member who is an alien, solely for that reason?

A. No. This is a violation of the Fourteenth Amendment equal protection clause.

Q. May a university governing board discharge a faculty member solely because of open and avowed membership in the Communist Party?

A. No. This would violate individual rights safeguarded by the First and Fourteenth Amendments.

Q. Is it a protected exercise of free speech if a teacher publishes a long letter to the editor in a local newspaper, criticizing the financial and other policies of the governing board, quoting statistics that are substantially accurate, and not intentionally false, or in disregard of truth, or maliciously motivated?

A. Yes. The U.S. Supreme Court has held that the teacher can not be discharged solely for that reason.

Q. Are state statutes prescribing lengthy "disclaimer" oaths of loyalty for teachers in public universities, colleges, or schools unconstitutional?

A. Yes. In state after state such statutes have been declared void by the U.S. Supreme Court, some lower federal courts, and some state courts. In some states, such statutes may yet survive because they have not been challenged in court. A prescribed oath that is no more than a brief and simple affirmation of allegiance to the state and the nation, such as is taken by elective officers, is not unconstitutional.

Q. Do faculty members have a constitutional right to join a teachers' union or other organization of their choice?

A. Yes, so long as the organization has no unlawful purposes, known as such to the faculty members.

Q. Is a "faculty strike" illegal?

A. Yes. Concerted withholding of services by public employees has thus far been held unlawful, under statutes and at common law. But if hundreds of teachers, almost the entire faculty of a public school system, concertedly submit bona fide written resignations, this is not unlawful and can not be penalized even if the same teachers eventually concertedly negotiate a return to work.

Q. Do the wage-hour provisions of the federal Fair Labor Standards Act apply to universities, colleges, schools, and hospitals?

A. Yes. The U.S. Supreme Court so decided in 1968.

Q. Where members of a university or school governing board are popularly elected, not at large, but from prescribed subdistricts within the whole constituency, does the principle of "one man, one vote" apply?

A. Yes. In 1970, the U.S. Supreme Court declared in a majority opinion by Mr. Justice Hugo L. Black, that "Whenever a state or local government by popular election selects persons to perform public functions, the Equal Protection clause (of the Fourteenth Amendment) requires that each qualified voter have an equal opportunity to participate in the election, and when members of an elected body are chosen from separate districts, each district must be established on a basis that as far as practicable will insure that equal numbers of voters can vote for proportionally equal numbers of officials."

## PROGRESS CONTINUES

The foregoing questions make up only a small sampling of the hundreds of issues touched upon in the 12 chapters in this volume. Many of the decisions vividly demonstrate that today's dissent may be tomorrow's law, as was long ago shown by the illustrious careers of such eminent jurists as Oliver Wendell Holmes and Louis D. Brandeis.

This volume not only records advances toward a humane law of higher education in the world's greatest Republic, but also corroborates the sage observations of former Associate Justice Abe Fortas, who, when writing of the widespread and complex changes that currently pervade the society, remarked that central to all these changes is "the Court's rediscovery of the human values which our Constitution states; and the Court's vindication of the individual's power to secure his human rights through litigation and the judicial mechanism." More bluntly, he spoke of "an acceptance of the revolutionary principle that everyone is entitled to civilization's benefits. . . . It is a revolution founded on the principle of entitlement, not grace or charity. It is a revolution based on the principle of human rights."

# CHAPTER 1

## INCEPTION OF THE CONTRACT

The experience of many years repeatedly demonstrates that no one has a contract with a college or university until the governing board has voted affirmatively on the question.[1] There are exceptions to the generalization. In comparatively rare instances the president is authorized by the board to commit the institution to contracts with academic employees in the lower ranks. More frequently, an officer known as director of personnel is empowered to complete contracts with non-academic employees not above a specified classification.[2]

But cases continue to get into the courts in which it is obvious that one or both parties are ignorant of the basic rule. It seems appropriate to look at two such recent cases—one in the supreme court of Minnesota; and one in the Fifth Circuit U.S. Court of Appeals, having arisen in Mississippi.

### No Contract Exists Except as Voted by Governing Board

Joseph Lenough Anderson received a letter dated February 27,

---

1. For example, see *Frances Brown* v. *State Board of Education*, 142 Mont. 547, 385 P. 2d 643 (1963), discussed at pages 77-78 in *The Colleges and the Courts, 1962-1966;* and *Sittler* v. *Board of Control of Michigan College of Mining and Technology*, 333 Mich. 681, 53 N.W. 2d 681 (1952).

2. See the chapter *infra* on non-academic employees.

1

1967, from M. L. Shane, dean of the faculties at Southwest Minnesota State College:

"With the approval of President Howard A. Bellows, I am pleased to offer you the position of chairman of the division of humanities at Southwest Minnesota State College. . . .

"While the length of this appointment is not stated in the attached form, it is assumed that the initial commitment by you and the College will be for a minimum period of four years, or the life-span of one class."

The accompanying form was captioned "Letter of Appointment" and purported to certify the appointment, with duties to begin August 1, 1967, and with remuneration to be $12,000 for the academic year of nine months and $1,400 for the summer session. It made no mention of any period longer than one year. It concluded with this statement:

"All appointments to the College Faculty are submitted to the Minnesota State College Board for final consideration. Meanwhile, this form duly signed constitutes a commitment for appointment by the College Administration. After action by the College Board, a formal contract will be issued."

On June 30, 1967, the college president wrote to Anderson: "At the meeting of June 20, 1967, the Minnesota State College Board appointed you . . . ," repeating the details as in the "Letter of Appointment" above, making no mention of any period longer than one year.

It turned out that, after two years, personality conflicts developed between Anderson and the dean of faculties and the president. There was no suggestion of lack of ability or diligence on the part of Anderson. During the Spring of 1969 the president and the dean notified him that he would not be continued as chairman of the division of humanities, but offered him appointment as associate professor of humanities for the academic year 1969-70, at a salary of $13,500. To this he apparently made no written response; and on July 28 the president withdrew the offer and advised Anderson that proceedings would be instituted to effect his discharge for cause.

This could be accomplished under Board Regulation 17 (b) which provided that a non-tenure teacher could be discharged for cause during any contract period. The regulation specified that, if such teacher requested reasons for his dismissal, the Board must give its reasons in writing within 10 days; and the teacher, within 10 days after receiving the same, might make a written request for a hearing before the Board, which must be provided.

On August 7 Anderson's attorney wrote the president: "We will request such hearing upon receipt of the written reasons for discharge if action is taken by the State College Board."

On September 24 the president wrote Anderson that the Board had adopted the earlier recommendation that he be removed as chairman of humanities and be appointed as associate professor for 1969-70, at $13,500. Anderson responded on September 30: "I do not accept the reassignment of responsibilities. . . . I will shortly file legal action to redress the wrongs. . . . In order to avoid any action which will injure the incoming students or deprive them of their course work, I will meet and teach classes as outlined by you until the court has determined the matter."

The county district court issued a writ of mandamus ordering the college to reinstate Anderson as chairman of the division of humanities, but the supreme court of Minnesota vacated the order and discharged the writ. Justice Robert J. Sheran, after reciting the facts at length and with care, stressed that a contract of employment does not come into existence until voted by the governing board, and that all prior correspondence or negotiations by college administrators are only preliminary; and he concluded: "There is nothing in the record before us to show that the State College Board ever offered, accepted, approved, or ratified an employment contract for any period beyond one year." And, "Dr. Anderson must be charged with knowledge that the exclusive authority for the execution of employment contracts rests, under our statutes, with the State College Board."[3]

Concluding: "Dr. Anderson, whose qualifications in his field as an instructor are apparently of the highest order, has voluntarily served as an associate professor for 1969-70, reserving his right to claim the chairmanship of the division of humanities on the theory that he had a 4-year employment contract. We have decided against him on this point of law. Under our analysis of the problem, the employment contract between Dr. Anderson and the college board was year to year. A proper notice has been given that it will not be renewed for the academic year 1970-1971. As to the academic year 1969-70, we do not believe that a hearing with respect to the reasons

---

3. *State ex rel. Anderson* v. *Bellows*, (Minn.), 179 N.W. 2d 307 (1970).

why he was not permitted to serve as chairman of the division of humanities during an already completed academic year is required or would serve any useful purpose."

## An Allegation That Appointment Is Denied on Unconstitutional Grounds Must Be Tried on the Merits, Holds the Fifth Circuit U.S. Court of Appeals

The contemporary federal case from Mississippi grew out of a convoluted set of facts. Dr. Kenneth T. Rainey, a white minister of the gospel, taught in Mississippi College, a predominantly white private college (Southern Baptist denomination) from 1965 to 1970. In January 1969 he testified in the Hinds County Court as to the literary and artistic merits of a film, "The Fox," where persons connected with its public exhibition were on trial for criminal obscenity. The event received much publicity unfavorable to him and to Mississippi College, and the college refused to place him on tenure for the academic year 1970-71—the year in which he would normally have been placed on tenure under the prevailing college rules.

In February 1970 he was designated by a private foundation as a Woodrow Wilson Teaching Intern for the academic year 1970-71. On April 1, Dr. John A. Peoples, president of Jackson State College, a predominantly black public institution, sent him a proposed contract as assistant professor of English for 1970-71. He signified his acceptance by signing and returning the papers April 13.

The written contract carried a *typed* signature of Dr. Peoples "on behalf of the Secretary of the Board" (Mississippi's Board of Trustees of State Institutions of Higher Learning), and also a rubber-stamped signature of Dr. Peoples as president of the college. Nowhere did the papers say the contract had been voted by the Board.

For the summer of 1970 an agreement was made June 8, under which Dr. Rainey taught English courses in the two 1970 summer sessions of Jackson State College. On August 6 Dr. Peoples sent his list of recommendations of faculty appointments for 1970-71 to the Board, including Rainey's name among others. The Board resolved that appointment of Rainey would not be in the best interests of the college or the state, and also removed the names of three other proposed appointees, saying it was necessary to abolish all four positions in order to increase the budget of the college security force.

On August 21 Dr. Peoples informed Dr. Rainey in writing that his contract for 1970-71 had been inadvertently mailed to him in April without having been submitted to the Board, and that the Board had now eliminated the position. On September 1 Rainey's counsel formally requested the Board to grant a hearing and received a prompt reply from the Executive Secretary of the Board saying the Board would not discuss the matter with Dr. Rainey. On the same day, he filed suit in U.S. District Court, alleging violation of Rainey's civil rights under 42 *U.S. Code* section 1983, with motions for a temporary restraining order and a preliminary injunction which would keep Rainey in his position under the contract until completion of the litigation.

Chief District Judge William Harold Cox dismissed the complaint for lack of jurisdiction, and appeal was immediately taken to the Fifth Circuit U.S. Court of Appeals, where the opinion was written by Circuit Judge Bryan Simpson, sitting with Circuit Judge Richard T. Rives and Judge Philip Nichols of the U.S. Court of Claims. Said Circuit Judge Simpson: "The complaint in unmistakable terms states that an opportunity to be employed by the State of Mississippi is being denied to appellant because he sought to exercise his First Amendment right of free speech." (Employment was denied in retaliation for his testifying for the defense in the criminal obscenity trial.)

For the college it was argued that Rainey at no time had a valid contract for 1970-71, and that he was not denied employment on unconstitutional grounds. The court disposed of these contentions with three statements: (1) "We do not decide on this appeal whether or not appellant will ultimately be entitled to any relief. We decide that he must have his day in court." (2) "The exhaustion of administrative remedies is not a prerequisite to the bringing of an action under section 1983." (3) *"Under the facts alleged in this case,* the federal court had jurisdiction and must proceed to hear the cause." Thus the judgment of dismissal was reversed and remanded, leaving standing the injunction of September 21, 1970, and keeping Rainey's alleged contract in force until his case could be decided on the merits.[4]

---

4. *Rainey* v. *Jackson State College*, (U.S.C.A., Miss.), 435 F. 2d 1031 (1970).

Obviously the emphasis was upon the constitutional civil rights aspect of the case. This aspect, in one form or another, will be found to be uppermost in many of the cases discussed in almost every chapter of this volume. It is the dominant motif of the times in this area.

*An Instance Wherein a University Board of Regents*
*Rejects an Applicant for a Position After He*
*Had Been Preliminarily Appointed and*
*Had Moved to the Vicinity*

At the University of Minnesota one McConnell had negotiated with the appropriate administrative authorities and agreed with them that he would be appointed and would accept the position of head of the cataloging division (with academic rank of instructor) of one of the university libraries. No contract of employment was ever perfected, however, because the appointment was rejected by the Board of Regents.

Normally, ratification of such contracts by the Board is routine; but in this instance it seems that McConnell, prior to ratification, had moved to St. Paul and become involved in much notoriety by publicly declaring himself a homosexual and applying for a marriage license to a male law student. Over the favorable recommendation of the academic staff, the Regents refused to approve the appointment, because "his personal conduct, as represented in the public and University news media, is not consistent with the best interest of the University."

In response to his plea that his rejection was arbitrary and discriminatory, and remediable under 42 *U.S. Code,* section 1983, U.S. District Judge Philip Neville enjoined the Regents from refusing to approve:

". . . It must be shown that there is an observable and reasonable relationship between efficiency in the job and homosexuality. The Regents are of necessity speculating and presuming. In the case at bar, of course, since plaintiff never has been permitted to enter on his duties, there is no history as to his performance or the possible claimed effect of his homosexuality. Plaintiff's position will not expose him to children of tender years who conceivably could be influenced or persuaded to his penchant. What he does in his private life, as with other employees, should not be his employer's concern unless it can be shown to affect in some degree his efficiency in the performance of his duties."

Elaborating: "An homosexual is after all a human being, and a citizen of the United States despite the fact that he finds his sex gratification in what most consider to be an unconventional manner. He is as much entitled to the protection and benefits of the laws and due process fair treatment as are others, at least as to public employment in the absence of proof and not mere surmise that he has committed or will commit criminal acts or that his employment efficiency is impaired by his homosexuality, *i.e.*, sexual propensity for persons of one's own sex and the commission of homosexual criminal acts. Homosexuality is said to be a broad term involving all types of deviant sexual conduct with one of the same sex, but not necessarily criminal acts of sodomy.

"Plaintiff does not have an inalienable right to be employed by the University but he has a right not to be discriminated against under the Fourteenth Amendment due process clause. He has a constitutional right that the terms of his public employment which he must meet be 'reasonable, lawful and non-discriminatory.' . . . A discriminatory deprivation of employment is a deprivation of liberty and property under the Fourteenth Amendment."[5]

This judgment was reversed by the Eighth Circuit U.S. Court of Appeals, where the judges found that the Regents' refusal to hire an activist homosexual could not be held to be unconstitutionally arbitrary and capricious. Excerpts from the opinion of the court, by Circuit Judge Roy L. Stephenson:

"It is our conclusion that the board possessed ample specific factual information on the basis of which it reasonably could conclude that the appointment would not be consistent with the best interests of the University. . . ."

And "(It is) a case in which the applicant seeks employment on his own terms; a case in which the prospective employee demands, as shown by the allegations of the complaint and by the marriage license incident as well, the right to pursue an activist role in implementing his unconventional ideas concerning the societal status to be accorded homosexuals, and, thereby, to foist tacit approval of this

---

5. *McConnell* v. *Anderson*, (U.S.D.C., Minn.), 316 F. Supp. 809 (1970); reversed in (U.S.C.A., Minn.), 39 *U.S. Law Week* 2167 (October 18, 1971).

socially repugnant concept upon his employer, who is, in this instance, an institution of higher learning. We know of no constitutional fiat or binding principle of decisional law which requires an employer to accede to such extravagant demands. We are therefore unable fairly to categorize the board's action here as arbitrary, unreasonable, or capricious."[6]

### In Practice, the Board's "Letter of Appointment" Is an Offer; and No Contract Exists Until the Recipient Accepts

At Eastern New Mexico University the custom was for the president to take his list of proposed personal service contracts, including specified salaries, for the next year to the Board of Regents for approval in March. Then the period up to June 30 could be used for the necessary communications and possible negotiations with the offerees. The Board was required by statute to have its budget complete by June 30.

At a meeting of the Board March 13, 1970, the president presented the detailed list (about 160 individuals listed by name and proposed salary, aggregating about $1,500,000), and the Board voted approval. On the same day these proposed salaries were put in the form of offers, signed by the president as agent of the Board, and mailed to the individuals concerned. Two student newsmen (editor and photographer for the student newspaper) attended the meeting and asked that the list be released to them. Their request was rejected. The local Roosevelt County district court granted a writ of mandamus to compel release of the papers. This judgment was reversed by the New Mexico supreme court.

The part of the opinion relevant here is in the words of Justice John B. McManus: "These procedures (of March 13) resulted in no contract. . . . A contract could only come into being upon acceptance of the offer by the individual faculty member. The offer might be accepted . . . or . . . refused, or a counteroffer transmitted. Negotiations might be had between the staff and the faculty member which might or might not result in a contract. All of these things normally occur between the time of the making of the offers and the June 30

_____

6. *McConnell* v. *Anderson*, (U.S.C.A., Minn.), 39 *U.S. Law Week* 2167 (1971).

deadline." The point of this statement is that "We believe that no useful purpose would be served by disclosing preliminary contractual negotiations between the board and its professional and other employees."

"We would not take away from petitioners the right to know about salary matters, but would merely suspend or defer the privilege of inquiry until the Board of Regents reaches its final conclusion, *i.e.*, the culmination of the contract between the board and the individual." This was the judgment of the majority, composed of Justice McManus, Chief Justice James C. Compton, and Justice Paul Tackett.[7] Justice LaFel E. Oman, joined by Justice Donnan Stephenson, dissented in a scholarly dissertation against secrecy in governmental activities, reviewing several decisions:

"The majority holds that 'no useful purpose' would be served by disclosing preliminary negotiations; that only ultimate actions should be accessible or that unreasonable interference with the business of government might result. . . . However, in our opinion, the fundamental and overriding principle to be served is preserving and protecting free access by citizens, including representatives of the media, to information regarding the conduct of governmental affairs, however saddening may be the results which ofttimes occur in individual cases."

Other decisions regarding salaries are discussed herein in Chapter 5, *infra*.

### If the Board's Offer Is Not Transmitted to the Offeree, No Contract Comes into Being

Another illustration of a failure to achieve a "meeting of the minds" culminating in an actual offer and acceptance is afforded by the case of Barbara Thomas at Kirkwood Community College at Cedar Rapids, Iowa. She was hired to work from August 22, 1968, to June 30, 1969, on a temporary part-time basis to accomplish specific internal research tasks, and was orally told, she alleged, that she would thereafter be offered a contract for full-time work as a director of research.

---

7. *Sanchez v. Board of Regents of Eastern New Mexico University*, (N.M.), 486 P. 2d 608 (1971).

On March 27, 1969, the governing board voted to employ her in a "new" position at an annual salary of $17,300. After the board's affirmative vote, her appointment was opposed by an assistant superintendent, Dr. Frank Malone. She was not offered the new contract, and her services were terminated June 30, upon the expiration of her part-time employment. She sued for violation of her civil rights because she had been given no reasons for termination nor any hearing thereon. She cited the decisions of U.S. Courts of Appeals in *Drown* v. *Portsmouth* (First Circuit) and *Ferguson* v. *Thomas* (Fifth Circuit), both of which are cited and discussed *infra* in Chapter 2.

Both of those cases involved teachers who had served several years on successive one-year contracts, and were held to have acquired an "expectancy of reappointment," whereas in this instance there had been only one year of expressly "temporary, part-time" employment. U.S. District Judge Edward J. McManus dismissed the case, and his judgment was affirmed by the Eighth Circuit Court of Appeals in an opinion by Circuit Judge Donald P. Lay, sitting with Circuit Judges Charles J. Vogel and Floyd R. Gibson.

Judge Lay was careful to point out that whether the alleged oral representations of the superintendent and the board's resolution to hire her for a new position might afford sufficient factual basis for a breach of contract suit was not before the court. He refrained from saying more on that, preferring to make clear that the present decision rested not on any alleged contract right, but solely on the asserted constitutionally protectible interest:

"Sufficient here is the fact that her position as a temporary employee affords her no right on which she might base a constitutionally protected "expectancy of interest.""[8]

---

8. *Barbara Thomas* v. *Kirkwood Community College*, (U.S.C.A., Iowa), 448 F. 2d 1253 (1971).

# CHAPTER 2

## TERMINATION OF NON-TENURE CONTRACTS: NEW CONCEPTS OF DUE PROCESS

It is well understood that teachers in universities, colleges, or public school districts may be classified in three general groupings as to the conditions of their employment:

1. Non-tenured, or simply employed for a specified short term, usually one year, with no stipulations about renewal of the contract at its expiration;

2. Probationary, or employed for a specified short term, usually one year, with the understanding that the contract will be allowed to lapse and not be renewed at its expiration if the services have not been satisfactory or if for any reason the services are not wanted further; but also that after a specified number of years in probationary status the employee will be eligible to be considered for tenure appointment;

3. Tenured, or employed under a "contract of indeterminate duration" which stipulates that it will be automatically renewed year after year as long as the services are satisfactory, or until the employee voluntarily resigns or retires or dies or becomes disabled or runs afoul of one of the specified causes for dismissal and is ordered dismissed by the governing board

11

after the stipulated due process. (Tenure rules or statutes also usually provide for some means of terminating the contracts of employees whose services may be no longer needed because of drastic financial limitations or of major changes in instructional programs necessitating the elimination of some positions.)

We begin in this chapter with the oldest and simplest situation: that of the non-tenured. The first major observation is that for centuries all courts agreed that to be rid of the short-term employee all the governing board had to do was simply to allow his contract to expire according to its own terms, at the termination date specified in it.

The dropped employee had no right to a statement of charges, or any sort of statement of the board's reasons; no hearing of any kind at which he could present his own side of the story. The only concession to him was a provision often inserted in the statutes of the state (for school boards) or in the ordinances of the college governing board that his contract could not be thus abruptly terminated unless the board had taken care to notify him in writing by some specified date in March or April that his contract would not be renewed. This is a humane effort to spare such employees the hardship of being informed at so late a date as to leave insufficient time to find another position for the next academic year.

Some college or university governing boards have adopted rules or practices requiring that the notice to employees who have served longer than one year must be earlier than March or April—often providing that the date be about four months earlier for each of two or three years of prior service. Such provisions have been urged, and with considerable success, by the American Association of University Professors.

## Minimum Fairness for the Professor Who Is to Be Dropped

Dr. William C. Ferguson came to Prairie View A & M College in 1958 as head of the department of business administration. In 1965 he ceased to be the department head but continued as a full professor. Difficulties arose during the academic year 1966-67 concerning various matters, including his management of a 20-student dormitory which he owned and his efforts to have business administration raised from the status of a department to that of a major school. After considerable controversy the president recommended to the Board of Regents of the Texas Agricultural and Mechanical University System that Dr. Ferguson's annual contract not be renewed at the end of the year 1966-67, and the Board so voted. He had never been given specific written causes and a fair opportunity to refute the alleged causes and present his side of the case. The Board gave him a perfunctory opportunity to speak extemporaneously, but refused to hear two members of the faculty whom he wished to call as witnesses. At the time there were no tenure rules in the Texas Agricultural and Mechanical University System.

The U.S. District Court later heard the case, including the two witnesses mentioned; and it turned out that their testimony strengthened the case against Dr. Ferguson, and his petition for relief was denied. In the Fifth Circuit Court of Appeals, Circuit Judge Charles Clark, joined by Circuit Judge David W. Dyer and writing for the majority of the court, said: "Since the very witnesses Dr. Ferguson wanted to present have now testified and it is clear from their testimony that their testimony would have greatly enhanced the basis of the Board's action in affirming his termination, it is not necessary for this cause to be remanded to the district court for referral back to the board of regents. Justice and fairness to all parties indicates that his termination may be affirmed here and now."

Circuit Judge Homer Thornberry dissented from that part of the majority decision: "The majority's holding reduces to the proposition that the Board was not required to afford Dr. Ferguson due process because Dr. Ferguson's case was weak.

"In my view the college was required to afford Dr. Ferguson due process regardless of the merits of his case, and because of its failure to do so this Court should not sustain the termination of his employment."

The Court was unanimous in setting forth the more general principles:

"Within the matrix of the particular circumstances present when a teacher who is to be terminated for cause opposes his termination, minimum procedural due process requires that:

"(a) he be advised of the cause or causes for his termination in sufficient detail to fairly enable him to show any error that may exist,

"(b) he be advised of the names and the nature of the testimony of the witnesses against him,

"(c) at a reasonable time after such advice he must be accorded a meaningful opportunity to be heard in his own defense, and

"(d) . . . hearing should be before a tribunal that both possesses some academic expertise and has an apparent impartiality toward the charges."[1]

The quoted statement is the durable contribution of the rather confusing record of the case. It has frequently been cited with approval by other courts in similar cases.

### When Is "Reasonable Expectation of Renewal" a "Protectible Interest"?

An additional issue that has had the attention of more than one U.S. Circuit Court of Appeals recently is the question of whether—and if so, under what circumstances—a non-tenured employee may acquire an "expectancy of reemployment," such as to entitle him to at least some elements of due process instead of the abrupt termination which had been the historic practice.

"This case is controlled by *Ferguson* v. *Thomas*," wrote Circuit Judge John C. Godbold for the Fifth Circuit Court of Appeals, composed of Senior Circuit Judge Warren L. Jones, Circuit Judge Griffin B. Bell, and himself, in a case arising in Mississippi involving a public school teacher who had no tenure and whose one-year contract had not been breached, but simply allowed to expire. The court concluded that "his long employment in continuing relationship through renewals of short-term contracts was sufficient to give him an expectancy of reemployment that constituted a protectible interest," and in these circumstances summarily dropping him "did not attain the most minimal due process standards" and could not be sustained.

At a public school in Bolivar County, Mississippi, certain members of the local Parent-Teacher Association had complained to the board of education about Lucas, a teacher, on account of remarks critical of the board he was said to have made. The board resolved not to reappoint him, but gave him neither the names of the malcontents nor

---

1. *Ferguson* v. *Thomas*, (U.S.C.A., Tex.), 430 F. 2d 852 (1970).

the substance of their complaints; nor was he given specific reasons for the decision to drop him, nor any hearing at which he could answer the complaints and defend himself.

One of the court's main concerns seemed to be adequate control of the flow of controversies from schools and colleges to the federal courts, with due solicitude for the constitutional civil rights of aggrieved faculty members. "All this simply underscores," wrote Judge Godbold, "that not only necessity but practicability, and the common sense fairness that rules in day to day dealings, require that if a teacher with a protectible interest opposes his termination he be told the reason and what supports the reason and given an opportunity to present his side if he desires."

Continuing, "The localized, less formalized, less adversary atmosphere of the board is the best forum to adjudicate and ameliorate problems of teacher re-hiring to the mutual acceptability, if not the full satisfaction, of board and teacher. Abdication to the courts may be the short way across, but it may be the long way around, as in this case. The rights of the individual teacher, of teachers in general, of the school system and those taught in it, and the community, all coalesce in the desirability of notice and hearing at the local level."

Turning to the civil rights aspect of the case (a teacher's freedom of speech in criticizing the board), there seemed also to be concern about saving local boards from too great a burden if hearings were required in all cases, by maintaining the distinction between constitutional issues and non-constitutional matters: "Our holding should not be misunderstood. In this instance we know from the District Court record that the asserted reason for termination involved a possible collision with Lucas' First Amendment rights. A hearing was mandatory, if desired by Lucas. But where the only matter in issue is a difference of view over a school board's exercise of judgment and discretion concerning matters non-constitutional in nature, the board is not required to conduct a hearing."

For this conclusion reliance was placed on the 1969 decision of the Eighth Circuit Court of Appeals in a case arising in Arkansas, where a local school board declined to reappoint six non-tenured black teachers, on the informal recommendation of the black principal, variously charging laziness, incompetency, insubordination, and inattention to duty. After the board had resolved to drop these teachers, it gave them hearings and refused to change its decision. In federal court the teachers asked an order to renew their contracts and a judgment against the board for damages and attorneys' fees. No issue of racial discrimination was pleaded. District Judge Oren Harris dismissed the case as presenting no federal question, and his judgment was affirmed in an opinion by Circuit Judge Floyd R. Gibson, with Circuit Judge Harry A Blackmun concurring without opinion and Circuit Judge Donald P. Lay dissenting vigorously.

Circuit Judge Gibson, after noting that Arkansas statutes did not provide for hearings in such cases, concluded: "We agree with the District Judge that there is no civil rights issue presented in this case, and that the disagreement between the teachers and the principal is an internal matter to be handled by the school board. Further, there is no federal due process issue presented."

Circuit Judge Donald P. Lay, dissenting, exposed some very flimsy and self-contradictory testimony by the black principal under questioning, and said sharply, "Constitutional rights of public school teachers are not conditioned upon state tenure laws." Also: "As long as a public school board chooses to set forth reasons for a teacher's exclusion and the stated grounds are damaging to professional reputation I submit the Constitution affords the protection of substantive due process."[2]

Reverting now to the Lucas case, we find Circuit Judge Godbold continuing: "There are in-between situations which are somewhat more difficult. If the board asserts a non-constitutional reason and the teacher claims it is a sham and that the real reason is one impinging on his constitutional rights, he must be afforded a hearing. Also, even in the area of non-constitutional reasons, the board's decision must not be wholly unsupported by evidence, else it would be so arbitrary as to be a constitutional violation."[3]

### The Burden of Proof of Violation of Civil Rights Is upon Him Who Alleges It

The Fifth Circuit Court of Appeals in 1971 decided another case in which violation of constitutional civil rights was alleged, but not

---

2. *Freeman* v. *Gould Special School District*, (U.S.C.A., Ark.), 405 F. 2d 1153 (1969). Certiorari denied, 396 U.S. 843, 90 S. Ct. 61, 24 L. Ed. 2d 93 (1969).

3. *Lucas v. Chapman*, (U.S.C.A., Miss.), 430 F. 2d 945 (1970).

proved, though a hearing on the matter had been held in the U.S. District Court. The opinion was by Circuit Judge Homer Thornberry, sitting with Circuit Judges Lewis R. Morgan and Charles Clark.

Willie Fluker and Richard Parsons, non-tenured assistant professors of history and art respectively at Alabama State University (formerly Alabama State College), each serving under his second annual contract for the academic year 1969-70, were notified in writing by President Levi Watkins on December 15, 1969, that their contracts would not be renewed for academic year 1970-71, without stating reasons. They did not request any explanation or hearing at the university, but went directly to the U.S. District Court, alleging that their employment was being terminated in violation of the First and Fourteenth Amendments because of their associations, activities, and expressions of opinion.

On March 31, 1970, the District Court held a hearing on the allegations and ordered the university to give Fluker and Parsons formal notice and specifications of the charges against them and a hearing on those charges within 30 days. President Watkins immediately complied with this order by writing letters to Fluker and Parsons, explaining the reasons for their upcoming termination and inviting them to attend a hearing on the matter scheduled for April 7, before the university's Advisory Committee on Faculty Personnel.

The president explained that Fluker was the only person in the history faculty not having tenure; that he was the last person employed in that department; that only one of the six members held a doctoral degree, and that in order to comply with the accreditation standards of the Southern Association of Colleges and Schools it would be necessary to bring in a new member holding a doctoral degree, and that this in turn would necessitate dispensing with the services of one present member. The situation of Parsons was somewhat similar. He was not on tenure and he was the member of the fine arts department with least training and experience. The department needed to acquire in his stead a new member holding the degree of Master of Fine Arts.

The hearing of April 7 was held as scheduled, with the parties present and represented by counsel. The testimony from both sides was devoted almost entirely to the adequacy of the reasons explained by the president, with almost nothing said about the alleged First Amendment activities of Fluker and Parsons. The Faculty Advisory Committee concluded that it was unable to reach a judgment on the legal adequacy of the reason explained, and merely recommended that, if the controversy could not be settled by the plaintiffs and the administration, it should be taken to a court of law. President Watkins was advised by the university's attorney that his position in the matter was legally correct, and he again notified Fluker and Parsons that their contracts would not be renewed; whereupon they returned to the District Court, whose first order had reserved jurisdiction over any remaining questions in the case.

Chief District Judge Frank M. Johnson conducted a second hearing for any "new additional testimony," and denied the university's motion to limit the hearing to a review of the record of the proceedings before the Faculty Advisory Committee. After this second hearing he concluded that "each of the plaintiffs has been accorded, fully and completely, any and all procedural rights to which they are entitled. . . . The evidence in the case convinces this Court that the action taken by the university was an altruistically motivated action to strengthen the faculty; it was based on educational and administratively sound principles and reasons. . . . "

Apart from the foregoing considerations, Judge Johnson was careful to say: ". . . even though the plaintiffs occupied a probationary status, even though they did not have any tenure, they are entitled to their constitutional protections—particularly their right not to be punished or to have sanctions imposed upon them by reason of their exercise of their First Amendment rights."

He noted that Fluker and Parsons seemed to contend that they had acquired some insulation from being selected for termination by virtue of activities in which they said they participated during the period of unrest on the Alabama State campus in May of 1969. He held that there was no basis in fact for their contention that those activities were the cause of their termination. It was a case simply of lack of evidence. He expressly refrained from making any findings on the question of whether the activities and attitudes of the plaintiffs would sustain the action of termination of their employment. It was unnecessary. Having made these findings, he denied any and all relief sought by both parties.

Upon appeal, Circuit Judge Homer Thornberry said: "The law in this Circuit is crystal clear that a non-tenured teacher alleging that he has been dismissed for constitutionally impermissible reasons 'must bear the burden' . . . of proving that a wrong has been done by the collegi-

ate action in not rehiring him," citing a recent Fifth Circuit decision.[4]
Also, as to the argument that the plaintiffs had "at least made a sufficient circumstantial showing to shift the burden of going forward onto
the university," Circuit Judge Thornberry noted that: "Under the law
of this Circuit, neither the burden of going forward nor the burden of
proof shifts to the State until it has been established by the complainant that he has been dismissed for exercising his constitutional rights. At
that point, the State assumes the burden of justifying its action by
showing that the complainant's activities 'materially and substantially
interfere with the requirements of appropriate discipline on the operation of the school,' " citing from other decisions of the Fifth Circuit and
of the Supreme Court.[5]

He also upheld as correct the ruling of District Judge Johnson that
the district court's holding of a hearing *de novo* cured any procedural
defects in the proceedings which had been conducted by the Faculty
Committee.

Turning to the factual issues, Circuit Judge Thornberry patiently
recited the several contentions of Fluker and Parsons and showed that
there was testimony in the record rendering each of these contentions
of doubtful credibility, and that in sum they were indeed insufficient to
prove that the termination was actually motivated by animus against
the teachers' attitudes toward the administration or against their exercise of constitutional rights. Accordingly the Circuit Court panel unanimously affirmed the judgment of the District Court.[6]

Comparable in some respects to the foregoing was a 1972 summary
judgment for the West Virginia Board of Regents by U.S. Chief
District Judge Robert Earl Maxwell, when four male and three female
faculty members at Fairmont State College who had been dropped at
the expiration of their one-year contracts, and denied any hearing, sued
for a remedy. One paragraph of their complaint recited: "Upon information and belief, the suspected reason for (the Regents') actions are
due to the plaintiffs' sex, their known sympathy with minority students, their verbal support of the anti-war protest movement, and their
just but harsh criticism of the College's administration, all of which ac-

---

4. *Sindermann v. Perry*, (U.S.C.A., Tex.), 430 F. 2d 939 (1970).
5. Including *Pickering* v. *Board of Education*, 391 U.S. 563, 88 S. Ct. 1731,
20 L. Ed. 2d 811 (1968).
6. *Fluker and Parsons* v. *Alabama State Board of Education*, (U.S.C.A., Ala.),
441 F. 2d 201 (1971).

tivities are permissible within the scope of the First and Fourteenth Amendments."

The court was not satisfied that the plaintiffs' pleadings included enough substantiated facts to justify a trial on the merits. They seemed to take the position that the facts could be taken for granted, and that the issues were questions of law. Twice they were invited to bring supporting facts into court. Some of them were dilatory in submitting affidavits, and at a pre-trial hearing they did not submit sufficient evidence to convince the court that the facts alleged were more than "suspected." Nevertheless, Judge Maxwell wrote a 10,000-word opinion, not only supporting his decision on the ground of defective pleadings, but also arguing at length that non-tenured faculty members in a case such as this are not entitled to a procedural right to a hearing.[7] (Compare and contrast with *Holliman* v. *Martin,* herein in Chapter 3; and with *Hetrick* v. *Martin,* at footnote 5 in Chapter 8 *infra.*) Note also the technical resemblance to *Fooden* v. *Board of Governors of State Colleges and Universities,* a decision of the supreme court of Illinois cited at footnote 8 in Chapter 3 herein. There is apparent judicial disagreement regarding the sufficiency of the pleadings when infringement of Constitutional rights is alleged. Should technical flaws in the pleadings prevent trial of the facts?

### Minimal Requirements of Procedural Due Process in Non-renewal of Contract of Non-tenured Public School Teacher Enunciated by U.S. District Court in Ohio but Reversed by Sixth Circuit

Thomas Justin Orr was employed during the 1969-70 school year as a teacher of tenth-grade English and history in Walnut Ridge High School, Columbus, Ohio. When notified that his contract would not be renewed for the next academic year, he asked the U.S. District Court to require the school board either to give him a statement of reasons and a hearing on them, or to order his contract renewed. U.S. District Judge Joseph P. Kinneary heard the complaint, and set out what he regarded as minimum requirements of due process in the non-renewal of the short-term contract of a non-tenured public school teacher:

7. *Chitwood* v. *Feaster, President of Fairmont State College,* (U.S.D.C., W. Va.), 54 Federal Rules Decisions 204 (1972).

1. Written statement of reasons for the proposed non-renewal, transmitted to the teacher prior to final action by the board.
2. Adequate notice of a hearing at which the teacher may respond to the stated reasons.
3. A hearing at which the teacher has an opportunity to present evidence controverting the stated reasons.
4. Delivery to the teacher of a copy of the reasons supporting its decision not to renew the contract, if the board makes such a decision.

These four essentials are, it will be noticed, somewhat similar to, but not identical with, the list of minimal requirements stated by the Fifth Circuit Court of Appeals in the case of *Ferguson* v. *Thomas*, as quoted near the beginning of this chapter. Taken together, the two listings serve to convey a general idea of what constitutes due process for non-tenured faculty members facing non-renewal of their contracts by a governing board which refuses to provide either reasons or a hearing. Neither list is intended to be all-inclusive or rigid or final, because apparently all judges believe the area is one within which a degree of flexibility should be maintained, permitting variations according to the nature and circumstances of different cases.

District Judge Kinneary issued orders directing the Columbus school board to deliver to the teacher's counsel a written statement of its reasons for not renewing his contract, set a hearing date and advise the teacher's counsel that he will have opportunity to present evidence relating to the reasons, and within 15 days after the hearing advise the teacher of its decision. A further clause of the court order directed that if the board chose not to comply within 30 days, then it must offer the teacher a contract for 1970-71 on terms not less favorable than those contained in his contract for the year 1969-70.[8]

This judgment was reversed by the Sixth Circuit Court of Appeals June 16, 1971, in an opinion by Chief Circuit Judge Harry Phillips, sitting with Circuit Judges William E. Miller and W. Wallace Kent.

This court wrote: "A non-tenured teacher's interest in knowing the reasons for non-renewal of his contract and in confronting the Board on those reasons is not sufficient to outweigh the interest of the Board in free and independent action with respect to the employ-

---

8. *Orr* v. *Trinter*, (U.S.D.C., Ohio), 318 F. Supp. 1041 (1970). Subsequently reversed by Sixth Circuit U. S. Court of Appeals in (U.S.C.A., Ohio), 444 F. 2d 128 (1971).

ment of probationary teachers"; and concluded: "In the present case Orr seeks to persuade this court to render a decision which would confer certain tenure privileges upon non-tenured teachers—in effect to amend the Ohio statute by judicial decree. This we decline to do."

The telegraphically worded digest reported in 40 *United States Law Week* 3126 (September 28, 1971) summarized the decision:

"Non-tenured Ohio public school teacher has no constitutional right to statement of reasons for school board's refusal to renew his employment contract and to hearing thereon." This decision seemed to align the Sixth Circuit with the Tenth Circuit (See *Jones* v. *Hopper*, herein near the end of Chapter 3) as the two Circuits standing for denial of either a statement of reasons or a hearing for non-renewed non-tenured teachers.

At the end of Chapter 3 herein there is a small tabulation of decisions in each of the 11 Circuits since 1965, bearing on these issues. By referring to the Table of Cases at the end of this volume, it is possible to locate in the text of this volume the discussion of each of the decisions named in the tabulation, and thus to gain an impression of the spectrum of opinions among the 11 Circuits prior to the decision of the United States Supreme Court in 1972 which is treated in Chapter 4.

### A Fair Hearing Is Vitiated If a Board Member Who Was Not Present Attends a Later Decisive Board Meeting and Casts the Deciding Vote Against Retention of the Teacher

Only twice in the earlier part of this chapter will be found judicial enumerations of the minimum essentials of a fair hearing. A 1971 decision of the U.S. District Court in New Hampshire made possible the addition of one further detail: The school committee of Manchester, with 13 of 15 members present, gave the teacher a suitable hearing. At its conclusion the board deliberated and took two votes on the question of retention. The first vote was 7 to 6 for retention and the second was 7 to 6 against. Neither instance represented a majority of the entire board, as required by the board's bylaw governing such cases. The board adjourned and met again a few days later. The later meeting was not a hearing; it was a meeting of the board to make its determination on the basis of the hearing that had already been completed. At this meeting a member who had been absent from the hearing was present, and cast the deciding vote (making a majority of the whole board) against retention.

This, thought U.S. District Judge Hugh H. Bownes, was a flagrant violation of due process; and he ordered the teacher reinstated forthwith, with his teaching assignment to be at the discretion of the school administration. The teacher's suit was against the individual board members, and not against the school district. Therefore Judge Bownes awarded no damages, because he saw no evidence of bad faith.[9]

## Due Process Is Violated by Arbitrary or Capricious
## Non-retention of Non-tenured Teacher on Basis of
## Unsubstantiated Rumors of Impropriety and
## Uncorroborated Complaints, Said U.S.
## District Court in New Hampshire

Again in 1971 U.S. District Judge Hugh H. Bownes decided the case of a high school teacher in a New Hampshire school district who was the victim of a 5 to 2 vote of the school committee not to renew his contract for the academic year 1970-71.

Donald R. Chase had a good record as a teacher in another New Hampshire school district. After that he had served three years as a radio announcer because the pay was better, but then returned to the teaching of English some three years before. His supervisors consistently gave him high ratings, and his principal recommended his retention. He initiated a meritorious system of instruction in the use of library resources, and he was developing a course in journalism appropriate for high school students.

His troubles had begun in 1968-69 when he accepted appointment by the local teachers' association as chairman of its negotiating committee, and in that capacity had heated debates with members of the school board in an attempt to negotiate a comprehensive contract between the board and the teachers. This antagonized some members of the board, and led to an impasse. Chase then resigned as chief negotiator, and the president of the association, who had appointed him, took up the job. During that year there were no complaints against Chase. One member of the board briefly mentioned an unspecified and unverified rumor from another town which seemed to have been derogatory.

---

9. *McDonough* v. *Kelly et al.*, (U.S.D.C., N.H.), 329 F. Supp. 144 (1971).

During 1969-70 three adolescent girls in the high school, one of whom was the daughter of a hostile school board member, made vague insinuations of improprieties. To one of these girls he had given a good deal of attention, to help her "catch up" after she had entered his class some weeks after the starting date. She thought he sometimes placed his arm on the back of her chair or touched her hand or her elbow unnecessarily. The others thought some of his remarks in class or directed to them were in the nature of the "double-entendre," capable of an innocuous interpretation but also susceptible of a lewd meaning. There was no accusation of actual misconduct of any kind, and no attempt to investigate or verify the innuendoes; but in March 1970 the board voted 5 to 2 not to renew his contract.

Judge Bownes wrote in his opinion: "The facts present a distressing example of how a competent, innovative, and outspoken teacher can have his entire career effectively blighted by a school superintendent's and school board's blatant disregard of his rights and of the most elementary concepts of justice and fair play." He ordered Chase reinstated forthwith, with entitlement to all the benefits appertaining to his employment for the academic year 1970-71, and with all reference to non-retention expunged from his record. He also awarded $2,550 in damages against the school district, and individually against the superintendent and the five school board members who voted against renewing the contract.[10]

In the meantime Chase has been unemployed until December 1970, when he got a job with the New Hampshire Education Association which paid better than his teaching job. In the spring of 1970 he had been elected moderator of the Town of Croyden, and in the fall he had been elected to the state legislature as representative of Croyden and Cornish.

*Published Phrase About "Practice of the University,*
*but Not Contractually Binding" Does Not Relieve*
*University of Obligation to Provide Fair Practice*

The faculty handbook of Howard University provided that it

---

10. *Chase* v. *Fall Mountain Regional School District,* (U.S.D.C., N.H.), 330 F. Supp. 388 (1971).

would be the practice of the university, without contractual obligation to do so, for deans to give written notice of non-reappointment not later than December 15, and for the board of trustees to give such notice directly following its January meeting. This handbook had been duly adopted by a vote of the board of trustees, and constituted a part of its rules.

Late in the spring certain non-tenured members of the faculty were suddenly notified that they would not be reappointed for the following academic year—they would be dropped for misconduct on account of their alleged participation in campus disorders of recent occurrence. They were given no fair opportunity to state their version of the events in which they were said to have been implicated. They were denied injunctive relief in the U.S. District Court. In the U.S. Court of Appeals for the District of Columbia the denial of injunctive relief was allowed to stand, but a remedy similar to that usually available for a breach of contract prior to its expiration was provided: the case was remanded to the District Court to permit any of the faculty appellants "to pursue, if he so chooses, a claim for monetary damage, if any, attributable to the non-reappointment."[11]

The opinion was by Circuit Judge Carl McGowan, joined by Circuit Judge J. Skelly Wright, with Circuit Judge Warren E. Burger not participating.

Precisely the same point was decided in similar manner by the New Mexico court of appeals when the Board of Regents of Eastern New Mexico University dropped a first-year assistant professor of art near the end of the academic year 1967-68 without proceeding in accord with the provisions of the faculty handbook regarding such matters. All parts of the handbook had been submitted to the board and approved by board vote. Therefore the provisions in the handbook were parts of the professor's contract, though not mentioned therein; and Judge Joe W. Wood, with Judges William R. Hendley and Lewis R. Sutin concurring without opinion, said bluntly that the attempted statement that these provisions are "not contractual" is untrue and pointless in these circumstances.

Therefore the professor's contract for 1967-68 was held to have been breached by the board, exactly as in the preceding Howard Uni-

---

11. *Greene* v. *Howard University*, (U.S.C.A., D.C.), 412 F. 2d 1128 (1969).

versity case. No issue regarding his possible reappointment for 1968-69 was involved in the appeal.[12]

*First Circuit Court of Appeals Held Non-tenured*
*Teacher Is Entitled to Detailed Statement of*
*Reasons for Non-renewal, but Not*
*to a Hearing by the Board*

The First Circuit Court of Appeals has held in a case arising in New Hampshire that, where the state statute requires notice of non-reappointment by March 15, a non-tenured teacher need not be given a hearing; but that the notice must contain an explanation in detail of the reasons for non-retention. The court reasoned that this kind of written notice would give the teacher opportunity to expose sham assertions or to correct erroneous statements, if any, as well as to benefit from the valid criticism of his own performance, at little or no inconvenience to the employer board.

The court seemed impressed by the cost in time and money of a quasi-judicial hearing for every teacher dropped from a large institution or system, and thought that the requirement of such a hearing in all such instances might tend toward results bad for the quality of teaching. The board might tend to tolerate incompetent teaching to avoid the inconvenience of a hearing; or both the board and its administrative employees might become over-cautious in employment recommendations and actual appointments, so that the schools would be left with a teaching force of "homogenized mediocrities."

It was also suggested that if and when teachers' organizations are parties to collective bargaining with the employing board, the procedures and conditions of employment and termination may be subject to agreements arrived at by that means.[13]

The same First Circuit Court of Appeals was consistent with its own decision in *Drown* v. *Portsmouth* in a more recent case wherein a non-tenured faculty member of Bridgewater State College in Massachusetts whose contract was not renewed for academic year 1971-72,

---

12. *Hillis* v. *Meister, President of Eastern New Mexico University,* (N.M. App.), 82 N.M. 474, 485 P. 2d 1314 (1971).
13. *Drown* v. *Portsmouth School District,* (U.S.C.A., N.H.), 435 F. 2d 1182 (1970).

alleged that his Fourteenth Amendment right to due process had been violated because he had not been given a statement of reasons for his non-renewal and had not been allowed access to his personnel file.

The U.S. District Court ordered the trustees to produce a statement of reasons, but then dismissed the case on the ground that the plaintiff had not alleged and probably would not be able to prove all the stated reasons invalid. In affirming this decision, the Court of Appeals said: "(In *Drown*) we laid down the standard for measuring a non-tenured teacher's challenge to a statement of reasons on the ground that they are arbitrary and capricious. We held that, to state a claim, a teacher must allege, and to prevail, he must prove, that each of the stated reasons is trivial, or is unrelated to the educational process or to working relationships within the educational institution, or is wholly unsupported by a basis in fact. . . .

Since the plaintiff (McEntaggart) does not, as he probably could not, challenge the conclusion that he is a threat to the harmony of the department, . . . he fails to claim under the third branch of the arbitrariness test that the reason is wholly unsupported by a basis in fact."[14] (The facts underlying "threat to harmony" might bear fuller investigation.)

Another U.S. District Court in Massachusetts, with a different set of facts before it, ordered Worcester State College not to terminate the employment of a non-tenured faculty member (Maurice M. Roumani, assistant professor of political science) until he had been provided with a particularized statement of the charges against him; an opportunity to be heard, with counsel, by the Board of Trustees; and written notice of the Trustees' decision. This seemed to go farther than the judgment of the First Circuit U.S. Court of Appeals in the *Drown* case, 435 F. 2d 1182 (1970), which had decided that the teacher was entitled to a statement of reasons, but not to a hearing.

A differentiating factor was that the faculty member at Worcester State College was in his second year and was entitled to notice of non-renewal by December 15; but actually had not received such notice until April 16, countermanding a notice of March 1 that he would be reappointed; all this ostensibly on the ground that the president had lately been informed that the faculty member's representations regarding his progress toward a doctoral degree were untrue. In May 1971,

---

14. *McEntaggart* v. *Cataldo*, (U.S.C.A., Mass.), 451 F. 2d 1109 (1971).

at the request of the president, the two men met and considered the evidence of his doctoral progress; but no further action was taken as to his reappointment. If the four-month delay in notice had not occurred, the case would probably have been controlled by the *Drown* decision, but U.S. District Judge W. Arthur Garrity, after studying *Birnbaum* v. *Trussel*, 371 F. 2d 672 (1966),[15] with its analysis of Supreme Court decisions, concluded that a public employee "can be removed neither on arbitrary grounds nor without a procedure calculated to determine whether legitimate grounds do exist."[16]

### Failure to Allege Consistently a Constitutional Violation Causes Plaintiff to Be Denied Court Hearing by the Fifth Circuit Court of Appeals

The case of a public school teacher in Miami turned out adversely to the teacher, although it was pursued to the Fifth Circuit Court of Appeals. Robert Thaw was dropped at the end of his third one-year contract on the recommendation of his principal, who reported that "on many occasions he left his class for a time . . . , and in several instances ignored the school's disciplinary procedures." Thaw asked the trial court to require the board to give him a hearing. U.S. District Judge Ted Cabot denied this request; and his decision was affirmed by the Circuit Court of Appeals in an opinion by Circuit Judge Homer Thornberry, sitting with Circuit Judges Lewis R. Morgan and Charles Clark. The rationale was that the court should not take jurisdiction because "in his complaint below, Thaw invoked jurisdiction of the court on the basis of the First and Fourteenth Amendments. Nowhere else in his complaint did he allege a First Amendment violation, however, and at oral argument he agreed that he was alleging none."[17]

The point is that if one is alleging no violation of a procedural or substantive constitutional right, but only a right derived from a contract, then under concepts which prevailed formerly, he would be expected to exhaust his administrative remedies and then seek redress

---

15. Sketched and cited herein in Chapter 6, footnote 1.
16. *Roumani* v. *Leestamper*, (U.S.D.C., Mass.), 330 F. Supp. 1248 (1971).
17. *Thaw* v. *Board of Public Instruction of Dade County, Florida*, (U.S.C.A., Fla.), 432 F. 2d 98 (1970).

in his state courts. A federal court would decline to take jurisdiction unless there were special reasons, such as diversity of citizenship or a sum involved in excess of $10,000. Contract rights belong only to parties with valid contracts, generally governed by state law; but federal Constitutional rights appertain to all U.S. citizens, and when infringements are *alleged* they are sufficient to invoke the jurisdiction of a federal court.

*Substantive Right Not to Be Terminated for*
*Constitutionally Impermissible Reason*
*Seems Settled; Procedural Entitlements*
*Not Yet Uniformly Established*

"I think it is well settled that the employment of a public school professor, instructor, or teacher may not be terminated for his exercise of constitutionally protected rights," said U.S. District Judge Hubert I. Teitelbaum in the case of Jerry A. Shields, an assistant professor of English at Slippery Rock State College in Pennsylvania. Shields served year-by-year from August 1967 to August 1970, when he was offered a one-year terminal contract for 1970-71 and notified that he would not be re-hired for 1971-72.

Shields alleged the reason for the non-renewal of his contract was his admitted participation in demonstrations during the "Vietnam Moratorium" of October 1969 and the Cambodia and Kent State sequelae of May 1970; in short, no more than his exercise of his First Amendment rights of free speech and assembly. He asked that the court require either an administrative hearing for him or order his reappointment. The requested relief was denied. In cases such as this the burden of proof is on the plaintiff, and Judge Teitelbaum found that the evidence offered in support of Shield's allegation was only tenuous and unpersuasive. Administrators concerned in the decision to terminate his contract testified that at the time the decision was made they were totally unaware of his participation in the demonstrations, and that the decision was uninfluenced by any such factor.

So, concluded Judge Teitelbaum: "In the circumstances of this case, including those of the non-tenured status of Mr. Shields and the year-in-advance notice of his termination, I find that the interest of the state outweighs that of the plaintiff, and conclude that procedural due process does not require an administrative hearing."[18]

It is important to observe that the court did not say an administrative hearing is never necessary, but only that it was not required in the circumstances of this case; and that the court was firm in its equal espousal of the substantive right not to be terminated for exercise of constitutional rights. In support of this it cited the opinion of District Judge James E. Doyle in the case of *Roth* v. *Regents of Wisconsin State Colleges* (affirmed by the Seventh Circuit Court of Appeals in 446 F. 2d 806 in 1971), a case to appear more than once in subsequent chapters in this volume.

A quotation from Judge James E. Doyle is of significance to us at this point: "This substantive constitutional protection is unaffected by the presence or absence of tenure. . . . Nor is it material whether employment is terminated during a given contract period, or not renewed for a subsequent period."

Thus there is little point in grouping the cases according to whether the aggrieved faculty members are non-tenured, probationary, or tenured, so far as the substantive constitutional rights are concerned. But as yet there is some differentiation among the decisions concerning the extent of procedural rights and what constitutes due process for the plaintiffs in different categories. In the present case Judge Teitelbaum was expressly somewhat influenced by Shields' "non-tenured status."

### U.S. District Courts in Wyoming and Alaska
### Decide to the Contrary

At Riverton, Wyoming, the local public junior college, only two years old in 1970, was known as Central Wyoming College. Two teachers who had completed two successive 9½-month contracts were given written notice February 27, 1970, that their contracts would not be renewed for the academic year 1970-71. They requested formal hearings before the board of trustees, but these were denied. However, both were invited to attend a regular meeting of the board to discuss the matter informally, and one of them did so. Their next step was to the court of U.S. District Judge Ewing T. Kerr, where they asked for an order of reappointment, and a judgment in damages. They included

---

18. *Shields* v. *Watrel*, (U.S.D.C., Pa.), 333 F. Supp. 260 (1971).

in their complaint an alleged "chilling effect" on their rights under the First and Ninth Amendments.

Naturally Judge Kerr was heavily influenced by the recent decision of the Tenth Circuit Court of Appeals in *Jones* v. *Hopper*,[19] which gave no countenance to allegations of civil rights violations in a case of this kind, and held the fort for the widest possible discretion for state and local educational governing boards, acting under state statutes. He seemed to equate the right to notice and hearing with tenure only, and made such statements as "The statutes of Wyoming do not provide tenure or continued employment for a faculty member with a community college," and "It is not within the province of this court to establish tenure at community colleges in Wyoming." He dismissed the complaint for lack of jurisdiction, and hence there was no trial.[20]

Hilton Wolfe was employed from year to year as assistant professor of English at the University of Alaska at Fairbanks, beginning in September 1969. In December 1970 he was notified that his appointment would be terminated upon the expiration of his current contract in May 1971. No reasons were stated. He sought recourse successively through the academic vice president, the university grievance committee (which first decided against him, then reversed itself and recommended he be reappointed), the president, and the Board of Regents. After giving him a hearing, the Board voted unanimously to sustain the president's decision to terminate his services.

In the court of U.S. District Judge James A. Von der Heydt, Professor Hilton alleged he was dropped because he had exercised his right of constitutionally protected free speech, and that he had not been afforded a proper hearing on that issue; and that the failure to notify him of the reasons for his termination was a violation of the due process clause and the equal protection of the law clause of the Fourteenth Amendment. He asked only for the equitable remedy of reinstatement, and an injunction against violation of his constitutional rights.

Judge Von der Heydt took jurisdiction and held that the complaint stated a proper cause of action under 42 *United States Code* 1983; and allowed the university an extension of time of 45 days to prepare and file an answer. He also held that the president and the board (in its

19. See herein, Chapter 3, text appertaining to footnote 11.
20. *Schultz* v. *Palmberg*, (U.S.D.C., Wyo.), 317 F. Supp. 659 (1970).

corporate collective capacity) are "persons" within the meaning of Section 1983, and not immune from suit; but allowed the board members in their individual capacities to be dismissed as parties in this suit.[21]

*Maryland's State Court of Last Resort Held State*
*College Can Drop a Non-tenured Teacher*
*Without a Formal Hearing When He Claims*
*No Violation of Academic Freedom*

Somewhat similarly, the Maryland Court of Appeals sustained the non-reappointment of a non-tenured teacher who was informed at the end of one academic year that he would be given employment for the next academic year, but it would be his terminal year. He erroneously thought a policy statement adopted by the governing board in February 1968 gave him a right to a statement of reasons and a hearing; but actually the statement only declared that if a teacher alleged a *prima facie* case of violation of academic freedom, then his case could be considered by a faculty committee and by the governing board. "The policy statement," said the court, "saddles him with the necessity of alleging 'a *prima facie* case of violation of academic freedom.' " This he had not undertaken to do. No such allegation appeared in his pleadings. Hence the court thought, after considering the pertinent Maryland statutes, the college had a right not to extend his employment without providing him either a statement of reasons or a formal hearing.[22]

This is typical of the earlier condition of the law in many states. In Chapter 3 we distinguish probationary faculty members under tenure systems from others having no probationary status under any tenure system. The distinction is of no consequence as to substantive constitutional rights; but it has some current significance as to procedural entitlements in some instances, though not fully settled.

---

21. *Wolfe* v. *O'Neill*, (U.S.D.C., Alaska), 336 F. Supp. 1255 (1972).
22. *Griffin* v. *Board of Trustees of St. Mary's College of Maryland*, Maryland Court of Appeals, Case No. 329 (June 2, 1970).

# CHAPTER 3

## TERMINATION OF THE CONTRACTS
## OF PROBATIONARY FACULTY
## MEMBERS

In the immediately preceding chapter all or most of the cases involved either teachers in institutions having no tenure rules, or teachers who individually had no tenure status, whether permanent or probationary. In this present chapter we observe some decisions affecting teachers serving their probationary years under tenure rules.

This does not mean that *all* cases involving probationary faculty members are grouped here. Some of them appear in other chapters because the principal issues around which those chapters are constructed seem to overshadow or outweigh the simple fact of probationary status.

The year 1965 may be said to be one of the "early" years in the current period of revolutionary change in the law of the appointment and reappointment of faculty members in universities, colleges, and secondary schools. The prime problem is to find the proper balance in each case between the legitimate interests of the state as protected in the terms of the contract, and the civil rights of the teacher as guaranteed in the United States Constitution. The balance may be affected by a variety of factors in different cases, and also by the date of the decision in a time when the climate of judicial opinion is changing.

*Fourth Circuit Decision Dealt with Contract Expressly*
*Terminable on Short Notice by Either Party*

In a case from Maryland in 1965 the Fourth Circuit Court of Appeals held that the terms of the probationary teacher's contract governed the controversy entirely, and gave no countenance to the plea that the employment was terminated without a hearing, and the allegation that the real reason was that he had assigned and discussed in class a book which the board of education had proscribed, in violation of freedom of speech.

Ray Elbert Parker was a first-year probationary teacher in a high school in Prince Georges County, Maryland, under a contract expressly providing that *either party could terminate it by giving the other party 30 days' notice.* This feature of the contract probably heavily influenced the court. Parker assigned and discussed in class the book *Brave New World* by Aldous Huxley. Thereupon an irate parent asserted the book was "atheistic, obscene, and immoral," and demanded that both Parker and the book be removed from the school. *Brave New World* was listed as "optional" on a long list of books officially issued, some of which were listed as "required," and some as "optional." The board of education removed the book from the library and resolved not to renew Parker's contract, and refused to give him a hearing.

In the U. S. District Court Chief Judge Roszel C. Thomsen flatly held that no constitutional rights were involved, and that the contract was in accord with Maryland statutes. He also noted that the state and county teachers' associations argued against Parker as *amici curiae*, because they wanted at all costs to protect the rights of tenured teachers, and to preserve and sharpen the distinctions between tenured and non-tenured.

Affirming the dismissal of the suit, Circuit Judges Albert V. Bryan and J. Spencer Bell, with Senior District Judge Alfred E. Barksdale sitting by designation, said *per curiam*: "Our decision rests entirely on the contract," and explicitly declined to pass upon any alleged constitutional issues.[1]

---

1. *Parker* v. *Board of Education of Prince Georges County*, (U.S.C.A., Md.), 348 F. 2d 464 (1965); affirming 237 F. Supp. 222 (1965). Certiorari denied, 382 U.S. 1030, 86 S. Ct. 653, 15 L. Ed. 2d 543 (1966); rehearing denied, 383 U.S. 939, 86 S. Ct. 1071, 15 L. Ed. 2d 857 (1966). Justices William O. Douglas and William J. Brennan would have granted certiorari.

It will be observed *infra*, in the case of *Johnson* v. *Branch*, that the same Fourth Circuit Court of Appeals reached a very different decision under different facts (teacher terminated because she was active in racial civil rights work, including voter registration). There the Circuit Court reversed the District Court judgment and directed it to order the teacher reinstated, and to determine damages due her. In that case the Circuit Court panel consisted of five judges, including J. Spencer Bell and Albert V. Bryan, with the addition of Chief Judge Clement F. Haynsworth and Circuit Judges Simon E. Sobeloff and Herbert S. Boreman. (See Chapter 7, "Discrimination: Race; Religion; Sex; Ideology.")

### Fifth Circuit Holds That Plea of Non-renewal Because of Exercise of Civil Rights Can Not Be Summarily Dismissed

Again in the Fifth Circuit Court of Appeals, Chief Circuit Judge John R. Brown, sitting with Circuit Judges Walter Pettus Gewin and Irving L. Goldberg, quickly recognized that probationary teachers alleging non-reappointment because they exercised their rights of association by participating actively in local teachers' organizations, were entitled to be heard in the U.S. District Court below.

Elenore Pred and Stanley Etersque, instructors in the Miami-Dade Junior College in Florida, were denied fourth-year contracts, tantamount to tenure, allegedly because both had exercised leadership in the teachers' association, and one was accused of speaking in the classroom of new desires for freedom on the campus. District Judge Emmett C. Choate summarily dismissed the complaint; but Chief Circuit Judge John R. Brown, growing weary of summary and unexplained dismissals of civil rights cases, spoke out astringently:

"This is another monument to needless waste of lawyer and Judge time, and, perhaps more important, client money. For now, after fourteen months, this case must go back to start the normal process of discovery leading to the production of facts or the demonstrated lack of them, on which, either before or after a conventional trial, the real merits of the case will be determined." Accordingly the summary judgment was reversed and remanded.[2]

---

2. *Pred* v. *Board of Public Instruction of Dade County, Florida*, (U.S.C.A., Fla.), 415 F. 2d 851 (1969).

He declared, "Simply because teachers are on the public pay-roll does not make them second-class citizens in regard to their constitutional rights"; and inveighed against judicial dismissal of cases "on barebones pleadings," characterizing them as "too quick, too soon, too enigmatic." He cited and quoted from recent U.S. Supreme Court decisions in *Keyishian*,[3] *Pickering*,[4] and *Tinker*.[5] From *Keyishian*: "Our nation is deeply committed to safeguarding academic freedom," and "To impose any strait-jacket upon the intellectual leaders in our colleges and universities would imperil the future of our Nation."

### Two U.S. District Courts in California Were Not in Complete Harmony in Two 1971 Decisions, Both Arising in the State College System

California's State College System, a conglomeration of 19 diverse institutions scattered over 500 miles—from the state's northern Pacific coast to the Mexican border—, literally stretches "from palm to pine," and is so large as to fall within different federal court districts.

For example, on November 25, 1970, five probationary employees were notified by the president of Fresno State College in central California that they would not be offered appointments for the academic year 1971-72. One other was offered appointment for 1971-72, but told that this appointment would be terminal for him at that institution.

These plaintiffs asked for relief from the U.S. District Court, relying heavily on the decisions in *Ferguson* v. *Thomas*, (U.S.C.A., Tex.), 430 F. 2d 852 (1970), and *Greene* v. *Howard University*, (U.S.C.A., D.C.), 412 F. 2d 1128 (1969), discussed *supra* in Chapter 2.

U.S. District Judge William T. Sweigert denied relief. His reasoning is neatly encapsulated: "Although tenured teachers are entitled to full due process before they may be dismissed, less demanding, less adversary, minimal process suffices for non-reappointment of probationary teachers."[6] He did not espouse, or at least did not emphasize, the view that constitutional rights appertain to all citizens alike. He pointed to the Executive Order No. 112 of the California State Col-

---

3. Cited herein in Chapter 9, "The Loyalty Oath Furor."
4. Cited herein in Chapter 8, "Freedom of Speech; Expression; Assembly; Petition."
5. Cited as 393 U.S. 511, 89 S. Ct. 739 (1969).
6. *Toney* v. *Ronald Reagan*, (U.S.D.C., Cal.), 326 F. Supp. 1093 (1971).

lege System, which provided for an elaborate "grievance procedure" which must be initiated by the grievant, adjudged this to be adequate and fair, and held that the plaintiffs must exhaust this administrative remedy before coming into court.

In the course of this opinion he made clear that he regarded certain features of the grievance procedure as meeting the requirements of due process in such cases. For example, the channel of appeal beyond the decision of the state college president was to a panel of three faculty members of the State College System, one chosen by the grievant, one by the college president, and one by the chancellor of the system. This panel would hold a hearing and make a recommendation to the chancellor, whose decision would be final. The panel hearing would not be open to the public, and no attorney-at-law would be allowed to be present. A tape recording of the proceedings would be confidential, except that the grievant would be allowed to obtain a copy of the transcript at his own expense.

In the same year, in an apparently similar case, a different U.S. District Court in a different part of the state reached markedly different conclusions.

Arnold J. Auerbach was appointed a full professor of sociology at San Fernando Valley State College (in Southern California), effective in September 1969. On March 1, 1970, he was reappointed for the academic year 1970-71 for his second probationary year. November 27, 1970, he was notified in writing by President James W. Cleary that he would not be offered a career appointment as a tenured professor and that his employment would terminate at the end of the academic year 1970-71.

This followed a series of negative recommendations by the various committees and individuals participating in an elaborate consultative process which was prescribed in the faculty handbook. The president, after repeated requests by Professor Auerbach, refused to state any reasons for this decision, and refused to offer him an impartial hearing "whereat he could attempt to establish that the reasons proffered were without foundation in fact, constitutionally impermissible, or otherwise wholly inappropriate for consideration."

It was found as a fact that "Nowhere in the applicable California statutes, rules of defendant Trustees or College consultative process is there any requirement that the president . . . or any of the committees or individuals making recommendations to him, inform the academic employee of the reasons for a negative decision or a negative advisory recommendation. . . . To the contrary, the personnel policies specifically provide that the College shall be under no obligation to explain its decision not to accord tenure or not to reappoint."

Auerbach declined to file a grievance under an internal grievance procedure that would offer no assurance that he would obtain a specification of reasons for his non-reappointment. He went to the U.S. District Court, pleading the well-known *42 United States Code section 1983*. U.S. District Judge Warren J. Ferguson found that "The decision . . . not to reappoint and accord tenure has caused and will continue to cause, unless restrained from enforcement, the plaintiff (Auerbach) damages to his professional reputation and standing and severely hamper his opportunities for employment at other institutions of higher learning, for which there is no other adequate remedy at law." Accordingly he held as a matter of law that there had been a denial of due process as guaranteed under the Fourteenth Amendment, and issued a permanent injunction directing that Auerbach be given a statement of reasons *and* a hearing; and retained jurisdiction until compliance with the order.[7]

### State Supreme Court Decisions in Illinois and Colorado

Illustrating that plaintiffs in constitutional civil rights cases may not always fare well in state courts is an Illinois supreme court case which must be taken as devoid of persuasive weight because the decision rests almost entirely on a procedural matter rather than on the merits of the issue, and because two of the Justices of the state supreme court dissented.

Ida Lalor and Benjamin Solomon, assistant professors in their second probationary year (pre-tenure) at Chicago State College, were notified in November 1968 by letter from the dean of the faculty that they would not be offered appointments for the academic year 1969-70.

They were joined by Jack Fooden, a professor and an officer of the Cook County Teachers' Union (Local 1600, American Federation of Teachers, AFL-CIO) in a suit asking for a declaration of the

---

7. *Auerbach* v. *Trustees of California State Colleges*, (U.S.D.C., Cal.), 330 F. Supp. 808 (1971).

rights of the parties and an order requiring the Board of Governors of State Colleges and Universities to offer Lalor and Solomon employment for the 1969-70 year.

They pleaded that "these teachers were unconstitutionally removed from the faculty because the true reason for their removal was their open leadership and activities on behalf of the Teachers' Union and because of their initiation and promotion of open discussion among members of the faculty concerning educational policies and programs for minority groups; and that the failure of the Board and its agent to assign reasons for their removal violated their constitutional rights of due process."

The Board had delayed five months (until April 18, 1969) before reviewing the case and approving the determination. It then entered a motion for summary judgment in the pending suit, supported by an affidavit of F. H. McKelvey, executive officer and secretary of the Board. McKelvey deposed that "under the bylaws, governing policies and practices of the Board" the Board's sole duty in this case was to provide the notice of non-retention by December of the current year, and this it had done. On this basis Judge Creel Douglass of the circuit court of Sangamon County granted summary judgment in favor of the Board.

The judgment was affirmed by the state supreme court in an opinion by Justice Thomas E. Kluczynski, with Justices Daniel P. Ward and Joseph H. Goldenhersh dissenting. The majority opinion declares that an affidavit from a competent source is a substitute for sworn testimony in open court, and must be taken as true unless refuted in similar manner by the adversary.

The averments of the teachers in their original complaint, said the court, were only "allegations made on information and belief" and were not a sufficient response to the "positive, detailed statements of fact" in the affidavit. Thus, by failing to file a counter-affidavit, or to respond with some such maneuver as a motion to strike all or part of the adversary pleadings, the teachers allowed themselves to be defeated in the circuit court. And the sufficiency of the affidavit or the competency of the affiant can not be challenged for the first time on appeal; hence it could not be argued in the supreme court.

In the view of Justice Kluczynski, the allegations that the teachers were improperly removed because of their union activities and expressions of views on public education did not raise a relevant issue of fact because they were only "pleaded conclusions"; and the court concluded that "there was no contractual obligation on the Board to announce its reasons for not re-employing Lalor and Solomon and therefore their employment could be properly terminated for any reason."

By emphasizing strictly procedural aspects of the case, the court saved the time and expense of a trial, and made sure that the issues raised by the teachers were neither argued nor decided, and avoided any forthright statement on its own responsibility regarding the constitutional facets of the case.[8]

Another Illinois case was rejected by a state court of appeals on purely technical grounds, and the record is so incomplete that it provides neither facts nor philosophy of much consequence. It is mentioned here to make this story as inclusive as possible. A teacher in a public junior college was asked to attend a closed meeting of the governing board to consider the question of renewing her contract. She did so. A week later at a public meeting of the board it was voted that her contract would not be renewed. The local district court sustained the action of the board, and an effort was made to get the case into the court of appeals by writ of certiorari. The court of appeals refused the writ because it is never granted except when the appellant has no other legal remedy. Here, said the court, the teacher had available the remedy of a suit for damages.[9]

## Seventh Circuit U.S. Court of Appeals Holds Statement of Reasons and Hearing Must Be Given When Teacher's Contract Is Not Renewed

Not only in *Roth* v. *Regents*, (U.S.C.A., Wis.), 446 F. 2d 806 (1971) (see *infra* at end of this chapter), but also in another 1971 decision involving non-renewal of the contract of a probationary high school teacher in Illinois, the Seventh Circuit went on record as holding that the teacher was entitled to not only a statement of

---

8. *Fooden v. Board of Governors of State Colleges and Universities of Illinois,* (Ill.), 268 N.E. 2d 15 (1971).

9. *Barden v. Illinois Junior College District 520, Kankakee,* (Ill. App.), 271 N.E. 2d 680 (1971).

reasons from the board, but also notice of a hearing at which she might respond to the stated reasons.[10]

In this case it appeared that the teacher had been vaguely admonished by being told she had not coordinated her teaching of German with that of another teacher of the same language in the same school; but there was conflict of testimony as to whether she had been invited to attend a board meeting and respond to this. The preponderance of evidence seemed to be to the contrary, and she did not attend the meeting at which it was decided not to renew her contract.

Circuit Judge Thomas E. Fairchild wrote the opinion, with Chief Circuit Judge Luther M. Swygert concurring without opinion. Circuit Judge John Paul Stevens dissented, expressing a profoundly conservative view of the function of the federal courts:

"I believe this interpretation of the due process clause will significantly enlarge the power and responsibility of the federal judiciary.

"Some years ago courageous and wise federal judges foresaw the potential harm that might flow from arbitrary actions by state government. On the assumption that the due process clause was more than a guarantee of fair procedure, they found a basis for substituting their views of sound policy for the 'arbitrary' decisions of state officials. Whether or not their policy judgments were correct, their expansive interpretation of the due process clause was fundamentally erroneous." Thus, with some acerbity, he denounced the trend of judicial opinion in this area.

*Tenth Circuit U. S. Court of Appeals, by Divided Vote,*
*Ignored Averment of Termination for Exercise*
*of Constitutional Rights*

Southern Colorado State College, at Colorado Springs, a four-

---

10. *Shirck* v. *Thomas,* (U.S.C.A., Ill.), 447 F. 2d 1025 (1971); reversing and remanding 315 F. Supp. 1124 (1970). The U.S.C.A. judgment was, however, vacated and remanded by the U.S. Supreme Court (141 *U.S. Law Week* 3003), June 29, 1972, for further consideration in light of the Supreme Court's decision in *Board of Regents* v. *Roth* (1972), which is fully discussed in Chapter 4, *infra* herein. This is a direction to the U.S. Court of Appeals to consider whether the two cases are "on all fours," and does not necessarily mean the ultimate outcome must be the same in both cases.

year institution recently developed from a former locally-supported two-year college, is governed by the Board of Trustees of State Colleges, together with four other state colleges of longer standing, the oldest and best-known of which is the former Colorado State College at Greeley, now renamed the University of Northern Colorado.

The Board of Trustees possesses by statute "power to appoint and remove all subordinate officers, professors, associate professors, teachers, assistants, employees or agents, in, or about, or concerning said college; to appoint or employ, discharge and suspend, contract and fail to renew contracts of employees and other subordinates. . . ." The language is unmistakably intended to convey the powers unqualifiedly and unequivocally, and it was probably written with no thought of any possible collision with First Amendment rights of teachers. The wording was construed literally and enforced by the majority of a seven-judge Tenth Circuit Court of Appeals in a 1969 case of a probationary college teacher who alleged that refusal to reappoint him after his second year was because he had exercised his constitutional rights to freedom of religious views, speech, and publication.

George Jones, Jr., an associate professor of philosophy, was notified in writing by the president of Southern Colorado State College in February 1966 that after the termination of his second probationary year in the following June, his contract would not be renewed.

Making his complaint specific, Jones alleged he was being dropped for four reasons: (1) He had objected to the disqualification of an applicant for his department because the applicant was an Oriental. (2) He had written to a student newspaper objecting to a certain textbook then in use in the English department. (3) He had founded an independent faculty-student publication carrying articles critical of the war in Viet Nam, objecting to monitored classrooms, and commenting on labor problems and pacifism. (4) He had supported a student, John Dean, who had attempted to register with his draft board as a conscientious objector, and whose parents had subsequently obtained a court order committing their son to a hospital.

Jones averred that he was a pacifist by religious conviction and that his oral and written views on this subject were an exercise of his religious freedom. He asserted that refusal to renew his contract because of the foregoing reasons unconstitutionally deprived him of a reasonable expectancy of continued employment, and asked $300,000 in damages.

U.S. District Judge Olin Hatfield Chilson dismissed the suit as stating no cause of action. Hence there was no trial. On appeal, the Tenth Circuit, in a *per curiam* opinion in which Chief Circuit Judge Alfred P. Murrah and Circuit Judges David T. Lewis, Jean S. Breitenstein, Delmas C. Hill, and John J. Hickey apparently concurred, affirmed the dismissal: "We believe the Trustees were exercising a discretion given them by the Colorado statute. The exercise of this discretion can not, under the facts alleged in the complaint, become unlawful conduct which would justify its falling within the ambit of the Civil Rights Act."[11]

Since this decision stands contrary to several judgments of U.S. Courts of Appeals in other Circuits, it is especially noteworthy to observe that a convincing dissent was entered by two of the Circuit Judges in this Tenth Circuit Court. Circuit Judge Oliver Seth, joined by Circuit Judge William J. Holloway wrote: "In my opinion the allegations are sufficient under the decisions of the Supreme Court for the case to be brought to trial." Later in the dissenting opinion: "Teachers of whatever status do not give up First Amendment rights by reason of their employment. *Pickering* expressly so holds. Nontenure teachers can not be held to have more limited constitutional rights than do others. They are on a temporary basis not for reasons related to the problems before us, but instead on the quality of their teaching."

Speaking of the authority of the Board of Trustees: "No matter how broad their discretion may be by statute or by custom, it can not be used to deprive teachers of their constitutional rights. This is what plaintiff has alleged, and this is sufficient. Whether he can prove it is indeed another matter, and a matter which has not yet been reached in this case."

"The balancing referred to in *Pickering* is done when the facts are in and not before. The Court there said:

'The problem in any case is to arrive at a balance between the interests of the teacher, as a citizen, in commenting upon matters of public concern and the interests of the State, as an employer, in pro-

---

11. *Jones* v. *Hopper*, (U.S.C.A., Colo.), 410 F. 2d 1323 (1969).

moting the efficiency of the public service it performs through its employees.'[12]

"We can not anticipate such a balancing of facts on this motion (to dismiss)."

The dissenting judges also made other statements too insightful into modern law to be overlooked: "The plaintiff could very well prove an 'expectancy' of continued employment to exist outside any specific contractual or statutory provision, if this be necessary; and secondly, the board's power to discharge can not be unlimited, as the holding of the majority assumes."

Conceding that college teachers are employees, the two judges reject the idea of recourse to the ancient rule of the master-servant relationship, that an employer "enjoys an absolute power of dismissing his employee, with or without cause." This, they say, "hardly fits the relationship between trustees of a college or university and the professors or the lesser teachers at such an institution."

For a few illustrations of what they mean, they cite four recent decisions of the U.S. Supreme Court touching the point: *Shelton* v. *Tucker*, 364 U.S. 479, 81 S. Ct. 247, 5 L. Ed. 2d 231 (1960); *Pickering* v. *Board of Education*, 391 U.S. 563, 88 S. Ct. 1731, 20 L. Ed. 2d 811 (1968); *Keyishian* v. *Board of Regents*, 385 U.S. 589, 87 S. Ct. 675, 17 L. Ed. 2d 629 (1967); *Wieman* v. *Updegraff*, 344 U.S. 183, 73 S. Ct. 215, 97 L. Ed. 216 (1952); and numerous other federal decisions.[13]

It may not be too much to say that Circuit Judges Seth and Holloway made an admirable effort to pull the Tenth Circuit into the second half of the twentieth century. Note again that the judgment of the majority which they inveighed against in this case stood almost alone. At that time (1969), the Tenth Circuit was apparently the only Circuit that held flatly and generally that First Amendment rights had no bearing on the case of a non-renewed non-tenured college teacher in a state whose antiquated statutes afforded him no claim.

Later, in mid-1971, the Sixth Circuit adopted a somewhat similarly adamant position in *Orr* v. *Trinter* (recited *supra*, Chapter 2, foot-

---

12. Mr. Justice Thurgood Marshall for the Court in *Pickering* v. *Township High School District 205, Will County, Illinois*. 391 U.S. 563, 88 S. Ct. 1731, 20 L. Ed. 2d 811 (1968).

13. The Wieman and Keyishian cases are discussed at pages 98-100 in *The Colleges and the Courts, 1962-66*. Danville, Illinois: The Interstate Printers & Publishers, Inc., 1967. 326 pp.

note 8); but there the pleadings did not concern First Amendment rights, but concerned only the right to due process of law.

### U.S. District Court in Virginia Held That Alleged Arbitrary Dropping of College Teacher Stated a Cause of Action

One of the most recently reported federal decisions of this type as this volume went to press was by U.S. District Judge Ted Dalton, involving Radford College in Virginia.

Mrs. Mary B. Holliman became an instructor of English there in 1965-66. The famous American Association of University Professors' "Statement on Academic Freedom and Tenure" of 1940 was expressly made a part of her contract. Each year thereafter for four years she received a letter offering continued employment and advising that she was still operating under the AAUP statement. During these years she was promoted to assistant professor and received pay increases aggregating $3,000. On February 12, 1969, she was told she would not be granted tenure and not be reappointed for 1970-71.

By letter she asked the dean's committee on tenure to reconsider; and asked the president of the college and the rector of its Board of Visitors to review the decision, all to no avail; and she received written notice that the Board of Visitors had voted to terminate her employment. Lastly she filed a list of charges against the administration with the "Faculty Committee on Academic Freedom and Tenure." This committee flubbed by responding that it had no power to investigate and compel testimony, and that she could not substantiate any of her claims by documentary evidence. She then went to the U.S. District Court, averring that "she had been the victim of arbitrary, malicious, and unfounded employment practices which violated her rights and privileges under the Constitution of the United States."

She claimed "the right to a full evidentiary adversary hearing concerning reasons for her non-retention . . . and that she must be afforded the right to confront her accusers and to put on evidence in her own defense at a hearing before the administrative body responsible for the decision."

"The question," said Judge Dalton, "is whether it is constitutionally permissible for a state college to conduct its hiring practices in an arbitrary way. Can such a decision be made on a basis wholly unreasoned, or without factual support, or based upon rumor, surmise, or vindictiveness?" Paying deference to the difficulty of the issue, he launched into a long analysis of the classic U.S. Supreme Court decisions in *Cafeteria and Restaurant Workers' Union Local 473 v. Mc-Elroy*, 367 U.S. 886, 81 S. Ct. 1743 (1961); *United Public Workers of America* v. *Mitchell*, 330 U.S. 75, 67 S. Ct. 556, 91 L. Ed. 754 (1947); and *Wieman* v. *Updegraff*, 344 U.S. 183, 73 S. Ct. 215, 97 L. Ed. 216 (1952); and concluded, "The focal point is the personal liberty to pursue one's employment without arbitrary vilification and reckless exclusion by the state."

He noted that the Fourth Circuit U.S. Court of Appeals had decided three cases bearing on this matter. (See the tabulation of the 11 Circuit Courts of Appeals at the end of this chapter.) He said: "To recognize this due process limitation on the hiring discretion of state universities is in no way to raise non-tenured positions to tenured status. Nor does it mean that the federal courts under the auspices of the Civil Rights Act will become a haven for every disgruntled professor whose contract is not renewed." His conclusion was that this complaint of Mrs. Holliman stated a cause of action meriting a finding of the facts by a jury in his court; and his order was, "This cause will be set for trial by jury for resolution of the factual issues involved, and thereupon the court will enter an appropriate order and judgment determining all legal and equitable issues involved."[14]

A case wherein there was no averment of any violation of First Amendment rights of free speech or expression, and no charge that the non-retention was the result of retaliatory motives, was that of George W. Derby, an instructor at the Parkside campus of the University of Wisconsin. When he sued the Regents of the University and the chancellor of Parkside for damages and an order of reinstatement, he simply alleged that the termination of his contract was "without any reason, justification of any sort, or basis in fact." He had been refused a hearing.

U.S. District Judge Myron L. Gordon at first denied relief, chiefly because of the absence of any First Amendment plea, and also because he was inclined not to agree with the *Roth* decision of District Judge James E. Doyle, holding that Roth was entitled to a hearing before the Regents as a procedural right under the due process clause

---

14. *Holliman* v. *Martin*, (U.S.D.C., Va.), 330 F. Supp. 1 (1971).

of the Fourteenth Amendment. Later, after Judge Doyle's judgment had been affirmed by the Seventh Circuit Court of Appeals, Judge Gordon felt bound by that decision, and denied the motion of the Regents of the University of Wisconsin for a dismissal of the case for no cause of action.[15] This was a few weeks prior to the June 29, 1972, decision by a narrowly divided U.S. Supreme Court reversing the *Roth* decision.[16] As to the eventual disposition of the *Derby* case, this deponent saith not.

## Contract Rights and Constitutional Rights

The contrast between the prevailing doctrine of a few years ago and that which is now coming into acceptance is well illustrated by another Texas case decided in 1970 by the Fifth U.S. Circuit Court of Appeals. In this instance the three-judge panel of the court did not include Circuit Judges Thornberry and Morgan, but was composed of Circuit Judges Charles Clark, John Minor Wisdom, and Robert A. Ainsworth. The opinion was by Judge Clark.

A junior college professor at Odessa Junior College in Texas was dropped, he alleged, because he had exercised his constitutional rights by promoting organization of the faculty and attending a meeting relating to statewide efforts of that kind, and also attended meetings of certain state legislative committees, even though this required his temporary absence from his duties, and administrative permission for the temporary absence had not been granted. U.S. District Judge Ernest Guinn found no violation of contract; and believing nothing more was involved, granted summary judgment to the college. Soon thereafter the U.S. Circuit Court of Appeals decided another case from Florida (the *Pred* case, recounted *supra*, footnote 2, this chapter) in which it classified "the rights of persons circumstanced such as the plaintiff, as constitutional rather than contractual." This, remarked Circuit Judge Charles Clark, "aligned this court with the Fourth Circuit (in *Johnson* v. *Branch*, recited *infra*, Chapter 7, footnote 3) and against the Tenth Circuit (in *Jones* v. *Hopper*, described *supra*, footnote 11, this chapter), in this as yet unresolved conflict between cir-

---

15. *George W. Derby* v. *University of Wisconsin*, (U.S.D.C., Wis.), 325 F. Supp. 163 (1971); and *Same*, 54 Federal Rules Decisions 599 (1972).

16. The convoluted progress of the *Roth* case is recounted at some length in Chapter 4, *infra*.

cuits." Consequently, said Judge Clark, "this renders Judge Guinn's summary judgment inappropriate and erroneous. We reverse for further development of the facts."[17]

In the companion case of *Roth*, then pending with *Sindermann* before the U.S. Supreme Court, a professor in the Wisconsin State University at Oshkosh was dropped without any statement of reasons or any opportunity to respond to them. The U.S. District Court decision was in his favor. In affirming this judgment, the Seventh Circuit Court of Appeals said:

"We think the district court properly considered the substantial adverse effect non-retention is likely to have upon the career interests of an individual professor and concluded, after balancing it against the governmental interest in unembarrassed exercise of discretion in pruning a faculty, that affording the professor a glimpse at the reasons and a minimum opportunity to test them is an appropriate protection." Moreover: "in the case of teachers, the government's interest goes beyond the promotion of fairness to the encouragement of an academic atmosphere free from the threat of arbitrary treatment."[18]

The dissenting judge questioned whether administrative bodies such as university governing boards should be required to hear and pass upon constitutional questions on which there is conflict of high-level legal authority. He suggested that the requirement of hearings in all such cases would overload the administrative bodies and also flood the federal courts. (It would seem that this would not necessarily follow if the boards learned to exercise their powers without infringing individual constitutional rights, which should not be too much to ask of them.)

### Expectancy of Continued Employment for a Probationary Teacher Was Recognized by the Second Circuit Court of Appeals As Early As 1947

A quarter of a century ago Circuit Judge Learned Hand, renowned as one of the most eminent among all federal jurists of his time, wrote

---

17. *Sindermann* v. *Perry*, (U.S.C.A., Tex.), 430 F. 2d 939 (1970). Then pending before U.S. Supreme Court, with companion case *Roth* v. *Regents of State Universities*, with expectation of decision during 1971-72 term.

18. *Roth* v. *Board of Regents of State Universities*, (U.S.C.A., Wis.), 446 F. 2d 806 (1971).

the opinion of the Second Circuit holding that a probationary public school teacher in New York who had been discharged allegedly because she accepted duty on a federal jury which necessitated absence from her classes for about four weeks, was entitled to a trial of the facts and the law in U.S. District Court.

Sitting with Circuit Judge Hand were Circuit Judges Thomas W. Swan and Charles E. Clark. Said the court:

"We assume that the discharge by the Board was not a breach of contract at all. Nevertheless it may have been the termination of an expectancy of continued employment, and this is an injury to an interest which the law will protect against invasion by acts themselves unlawful, such as the denial of a federal privilege."[19] (Federal jury duty was optional for women; they were eligible, but were to be excused on their own request without further ado.)

At this point we enter a simple tabulation of recent cases touching upon the issues of the types discussed in chapters 2 and 3, within each of the 11 Circuits of the United States Courts of Appeals. This affords a key to the points of consensus and the areas of differences among the Circuits. By the convenient expedient of turning to the Table of Cases at the end of this volume, and finding each caption within its state of origin, the reader will find the page in this volume whereon the case is discussed. Not all will be found within chapters 2 and 3; some will be found in other chapters where their major thrust places them in a different grouping.

Thus is afforded a glimpse of the landscape which the high tribunal had before it prior to its decision of mid-1972.

No mathematical or minute topical treatment of the decisions is proffered here, because the diversities among the sets of facts and the pleadings, as well as among the nuances of the judicial opinions, make it inadvisable to attempt any foreshortened and cryptic summarization. It is better to give attention to the unique features of each case, and not to assume that each is a simplistic matter of "open or shut," susceptible of useful numerical manipulation.

The reader will be aware that the faculty member's right to a statement of reasons and a formal hearing, if not before the governing board then in a federal court, when a violation of substantive consti-

---

19. *Bomar* v. *Keyes*, (U.S.C.A., N.Y.), 162 F. 2d 136 (1947). Certiorari denied, 332 U.S. 825, 68 S. Ct. 166, 92 L. Ed. 400 (1947).

SOME DECISIONS IN THE 11 CIRCUITS OF THE U.S. COURTS OF APPEALS, TOUCHING THE CONSTITUTIONAL RIGHTS OF FACULTY MEMBERS AS TO THEIR APPOINTMENT, RETENTION, AND DISCHARGE*

| Year | D C Cir | 1 Cir | 2 Cir | 3 Cir | 4 Cir | 5 Cir | 6 Cir | 7 Cir | 8 Cir | 9 Cir | 10 Cir |
|---|---|---|---|---|---|---|---|---|---|---|---|
| 1972 | | | | | | SINDERMANN U.S. S.Ct. affirmed, June 29. | ORR v. TRINTER (Ohio) | ROTH v. REGENTS U.S. S.Ct. reversed, June 29. | | | SCHULTZ v. Palmberg (Wyo.) |
| 1971 | | McENTAGGART v. CATALDO (Mass.) MAILLOUX v. KILEY (Mass.) | | SHIELDS v. WATREL (Pa.) | Holliman v. Martin (Va.) | FLUKER v. ALA. BD. ED. (Ala.) | Hetrick v. Martin (Ky.) | ROTH v. REGENTS (Wisc.) | Rozman v. Elliott (Nebr.) | TONEY v. REAGAN (Calif.) Auerbach v. St. Coll. (Calif.) | |
| 1970 | | DROWN v. PORTSMOUTH (N.H.) | | | | SINDERMANN (Tex.) THAW v. BD. (Fla.) LUCAS v. CHAPMAN (Miss.) FERGUSON v. THOMAS (Tex.) | | SHIRCK v. THOMAS (Ill.) | | | |
| 1969 | GREENE v. HOWARD U. (D.C.) | KEEFE v. GEANAKOS (Mass.) | | | | PRED v. BOARD (Fla.) | | | FREEMAN v. GOULD (Ark.) | | JONES v. HOPPER (Colo.) |
| 1968 | | | | | | | | McLAUGHLIN v. TILENDIS (Ill.) | | | |
| 1967 | | | | | | | | | ARK. A&M v. DAVIS (Ark.) | | |
| 1966 | | | BIRNBAUM v. TRUSSELL (N.Y.) | | FRANKLIN v. GILES (Va.) JOHNSON v. BRANCH (N.C.) | HENRY v. COAHOMA (Miss.) | | | | | |
| 1965 | | | | | PARKER v. BOARD (Md.) | | | | | | |

* District Court decisions, within the Circuit, are shown in initial capitals and lower case letters; Court of Appeals decisions are in solid capitals. (The Table of Cases at the end of this volume indicates the page on which each case is discussed herein.)

tutional rights such as freedom of speech, assembly, expression, association, or petition, or unconstitutional discrimination on account of race, religion, or sex is alleged, has come to be universally upheld. In the absence of any such allegation, there is a demonstrable tendency toward construing procedural due process as requiring a written statement of the board's reasons and a formal administrative hearing. This tendency may be somewhat decelerated by the divided decision of the U.S. Supreme Court on June 29, 1972, discussed in Chapter 4 herein; but this author predicts that its progress will eventually be resumed.

# CHAPTER 4

## THE TWO DECISIONS OF THE
## U. S. SUPREME COURT,
## JUNE 29, 1972

This chapter is devoted to the *Roth* case and the *Sindermann* case, both of which have already been cited and briefly discussed in Chapter 3. Both were dealt with by the United States Supreme Court, as companion cases, in decisions handed down June 29, 1972. It seems appropriate first to offer an exhibit of the *Headnotes* of these two decisions in parallel columns, to facilitate comparisons and distinctions. Such an exhibit begins on the next page.

Throughout the chapter we have heavily quoted directly from the words of the Justices, because the exact language is all-important to an understanding of the reasoning, and no good purpose would be served by loose paraphrasing where precision is essential.[1]

---

1. One liberty has been taken with the words of the Justices: wherever they speak of "the respondent," the name of the individual has been substituted (Roth or Sindermann, as the case may be) in order to ease the difficulties of the lay reader. These substitutions have been made throughout this chapter, in quotations from all the Justices who wrote opinions in these two cases.

HEADNOTES OF THE *ROTH* AND *SINDERMANN* DECISIONS
IN PARALLEL COLUMNS,
to facilitate comparisons and distinctions

*ROTH*
U.S. S. Ct. No. 71-162, 40 *U.S.L.W.*
5079, June 29, 1972.

"David F. Roth, hired for a fixed term of one academic year to teach at a state university, was informed without explanation that he would not be rehired for the ensuing year. A statute provided that all university teachers would be employed initially on probation and that only after four years' continuous service would teachers achieve permanent employment 'during efficiency and good behavior,' with procedural protection against separation. University rules gave a non-tenured teacher 'dismissed' before the end of the year some opportunity for review of the 'dismissal,' but provided that no reason need be given for nonretention of a nontenured teacher, and no standards were specified for re-employment. Roth brought this action claiming deprivation of his Fourteenth Amendment rights, alleging infringement of (1) his free speech right because the true reason for his nonretention was his criticism of the university administration, and (2) his procedural due process right because of the university's failure to advise him of the reason for its decision. The District Court granted summary judgment for Roth on the *procedural* issue. The Court of Appeals affirmed."

*Held*: "The Fourteenth Amendment does not require opportunity for a hearing prior to the nonrenewal of a nontenured state teacher's contract unless he can show that the nonrenewal deprived him of an interest in 'liberty' or that he had a 'property' interest in continued employment, de-

(Continued)

*SINDERMANN*
U.S. S. Ct. No. 70-36, 40 *U.S.L.W.*
5087, June 29, 1972.

"Robert P. Sindermann was employed in a state college system for ten years, the last four as a junior college professor under a series of one-year written contracts. The Regents then declined to renew his employment for the next year, without giving him an explanation or prior hearing. Sindermann then brought this action in the District Court, alleging that the decision not to rehire him was based on his public criticism of the college administration and thus infringed his free speech right, and that the Regents' failure to afford him a hearing violated his procedural due process right. The District Court granted summary judgment for the Regents, concluding that Sindermann's contract had terminated and the junior college had not adopted the tenure system. The Court of Appeals reversed on the grounds that, despite lack of tenure, nonrenewal of Sindermann's contract would violate the Fourteenth Amendment if it was in fact based on his protected free speech, and that if Sindermann could show that he had an 'expectancy' of re-employment, the failure to allow him an opportunity for a hearing would violate the procedural due process guarantee."

*Held*: "(1) Lack of a contractual or tenure right to re-employment, taken alone, did not defeat Sindermann's claim that the nonrenewal of his contract violated his free speech right under the First and Fourteenth Amendments. The District Court therefore erred in foreclosing deter-

(Continued)

## HEADNOTES OF THE *ROTH* AND *SINDERMANN* DECISIONS
## IN PARALLEL COLUMNS (Continued)

*ROTH* (Continued)

spite the lack of tenure or a formal contract. Here the nonretention of Roth, absent any charges against him or stigma or disability foreclosing other employment, is not tantamount to a deprivation of 'liberty,' and the terms of Roth's employment accorded him no 'property' interest protected by procedural due process. The courts below therefore erred in granting summary judgment for Roth on the procedural due process issue."

*SINDERMANN* (Continued)

mination of the contested issue whether the decision not to renew was based on Sindermann's exercise of his right of free speech. (2) Though a subjective 'expectancy' of tenure is not protected by procedural due process, Sindermann's allegation that the college had a *de facto* tenure policy, arising from rules and understandings officially promulgated and fostered, entitled him to an opportunity of proving the legitimacy of his claim to job tenure. Such proof would obligate the college to afford him a requested hearing where he could be informed of the grounds for his nonretention and challenge their sufficiency."

### The State of the Law in Mid-1972

From the decisions cited and discussed in chapters 2 and 3 herein, two issues emerge clearly:

1. First is the question of whether a faculty member whose contract is not renewed upon its expiration is entitled to a statement of reasons for his non-retention and an administrative or academic hearing on the facts, *if he alleges that the real reason was his exercise of some constitutionally protected right*, such as that of free speech and expression; freedom of assembly, association, or petition; or freedom of religion—all of which are guaranteed against federal encroachment by the First Amendment. (These safeguards apply against the states by virtue of having been interpolated into the Fourteenth Amendment.)

   The near-unanimous affirmative consensus on that issue was strengthened and confirmed by the U.S. Supreme Court in the two decisions of June 29, 1972, that are the subject of this chapter. The principle applies alike whether the teacher is temporary, non-tenured, probationary, or tenured; and without regard to whether he is dropped by allowing his contract to expire, or discharged before its expiration. Constitutional rights are the same for all. On this point the decisions of June 29, 1972, capping a long series of federal and state court judgments, serve an important purpose.

2. The second question is that of whether a faculty member whose contract is not renewed upon expiration, and who *does not claim that the cause of his non-retention was his exercise of any constitutional right*, is entitled to a statement of reasons and a hearing at which he can respond. Here an affirmative answer would say the Fourteenth Amendment "due process clause," proscribing as it does any deprivation of "liberty or property without due process of law," protects the teacher in such circumstances from loss of property interest in the occupation by which he earns his livelihood, occasioned by diminution of his reputation and consequent difficulty in obtaining like employment in another institution or another state.

It would further say that the same clause also protects not only the teacher, but also the students and the public from an atmosphere of oppression, unfairness, and star-chamber concealment in the school or university, which inhibits academic freedom and runs counter to the liberty guaranteed by the Fourteenth Amendment.

We have already observed that a considerable number of federal courts have given this affirmative answer, and would positively add to the growing list of safeguards for public employees a constitutional right not to have their employment terminated for no reason, or for reasons that may be based on mistake of fact, or that may be arbitrary or capricious or motivated by malice, without opportunity to receive a written statement of reasons and to respond to them at some sort of hearing prior to the decision.[2] This is called *"procedural* due process" in distinction from instances where a substantive right such as freedom of speech is involved and its protection is said to be *"substantive* due process."

---

2. See, for example, in Chapter 2, *supra:*
*Ferguson* v. *Thomas*, (U.S.C.A., Tex.), 430 F. 2d 852 (1970); and *Lucas* v. *Chapman*, (U.S.C.A., Miss.), 430 F. 2d 945 (1970).
And in Chapter 3, *supra:*
*Pred* v. *Board of Public Instruction*, (U.S.C.A., Fla.), 415 F. 2d 851 (1969); *Auerbach* v. *Trustees of State Colleges*, (U.S.D.C., Cal.), 330 F. Supp. 808 (1971); and *Shirck* v. *Thomas*, (U.S.C.A., Ill.), 447 F. 2d 1025 (1971).

We have also noticed that some courts have given a negative answer, holding that the entitlement to a statement of reasons and a hearing, if it exists, is derived wholly from the teacher's contract and the pertinent statutes of the state. In this view, no federal constitutional question is present. The issues of fact and law, if they must be litigated, should first be tried in state courts, and brought into federal courts only if and when the state statutes are alleged to be in conflict with the federal constitution.

We shall see that this negative answer was given in the *Roth* v. *Regents* case from Wisconsin, by a bare majority of the Supreme Court, thus reversing the favorable judgment of the U.S. District Court and the Seventh Circuit U.S. Court of Appeals; noting at the same time that the separate issue of the "substantive due process" aspect of the case (invasion of Roth's right of free speech) *was not before the court and was not decided* because the lower court had thought best to stay its own action on that issue at least until the appeal on the "procedural due process" aspect had been heard and decided. Thus the high court's decision gives a negative answer to one of the two major elements of the case, and *does not decide the other* (though it seems to assure that if Roth can go into court and prove that his non-retention was in fact wholly in retaliation against him for exercising his protected right of free speech, he will be entitled to a remedy).

## What the U.S. Supreme Court Decided, and What It Did Not

Before examining the two decisions separately and in some detail, let us look at the summarizing words of Mr. Chief Justice Warren Burger, who was a member of the majority in both cases, and who also added a brief concurring opinion expressly applicable to both:

"The Court holds today only that a state-employed teacher who has a right to re-employment under state law, arising from either an expressed or implied contract, has, in turn, a right guaranteed by the Fourteenth Amendment to some form of prior administrative or academic hearing on the cause for non-renewal of his contract."[3]

---

3. This is an accurate and truthful statement cleverly emphasizing the positive aspect of an essentially *status quo* decision, because it scarcely changes the law as it has stood in the states for many decades, and allows pertinent state statutes to override the Fourteenth Amendment guarantee of due process.

Actually, the majority of the Court reversed and remanded a summary judgment by the District Court, affirmed by the Circuit Court of Appeals, which held that Roth was entitled to a statement of reasons and a hearing on his non-retention. The rationale of the majority was that Roth did not have the right of which the Chief Justice speaks, "to re-employment under state law, arising from either an expressed or implied contract, . . ." Hence the negative decision on that issue. Roth had only a one-year contract which by its own terms and by state law expired on June 30 and said nothing whatever about any renewal. The holding of the Supreme Court was that on that issue alone, in the absence of the other wing of his plea (that the real reason for his non-retention was to punish him for exercise of his constitutionally-protected right of free speech), his prayer must fail. This is the law as it was for many decades. It was a standstill negative decision, tending to decelerate a progressive trend.

The companion case of *Sindermann* v. *Odessa Junior College*, from Texas, was somewhat different. Here the faculty member had gone to the U.S. District Court and been met by summary judgment against him. On appeal to the Fifth Circuit Court of Appeals, the case was reversed and remanded for trial of the facts, because on the record it was a clear case of "total dispute" as to whether the faculty member had been dropped for good cause under Texas statutes, or whether the real reason was in retaliation against him for exercising constitutionally-protected free speech. The Supreme Court affirmed the judgment of the Court of Appeals.

The majority also concluded that Sindermann, in contrast with Roth, could be considered as holding the equivalent of a tenured position, by virtue of the fact that he had served 4 years at Odessa and a total of 10 years in the Texas system of higher education; and although the Odessa institution had no *de jure* tenure plan, nevertheless it had a statement in its *Faculty Guide* which strongly expressed the spirit if not the exact letter, of a tenure plan; and it was held that Sindermann might well claim *de facto* tenure, which would make his status different from that of Roth in Wisconsin.

Hence, from the words of the Chief Justice already quoted, as well as from the expressions of Mr. Justice Potter Stewart, who wrote the majority opinions in both cases, it appears that the majority saw the right to substantive due process—as, for example, when free speech is involved—as belonging to all public employees, including faculty members whether on tenure or probationary or non-tenured or temporary. But the right to *procedural due process*, apart from any other substantive constitutional right, was apparently seen as belonging only to tenured faculty members, or any faculty members who are discharged before the expiration of their current contracts; and not to those who are merely dropped upon the expiration of their contracts, unless state statutes provide otherwise.

## Both Cases Went Back to Lower Federal Courts; the Judgments of the High Court Do Not Instantly Settle All the Issues

It is noteworthy that in both of these cases the respective U.S. District Courts rendered *summary judgments*. This means that there was no trial of the facts. As we have seen, both cases went up through the Circuit Courts of Appeals to the U.S. Supreme Court. Both then went back for further proceedings in the lower courts—*Sindermann* by affirmance of a Circuit Court order to try the facts, and *Roth* on remand "for further proceedings consistent with this opinion."

*The Supreme Court did not decide whether either Sindermann or Roth was entitled to reappointment.* In keeping with its function as the highest appellate tribunal, it only stated its version of the law of the cases, and sent them to the courts below for fact-finding and application of the law to the facts.

There are other circumstances which make it easy to exaggerate the total impact of the two high court decisions of June 29, 1972. Both were decisions by a bare majority of the Justices. Mr. Justice Potter Stewart wrote both opinions, and was joined in each case by Mr. Chief Justice Warren Burger and Justices Byron R. White, Harry A. Blackmun, and William H. Rehnquist. Mr. Justice Lewis Franklin Powell took no part in either case. In both cases Justices William O. Douglas, William J. Brennan, and Thurgood Marshall entered cogent dissenting opinions. The Chief Justice, besides signing the majority opinion, wrote a brief concurring opinion of his own.

Almost everyone knows that dissenting opinions often become the law of the land a few years later, after inevitable changes in the membership of the Court, shifts in the political climate, and the arrival of new concepts and new practices in social and economic organization. In all decisions by a divided court, especially if the vote is close, there is considerable probability that the minority opinion may subsequently be adopted by the court in later cases, thus overruling its own prior decision. This indicates flexibility and a degree of progressiveness, but it runs contrary to the virtue of stability.

One of the outstanding examples of speedy change was the decision written for the court by Mr. Justice Robert H. Jackson in 1943, holding that West Virginia school authorities could not lawfully expel a pupil from a public school for refusing to participate, on religious grounds, in the ritual of the "pledge of allegiance and flag salute," and flatly overruling a contrary decision rendered by the same court only three years before.[4]

Another instance of similar type is that of the 1951 decision of the U.S. Supreme Court sustaining the constitutionality of Maryland's *Ober Act*, a conspicuous example of the hysterical postwar and cold-war "witch-hunting" legislation, which was effectively overruled by the same court 13 years later in *Baggett* v. *Bullitt*, 377 U.S. 360, 84 S. Ct. 1316, 12 L. Ed. 2d 377 (1964).[5] Justices Tom Clark and John M. Harlan dissented, believing the overruling of its own decision after only 13 years would make the court seem erratic or unstable, and would not "command the dignity and respect due to the judicial process." But the strong swing toward rationality in the political climate made the decision seem necessary to the majority of the court.

Other than the tendency of dissents later to become the law, there are further reasons for caution about assessing the effects of Supreme Court decisions. One of these is the danger of "over-interpreting," which sometimes leads laymen and lawyers—and even on occasion judges in high echelons—to overestimate what the high tribunal has actually decided.

*The Impact of the Two Decisions of June 29, 1972,*
*Should Be Astringently Appraised, and*
*Not Loosely Exaggerated*

Often a Supreme Court decision comes many months, or even

---

4. *West Virginia State Board of Education* v. *Barnette*, 319 U.S. 624, 63 S. Ct. 1178, 87 L. Ed. 1628, 147 A.L.R. 674 (June 14, 1943); overruling *Minersville* v. *Gobitis*, 310 U.S. 586, 60 S. Ct. 1010, 84 L. Ed. 1375, 127 A.L.R. 1493 (June 3, 1940).

5. Effectively overruling *Gerende* v. *Maryland Board of Supervisors of Elections*, 341 U.S. 56, 71 S. Ct. 565, 95 L. Ed. 745 (1951).

some years, after the litigated questions have been passed upon in lower federal courts or in state supreme or appellate courts. When a considerable heterogeneity of opinion develops among these courts, and especially if there are distinct conflicts among the judgments of the 11 Circuits of the U.S. Courts of Appeals, the Supreme Court sometimes consents to review an appealed case which it deems typical, so that its decision will add something to the harmony and consistency of the law throughout the nation.

As soon as the high tribunal has "noted probable jurisdiction," "granted certiorari," or otherwise signified its intent to review a particular case, many lower court judges having similar issues before them purposely postpone decision until after the Supreme Court has pronounced its judgment. This is in a certain sense an abdication of judicial independence, and from that standpoint is questionable. When a backlog of such deferred decisions awaits, and the high tribunal finally breaks the log-jam, conditions are favorable for hasty and sometimes "over-interpreted" conceptions of the ruling principles by some judges, many lawyers, and myriads of laymen.

Educators, most of whom are "laymen" from the standpoint of the legal profession, are largely dependent upon the newspaper and periodical press and the electronic media for prompt reports of court decisions; most of these reports are necessarily brief and fragmentary, and often touched with the aura of sensationalism that is thought necessary in the newsman's idea of "news." The high points of the court's majority opinion may receive reasonably accurate presentation, but dissenting opinions only rarely receive any attention at all. It is therefore advisable to scan most press reports with full knowledge that they do not, on account of limitations of the media, tell the full story and that almost always they fall short of a comprehensively accurate report of what the court has decided. A spirit of inquiry is better than a resigned and uninquisitive awe at the announcement of a high court decision.

### The Decision in the Roth Case Turned Entirely on the Question of Procedural Due Process

"The District Court granted summary judgment for Professor David F. Roth on the procedural issue, ordering the university officials to provide him with reasons and a hearing. 310 F. Supp. 972. The Court of Appeals, with one judge dissenting, affirmed this partial summary judgment. 446 F. 2d 806. We granted certiorari. 404 U.S. 909. The only question presented to us at this stage is whether Professor Roth had a constitutional right to a statement of reasons and a hearing on the university's decision not to rehire him for another year. We hold that he did not."[6]

Thus tersely wrote Mr. Justice Potter Stewart in an introductory paragraph of his opinion for the majority of the Supreme Court in the *Roth* case. He continued: "We must look to see if the interest is within the Fourteenth Amendment's protection of liberty and property."[7]

Quoting from the eloquent dissenting opinion of Mr. Justice Felix Frankfurter in the case of *National Insurance Company* v. *Tidewater Company*, 337 U.S. 582 (1948): "'Liberty' and 'property' are broad and majestic terms. They are among the great constitutional concepts . . . purposely left to gather meaning from experience. . . . They relate to the whole domain of social and economic fact, and the statesmen who founded this Nation knew too well that only a stagnant society remains unchanged.

"Yet, while the Court has eschewed rigid or formalistic limitation on the protection of procedural due process, it has at the same time observed certain boundaries. . . . In a Constitution for a free people, there can be no doubt that the meaning of 'liberty' must be broad indeed.

"There might be cases in which a State refused to re-employ a person under such circumstances that interests in liberty would be implicated. But this is not such a case.

"The State, in declining to rehire Professor Roth, did not make any charge against him that might seriously damage his standing and

---

6. *Board of Regents of Wisconsin State Colleges* v. *David F. Roth*, (U.S. S. Ct.), No. 71-162, 40 *U.S. Law Week* 5079 (June 29, 1972).

7. Early in the opinion Mr. Justice Stewart had said in a footnote: "The courts that have had to decide whether a nontenured public employee has a right to a statement of reasons or a hearing upon nonrenewal of his contract have come to varying conclusions. Some have held that neither procedural safeguard is required. *Orr* v. *Trinter*, 444 F. 2d 128 (CA 6); *Jones* v. *Hopper*, 410 F. 2d 1323 (CA 10); *Freeman* v. *Gould Special School Districts*, 405 F. 2d 1153 (CA 8). At least one court has held that there is a right to a statement of reasons but not a hearing. *Drown* v. *Portsmouth School Districts*, 435 F. 2d 1182 (CA 1). And another has held that both requirements depend on whether the employee has an 'expectancy' of continued employment. *Ferguson* v. *Thomas*, 430 F. 2d 852, 856."

The facts and the judgments in all these cases, along with those of other similar cases, are sketched in chapters 2 and 3, *supra*, herein.

associations in his community. It did not base the nonrenewal of his contract on a charge, for example, that he had been guilty of dishonesty or immorality. Had it done so, this would be a different case. For 'where a person's good name, reputation, honor or integrity is at stake because of what the government is doing to him, notice and an opportunity to be heard are essential.'" (Citing *Wisconsin* v. *Constantineau*, 400 U.S. 433 (1971) and several other germane decisions.)

"To be sure, Roth has alleged that the nonrenewal of his contract was based on his exercise of his right to freedom of speech. *But this allegation is not now before us.* The District Court stayed proceedings on this issue, and Roth has yet to prove that the decision not to rehire him was, in fact, based on his free speech activities.

"Hence, on the record before us, all that clearly appears is that Roth was not rehired for one year at one university. It stretches the concept too far to suggest that a person is deprived of 'liberty' when he simply is not rehired in one job but remains as free as before to seek another. . . ."

Finally, "The important fact in this case is that the terms of the appointment specifically provided that it was to terminate on June 30, 1969. They did not provide for contract renewal absent 'sufficient cause.' Indeed, they made no provision for renewal whatsoever. . . . They supported absolutely no possible claim of entitlement to re-employment."

The judgment of the high court expressly did not decide Professor Roth's alleged rights under First Amendment freedom of speech and left the door open for a resumption of his plea on that aspect of the case. It was reported that a pre-trial conference would be held in Wisconsin on April 23, 1973, and it was thought probable that new pleadings might be filed on that phase of the action.

### The Dissenting Opinion of Mr. Justice
### William O. Douglas

A key element in understanding the dissent of Mr. Justice Douglas is his quotation, with approval, from the opinion of U.S. District Judge James E. Doyle of Wisconsin in making the first adjudication of this case:

"Substantive constitutional protection for a university professor against non-retention in violation of his First Amendment rights is useless without procedural safeguards. *I hold that minimum procedural due process includes a statement of reasons why the university intends not to retain the professor, notice of a hearing at which he may respond to the stated reasons, and a hearing if the professor appears at the appointed time and place.* At such hearing the professor must have a reasonable opportunity to submit evidence relevant to the stated reasons. The burden of going forward and the burden of proof rest with the professor. Only if he makes a reasonable showing that the stated reasons are wholly inappropriate as a basis for decision or that they are wholly without basis in fact would the university administration become obliged to show that the stated reasons are not inappropriate or that they have a basis in fact."

Said Mr. Justice Douglas: "It was this procedure that the Court of Appeals approved. 46 F. 2d 806. The Court of Appeals also concluded that though the section 1983 action was pending in court,[8] the court should stay its hand until the academic procedures had been completed. . . . That is a permissible course for District Courts to take, though it does not relieve them of the final determination whether nonrenewal of the teacher's contract was in retaliation of the exercise of First Amendment rights.

"I would affirm the judgment of the Court of Appeals."

Earlier statements in the same dissenting opinion of Mr. Justice Douglas are pertinent:

"In the case of teachers whose contracts are not renewed, tenure is not the critical issue. . . . Careful fact-finding is often necessary to know whether the given reason for nonrenewal of a teacher's contract is the real reason or a feigned one. . . .

"As we held in *Speiser* v. *Randall* (1958) 357 U.S. 513, when a state proposes to deny a privilege to one who it alleges has engaged in unprotected speech, *Due Process requires that the State bear the burden of proving that the speech was not protected.* 'The protection of the individual against arbitrary action . . . is the very essence of due

---

8. The "Section 1983" is *United States Code*, Title 42, Section 1983:

"Every person who, under color of any statute, ordinance, regulation, custom, or usage, of any State or Territory, subjects, or causes to be subjected, any citizen of the United States or other person within the jurisdiction thereof to the deprivation of any rights, privileges, or immunities secured by the Constitution and laws, shall be liable to the party injured in an action at law, suit in equity, or other proper proceeding for redress."

process.' *Slochower* v. *Board of Higher Education of the City of New York*, 350 U.S. 551 (1956); but where the State *is allowed to act secretly behind closed doors and without any notice to those who are affected by its actions, there is no check against the possibility of such 'arbitrary action.'* "

"Moreover," wrote Mr. Justice Douglas, "where 'important interests' of the citizen are implicated, they are not to be denied or taken away without *Due Process*. (Here citing recent decisions of the Supreme Court regarding arbitrary disqualification for unemployment compensation, discharge from public employment, denial of tax exemption, withdrawal of welfare benefits, and others.) *We should now add that nonrenewal of a teacher's contract, whether or not he has tenure, is an entitlement of the same importance and dignity.*

"Nonrenewal of a teacher's contract is tantamount in effect to a dismissal, and the consequences may be enormous. Nonrenewal can be a blemish that turns into a permanent scar and effectively limits any chance the teacher has of being rehired as a teacher at least in his State.

"If this nonrenewal implicated the First Amendment, then Roth was deprived of constitutional rights (a) because his employment was conditioned on a surrender of First Amendment rights and (b) because he received no notice and hearing of the adverse action contemplated against him. Without a statement of reasons for the discharge and an opportunity to rebut those reasons—both of which were refused by the university—there is no means short of a lawsuit to safeguard the right not to be discharged for the exercise of First Amendment guarantees."

A footnote comment should be interjected here from the majority opinion by Mr. Justice Potter Stewart, touching the actions of the District Court (District Judge James E. Doyle), and the Seventh Circuit Court of Appeals (Opinion by Circuit Judge Thomas E. Fairchild). "In the present case," said the District Court, "it appears that a determination as to the actual basis of decision must await amplification of the facts, at trial. . . . Summary judgment is inappropriate." Hence it temporarily stayed action on that aspect of the case, but granted summary judgment for Roth on the pure procedural due process aspect. This was affirmed by the Seventh Circuit Court of Appeals.

Commented Mr. Justice Potter Stewart: "The Court of Appeals, nonetheless, argued that opportunity for a hearing and a statement of reasons were required here 'as a prophylactic against nonretention decisions improperly motivated by exercise of protected rights.' 446 F.

2d at 810. While the Court of Appeals recognized the lack of a finding that Roth's nonretention was based on exercise of the right of free speech, it felt that Roth's interest in liberty was sufficiently implicated here because the decision not to rehire him was made 'with a background of controversy and unwelcome expressions of opinion. . . .' "

Mr. Justice Stewart concluded this comment with: "Whatever may be a teacher's rights of free speech, the interest in holding a teaching job at a state university, *simpliciter,* is not itself a free speech interest."

Compare this with excerpts from Mr. Justice Douglas' dissenting opinion already quoted, and especially with the broader statements Justice Douglas made in his opening paragraphs:

*"No more direct assault on academic freedom can be imagined than for the school authorities to be allowed to discharge a teacher because of his or her philosophical, political, or ideological beliefs. . . .* Mr. Justice Frankfurter stated the constitutional theory in *Sweezy* v. *New Hampshire,* 354 U.S. 234, 261-262, concurring opinion (1957):

" 'Insights into the mysteries of nature are born of hypothesis and speculation. The more so is this true in the pursuit of understanding in the groping endeavors of what are called the social sciences, the concern of which is man and society. . . . For society's good—if understanding be an essential need of society—inquiries into these problems, speculations about them, stimulation in others of reflections upon them, must be left as unfettered as possible. Political power must abstain from intrusion into the activity of freedom, pursued in the interest of wise government and the people's well-being, except for reasons that are exigent and obviously compelling.'

"We repeated that warning in *Keyishian* v. *Board of Regents,* 385 U.S. 589, 603 (1967): 'Our Nation is deeply committed to the safeguarding of academic freedom, which is of transcendent value to all of us and not merely to the teachers concerned. That freedom is therefore a special concern of the First Amendment, which does not tolerate laws that cast a pall of orthodoxy over the classroom.' "

### The Dissenting Opinions of Justices Thurgood Marshall and William J. Brennan

The differences between the views of Justice Stewart and Justice Thurgood Marshall related to the definition and scope of "liberty" and "property" as used in the due process clause of the Fourteenth Amendment. In his dissenting opinion, Mr. Justice Marshall said:

"This Court has often had occasion to note that the denial of public employment is a serious blow to any citizen. . . . Thus, when an application for public employment is denied or the contract of a public employee is not renewed, *the government must say why*, for it is only when the reasons underlying government action are known that citizens feel secure and protected against arbitrary government action. . . ."

Here Mr. Justice Marshall quoted from the 1964 opinion of the Fifth Circuit Court of Appeals in *Hornsby* v. *Allen*, 326 F. 2d 610: "The public has the right to expect its officers . . . to make adjudications on the basis of merit. The first step toward insuring that these expectation are realized is to require adherence to the standards of due process; *absolute and uncontrolled discretion invites abuse*." These were the words of the eminent Chief Circuit Judge Elbert Parr Tuttle, of the Fifth Circuit.

Continued Mr. Justice Marshall: "It may be argued that to provide procedural due process to all public employees or prospective employees would place an intolerable burden on the machinery of government. . . . The short answer to that argument is that *it is not burdensome to give reasons when reasons exist*. . . .

"It is only where the government acts improperly that procedural due process is truly burdensome. And that is precisely when it is most necessary. . . . A requirement of procedural regularity at least renders arbitrary action more difficult." Here he quoted from the 1963 Supreme Court opinion in *Silver* v. *New York Stock Exchange*, 373 U.S. 341, 366: "Experience teaches . . . that the affording of procedural safeguards, which by their nature serve to illuminate the underlying facts, in itself operates to prevent erroneous decisions on the merits from occurring." The quoted words are those of Mr. Justice Arthur J. Goldberg.

Mr. Justice William J. Brennan wrote a dissenting opinion in which he was joined by Mr. Justice William O. Douglas, and in which he dealt with both cases (*Roth* and *Sindermann*). The point of his dissent is therefore best observed after we have digested *Sindermann*, to which we now turn.

*The Decision in the* Sindermann *Case Held That Lack of*
*a Contractual or Tenure Right to Re-employment,*
*Taken Alone, Does Not Defeat a Claim That*
*Non-renewal Violates the First and*
*Fourteenth Amendments*

After briefly sketching the facts alleged in the *Sindermann* case, which originated at Odessa Junior College in Texas, where Professor Sindermann's contract was not renewed, Mr. Justice Potter Stewart, writing for the majority of the Court, opened the first section of his opinion with a positive holding:

"The first question presented is whether Sindermann's lack of a contractual or tenure right of re-employment, taken alone, defeats his claim that the nonrenewal of his contract violated the First and Fourteenth Amendments. We hold that it does not."[9]

Justice Stewart documented this by explaining: ". . . There are some reasons upon which the government may not act. It may not deny a benefit to a person on a basis that infringes his constitutionally protected interests—especially, his interest in freedom of speech. . . ." Here he cited many prior decisions of the high court (mostly judgments striking down overbroad and too-restrictive "loyalty oath" statutes of various states).[10] He pointed out that the principle is applied without regard to the exact nature of the contractual or other claim to the job, as evidenced by comparison, for example, of *Pickering* v. *Board* with *Shelton* v. *Tucker*.

"Indeed," he said, "twice before this Court has specifically held that the nonrenewal of a nontenured public school teacher's one-year contract may not be predicated on his exercise of First and Fourteenth Amendment rights. (Citing *Shelton* v. *Tucker* and *Keyishian* v. *Regents*.) We reaffirm those holdings here.

---

9. *Charles R. Perry* v. *Robert P. Sindermann*, (U.S. S. Ct., No. 70-36), 40 *U.S. Law Week* 5087 (June 29, 1972).

10. *Wieman* v. *Updegraff*, 344 U.S. 183, 192 (1952); *Shelton* v. *Tucker*, 364 U.S. 479, 485-486 (1960); *Cramp* v. *Board of Public Instruction*, 368 U.S. 278, 288 (1961); *Baggett* v. *Bullitt*, 377 U.S. 360 (1964); *Elfbrandt* v. *Russell*, 384 U.S. 17 (1966); *Keyishian* v. *Regents*, 385 U.S. 589, 605-606 (1967); *Whitehall* v. *Elkins*, 389 U.S. 54 (1967); and *Pickering* v. *Board of Education*, 391 U.S. 563 (1968).

The last-named case is discussed herein in Chapter 8 and elsewhere. All the others cited are discussed or mentioned herein, chiefly in Chapter 9, which carries forward the story of "the loyalty oath furor."

"Sindermann has alleged that his non-retention was based on his testimony before legislative committees and his other public statements critical of the Regents' policies. . . . Plainly, these allegations present a *bona fide* constitutional claim . . . (citing *Pickering*). For this reason we hold that the grant of summary judgment against Sindermann, without full exploration of this issue, was improper." Thus he ended the first section of the opinion on a positive and progressive note.

### A New Concept of "De Facto Tenure"

Beginning the second section of the opinion of the majority, Mr. Justice Potter Stewart continued:

Sindermann's lack of formal contractual or tenure security in continued employment at Odessa Junior College, though irrelevant to his free speech claim, is highly relevant to his procedural due process claim. But it may not be entirely dispositive.

"We have held today in *Regents* v. *Roth* that the Constitution does not require opportunity for a hearing before the nonrenewal of a non-tenured teacher's contract, unless he can show that the decision not to rehire him somehow deprived him of an interest in 'liberty' or that he had a 'property' interest in continued employment, despite the lack of tenure or a formal contract. . . . Sindermann has yet to show that he has been deprived of an interest that could invoke procedural due process protection. As in *Roth*, the mere showing that he was not rehired in one particular job, without more, did not amount to a showing of a loss of liberty. Nor did it amount to a showing of a loss of property.

"But Sindermann's allegations—which we must construe most favorably to him at this stage of the litigation—do raise a genuine issue as to his interest in continued employment at Odessa Junior College. He alleged that this interest, though not secured by a formal contractual tenure provision, was secured by a no less binding understanding fostered by the college administration. In particular, Sindermann alleged that the college had a *de facto* tenure program, and that he had tenure under that program. He claimed that he and others legitimately relied upon an unusual provision that had been in the college's official *Faculty Guide* for many years:

" '*Teacher Tenure*: Odessa College has no tenure system. The administration of the College wishes the faculty member to feel that he has permanent tenure as long as his teaching services are satisfactory and as long as he displays a cooperative attitude toward his co-workers and his superiors, and as long as he is happy in his work."

"Thus Sindermann offered to prove that a teacher with his long period of service at this particular public college had no less a 'property' interest in continued employment than a formally tenured teacher at other colleges, and had no less procedural due process right to a statement of reasons and a hearing before college officials upon their decision not to retain him.

"Just as this Court has found there to be a 'common law' of a particular industry or of a particular plant that may supplement a collective bargaining agreement, *Steelworkers* v. *Warrior & Gulf Company*, 363 U.S. 574 (1960), so there may be an unwritten 'common law' in a particular university that certain employees shall have the equivalent of tenure. This is particularly likely in a college or university like Odessa Junior College, that has no explicit tenure system even for senior members of its faculty, but that nonetheless may have created such a system in practice."

At this point Justice Stewart placed a footnote to emphasize that the question is a matter of state law, saying "If it is the law of Texas that a teacher in Sindermann's position has no contractual or other claim to job tenure, Sindermann's claim would be defeated."

Concluding the opinion of the court, Mr. Justice Stewart added: "We disagree with the Court of Appeals insofar as it held that a mere subjective 'expectancy' is protected by procedural due process, but we agree that Sindermann must be given an opportunity to prove the legitimacy of his claim to such entitlement in light of 'the policies and practices of the institution.'

". . . Proof of such a property interest would not, of course, entitle him to reinstatement. But such proof would obligate college officials to grant a hearing at his request, where he could be informed of the grounds for his nonretention and challenge their sufficiency.

"Therefore, while we do not wholly agree with the opinion of the Court of Appeals, its judgment remanding the case to the District Court is affirmed."

As noted earlier herein, this case was settled out of court in December 1972, with Odessa Junior College paying Robert P. Sindermann $48,000 for back pay and attorneys' fees, and offering him reinstatement as a faculty member, which he declined.

*Apparently These Decisions Would Relegate Faculty
Members to State Courts on the Narrow Issue of
"Reasons and Hearing" Where No Violation of
Substantive Constitutional Rights Such as Free
Expression Is Alleged*

Not only did Mr. Justice Stewart emphasize that Sindermann's contractual status was a matter of Texas law; the same point was also strongly stressed by the Chief Justice in his brief concurring opinion with the two cases, already quoted in part earlier in this chapter under the rubric, "What the U.S. Supreme Court decided, and what it did not." The remainder of Mr. Chief Justice Burger's words were:

"Thus whether a particular teacher in a particular context has any right to such administrative hearing hinges on a question of state law. . . .

"Because the availability of the Fourteenth Amendment right to a prior administrative hearing turns in each case on a question of state law, the issue of abstention will arise in future cases contesting whether a particular teacher is entitled to a hearing prior to renewal of his contract. If relevant state contract law is unclear, a federal court should, in my view, abstain from deciding whether he is constitutionally entitled to a prior hearing, and the teacher should be left to resort to state courts on the questions arising under state law."

With all respect to the Chief Justice and to the Court, it must be noted that abstention would almost certainly decelerate the rate of progressive change in this crucial area of the law, and that it is indeed a standstill conservative view.

Needless to say, it is diametrically opposed to the conclusions of the three dissenting Justices in these cases, which were expressed in a brief dissenting opinion applying to both cases by Mr. Justice William J. Brennan, in which he was joined by Mr. Justice William O. Douglas, and in which he expressed agreement with the opinion of Mr. Justice Thurgood Marshall:

"Although I agree with Part I of the Court's opinion in *Sindermann*, I also agree with my Brother Marshall that Roth and Sindermann were denied due process when their contracts were not renewed and they were not informed of the reasons and given an opportunity to respond. Since Roth and Sindermann were entitled to summary judgment on that issue, I would affirm the judgment of the Court of Appeals in

*Roth,* and, to the extent indicated by my Brother Marshall, I would modify the judgment of the Court of Appeals in *Sindermann.*"

In his dissent in *Sindermann,* Mr. Justice Thurgood Marshall said, "When the government knows it may have to justify its decisions with sound reasons, its conduct is likely to be more cautious, careful, and correct," and "I would modify the judgment of the Court of Appeals to direct the District Court to enter summary judgment for Sindermann entitling him to a statement of reasons why his contract was not renewed and a hearing on disputed issues of fact."

Thus stood the judgment of the high tribunal, with five of the Justices taking the conservative stance on this issue, and three of the Justices on the progressive side, in mid-1972; and the issue could scarcely be said to have been permanently settled. One who has any acquaintance with the law of a generation ago, or even of a decade ago, must know that the litigation in many lower federal courts during the past seven years has exhibited a slowly accelerating tendency toward the progressive vision of the three dissenting Justices. Such a trend, even if slowed down for a time, is almost certain to continue eventually, as inevitable political, social, and economic changes occur.[11]

### "Justice Delayed Is Justice Denied"

Finally, contemplate again that each of these two cases was sent back to its respective U.S. District Court for trial of the facts, although apparently both cases had been in course of litigation for approximately three years. How many more months or years may elapse before the litigants learn what the outcome is can only be a matter of conjecture. Possibly one beneficial result of these two decisions in mid-1972 by a sharply divided U.S. Supreme Court will be to alert more members of the great body of U.S. Circuit Judges and U.S. District Judges throughout the nation, as well as judges of state courts, as to both the novelty and the significance of the issues involved, and thus tend to reduce the

---

11. Late in 1972 the press reported that the Sindermann case had been settled out of court, with Odessa College paying Professor Sindermann $48,000 to cover back pay and attorneys' fees, and offering him reinstatement, which he declined.

One of Sindermann's lawyers has been quoted as speaking somewhat irreverently of the *Roth* and *Sindermann* decisions of the Supreme Court as having "taken a situation where the lower courts were in confusion and, in two relatively brief opinions, turned confusion into utter chaos."

number of too-hasty summary judgments which often lead to years of litigation with its accompanying long-drawn suspense and uncertainty, expensive in many ways—not only in money but in deleterious effects upon the progress of public higher education.

# CHAPTER 5

## TENURE; PROMOTION; SALARIES;
## LEAVES OF ABSENCE;
## "MOONLIGHTING"

Decisions of the higher courts regarding the administration of faculty tenure rules in universities and colleges are not numerous. A few involving discharges for cause, not apparently of any earth-shaking significance, appear in Chapter 6 herein.

The subject of academic promotions is generally not a suitable one for adjudication in the courts. A small quota of disputes about salaries, mostly of trivial consequence, always appears.

Leaves of absence are of numerous types, including, among others, "sabbaticals" and maternity leaves. This area gradually becomes more important as the whole complex of "fringe benefits" for faculty members, already substantial, seems destined to grow in the interest of a better quality of educational service.

A perennial and largely unsolved question is that of what constitutes appropriate and inappropriate "outside work" for professors, meaning part-time employment either related or unrelated to their regular university or college work. Of course the cardinal rule is that it must not be excessive in quantity or such as to create a "conflict of interest" or otherwise interfere with the professor's proper discharge of his contracted obligation to the institution. Myriads of other related questions can and do arise.

### Junior College Teacher in California Who Had Taught Equivalent of Full Load for 10 Years, on "Hourly Basis," Ordered to Be Given Tenure as Full-Time Employee, Retroactive to 1965

Zelda X. Vittal was a part-time teacher of English as a second language at Long Beach City College (a public junior college) continuously after the academic year 1956-57. Each year from 1959 she sought to be given tenure as a permanent employee, appealing to the deans successively and the president without avail, and finally to the teachers' association. She was on an "hourly basis" and taught more than 75 per cent of the hours of a full-time teacher, but less than 75 per cent of the days of the school year. There was undisputed evidence that for 10 years she had carried a "teacher load" equivalent to or greater than the permanent teachers in the same program. In September of 1967 her hours of teaching were reduced by half, allegedly to punish her for asserting her claim and to prejudice her chances of being given the status of a permanent employee.

The trial court found the allegation to be true, and called the board's action "capricious and without justification." The court of appeals agreed, and ordered the college to classify her as a full-time permanent employee as of the year 1967, retroactive to September, 1965.[1] Apparently her petition for arrearages in salary was not granted.

The case is illustrative of a nationally widespread need for college governing boards and administrations to be considerate in adjusting the status and perquisites of part-time faculty members; especially those who render long, regular, and continuous service.

### State Tenure Acts in Arizona and Michigan Not Applicable to Junior Colleges

Teachers' tenure statutes enacted by state legislatures to apply to

---

1. *Zelda X. Vittal* v. *Long Beach Unified School District*, 8 Cal. App. 3d 112, 87 Cal. Rptr. 319 (1970).

all elementary and secondary school districts, or to selected classes of such districts, generally are irrelevant in higher education. (The nine Wisconsin State Universities are an exception.) In universities and four-year colleges, a tenure plan for faculty members, if it exists, generally rests upon a set of rules or ordinances adopted by the governing board of the particular institution.

Public junior colleges in their earlier days were sometimes regarded as extensions of secondary education, but certainly not as "high schools" or "elementary schools," and hence were often excluded by the explicit wording of statewide tenure statutes. In a sense, they were "neither fish nor fowl"; but they are now universally regarded as units of higher education. There is a tendency, especially in California, for them to drop the adjective "junior," and to abandon the later and more popular "community college" designation, and to be named simply "college," as in "Solano College." There is also a tendency to establish for state-wide networks of two-year colleges a state board to which statutory powers of governance are given to varying extents. Where the local public two-year colleges also have local boards of trustees (actual governing bodies, not mere advisory boards), there is thus a division of the powers of governance between the state and local levels. This situation is illustrated by a 1972 case in Arizona courts.

Dr. Dean L. Sinclair was hired May 4, 1970, to teach physical sciences for the academic year 1970-71 at Pima College in Arizona. The president of the college notified him in writing on March 11, 1971, that his contract would not be renewed for the year 1971-72, without stating any reasons. Sinclair's petition to the local trial court for a writ of mandamus to command the issuance of a new contract for 1971-72 was granted, and this judgment was affirmed by the Arizona court of appeals.[2]

Although each junior college had its own "county board of governors," retaining substantial powers of governance, a state statute (*Arizona Revised Statutes*, section 15-600) authorized the State Board of Directors for Junior Colleges to "enact ordinances for the government of the institutions under its jurisdiction"; and that board had adopted in 1961 a resolution directing county boards of governors to "establish and implement a policy" embodying the essentials of a tenure system. (This resolution is quoted in full in connection with the case of *Kaufman* v.

---

2. *Pima College* v. *Sinclair*, (Ariz. App.), 496 P. 2d 639 (1972).

*Pima Junior College Governing Board,* discussed *infra* in Chapter 12, "The President; Administrative Staff; Board Members.")

Officers of Pima College testified that Pima College had not devised any set of tenure rules of its own, but that it complied with that directive in a sense by simply adhering generally to the provisions of the state teachers' tenure statute, *except* that the college established March 1 as the notification date, instead of March 15, as in the statute. Pima's handbook for the faculty stated: "A faculty member who wishes to teach at Pima College after the termination of a contract year may assume he is invited to do so unless he is notified to the contrary by the president of the college prior to March 1 of the contract year." With these features of the case clearly stated, the trial court and the court of appeals were in agreement that Sinclair's contract was automatically renewed March 1, 1971, by operation of law, "even though Pima College has no formally adopted tenure policy"; and the writ of mandamus he asked for was properly issued.

The reasoning in this case bears resemblance to the theory of "*de facto* tenure" suggested by Mr. Justice Potter Stewart of the United States Supreme Court in the June 29, 1972, disposition of the case of *Charles R. Perry* v. *Robert P. Sindermann,* discussed *supra* herein in Chapter 4. It can be said that the idea of *de facto* tenure represents an advance toward a humane and equitable stance toward faculty members. The earlier tendency of most courts was to adhere unimaginatively to the blackletter of the pertinent formal ordinances of college governing boards: "No tenure ordinance, no tenure."

A contemporary Michigan case is entangled with the additional complication of "teacher certification." This kind of credentialing is universally required for teaching in public elementary and high schools, but never for teaching in universities and four-year colleges. Here again, there has been some temporary confusion in coming to a clear conclusion as to where the junior colleges belong.

Hazel C. Shaw was Coordinator of Nursing at the Macomb County Junior College in Michigan from February 1965 through June 1967. In 1969 she began an action for damages for breach of contract, relying on the state Tenure Act. The act applied only to "certificated" teachers. There was no provision for "certification" of junior college teachers. The attorney general had ruled that the State Board of Education could not validly promulgate rules on that subject. (*Michigan O.A.G., 1961-62,* No. 3478, p. 239.) The Tenure Act did not apply to institutions organized under the Community College Act of 1966. The State Board of Education had statutory authority to define "certificated," and it had defined it as "a person who holds a certificate valid for the position to which he is assigned." Therefore it was immaterial that Shaw held a certificate for all subjects in grades 7 and 8, and health and social science in grades 9 through 12.

Even if it had been cognizable under the Tenure Act, the suit for damages would have failed because the Tenure Act authorizes no remedy except reinstatement and back pay. For these reasons the trial court's judgement of dismissal was affirmed by the Michigan court of appeals.[3]

### Denying Tenure to College Teachers Because They Are Aliens Violates the "Equal Protection Clause" of the Fourteenth Amendment

Mohammed Younus and Pete Alexopoulos, respectively citizens of India and Greece, were admitted for permanent residence in the United States in 1967 and 1968. They became teachers in Southwest College, one of the units of the Chicago City College system (officially Junior College District No. 508, Cook County, Illinois), and became eligible for tenure in September 1970 and February 1971.

They alleged in U.S. District Court that the chairmen of their respective departments recommended tenure for them, and that the president of their college concurred. They were denied tenure solely because they were aliens. This was in accord with Paragraph 3 of Appendix D of an agreement with the Cook County Teachers' Union, Local 1600; but at the time of trial this item had been superseded in a new agreement which stipulated that in such cases the Board would make its decision on tenure by December 31, 1971. This, even if the decisions were favorable, said District Judge Bernard M. Decker, did not make their case moot or give them relief, because each had been deprived of the benefits of tenure for a considerable time after his date of eligibility, solely for an unconstitutional reason. It is well established that this kind of discrimination against aliens is in violation of the equal protection

---

3. *Shaw* v. *Board of Trustees of Macomb County Community College,* 37 Mich. App. 96, 194 N.W. 2d 558 (1971).

clause of the Fourteenth Amendment, and "has no rational relationship
to any legitimate state end."

Therefore Judge Decker ordered that Younus and Alexopoulos be
awarded all privileges which accompany tenure status, including extra
pay, retroactive to their respective dates of eligibility and up to December 31, 1971.[4]

### Academic Promotions Are Not Ordinarily Justiciable

"The judiciary is not the appropriate forum for decisions involving
academic rank. A professor's value depends upon his creativity, his rapport with students and colleagues, his teaching ability, and numerous
other intangible qualities which can not be measured by objective standards." Thus wrote U.S. District Judge Bernard M. Decker in his opinion granting summary judgment to Chicago State College in the case
where Cary B. Lewis, a black associate professor of business administration, sought an order to promote him to full professor, alleging racial
discrimination.

Recommendations for promotion originate in the departments, and
go thence to the APTS faculty committee, which reviews them and
forwards its suggestions to the president of the institution. He screens
them and presents his recommendations to the Board of Governors of
State Colleges and Universities, which makes the final decisions. In 1967
the APTS committee recommended Lewis and four white associate professors be promoted to full professors. The president returned all five,
asking the committee "to examine the criteria for such promotions . . .
and also to study the issues relating to the appropriate number and percentage of full professors." The committee resubmitted two of the original names, but did not include Lewis.

The next year, the APTS committee's recommendations did not
include Lewis, but they successfully recommended that another black
associate professor be promoted to full professor.

Lewis had been an associate professor for 6 years, and had been
at the college 11 years. Of the other 41 associate professors, 7 had been
in that rank for as long or longer than Lewis, and 5 had been employed
by the college for longer than 11 years. One had been at the college 15
years, and 9 years in his present rank. All these having longer service

---

4. *Younus* v. *Shabat*, (U.S.D.C., Ill.), 336 F. Supp. 1137 (1971).

and more time in rank were white. In 1969, 25 of the 297 faculty members were black, including 2 full professors out of 39, 2 associate professors out of 45, 14 assistant professors out of 119, 3 instructors out of 70, and 4 faculty assistants out of 24.

The opinion contains a good deal more statistical information of this type, and also mentions affidavits submitted by the president and all 10 members of the APTS committee for 1967 and 1968, affirming that their actions concerning Lewis were unrelated to his race; that his race was never mentioned; but that "while Professor Lewis was a valuable member of the faculty he did not meet the criteria established by the APTS committee and the president of the college for elevation to full professor."

The court found no convincing evidence of racial discrimination in the case before it, and granted summary judgment for the college.[5] For another case involving promotion, with an averment of discrimination on the ground of sex, see Chapter 7, *infra*.

## Oregon State Board of Higher Education Has Wide Discretionary Elbow-Room as to Salary Scales

William Vandever was hired in September 1964 as TV-radio producer-director in the Division of Continuing Education (of the Oregon State System of Higher Education) at station KOAP-TV at Portland. His written notice of appointment said he would have the academic rank of instructor at the yearly salary of $7,500 (later corrected to $7,200). Each year thereafter he was reappointed with the rank of assistant professor, and given merit increases in salary, but no tenure.

His salary was at all times less than the minimum specified for an assistant professor in the Board's general classification and compensation plan. In June 1968 he discovered this for the first time, and made efforts to have his salary increased. Finally refused by the chancellor of the system in January 1970, he sued for a declaratory judgment as to the power of the Board, injunctive relief, and a money judgment for additional salary allegedly due.

In the Oregon court of appeals Judge Robert Y. Thornton, after scrutinizing the applicable statutes, concluded that it was the plain legislative intent to give the Board wider discretion than other state

---

5. *Lewis* v. *Chicago State College*, (U.S.D.C., Ill), 299 F. Supp. 1357 (1969).

agencies in the management of its unclassified personnel; and that the Board had specific authority to adopt, as it did in 1956, a regulation allowing it to make exceptions to its general plan. Accordingly, it was within its powers in hiring Vandever at a salary less than the general minimum for his rank.[6]

### "Intent of the Parties" Is the Cardinal Rule for Interpretation of Contracts; and in a Rare Case It Governs Even When the Agreement Does Not Specify Salary

At the Detroit Institute of Technology (a private institution), an assistant professor of economics and finance was appointed for the year 1959-60 at a salary of $5,800. Each year thereafter up to 1965 he entered into a new contract, with a salary increase. In 1965 he was given a two-year contract, which he accepted April 28, in which the words were: "Salary for 1965-66 will be $7,500. Salary for academic year 1966-67 will be reviewed at a later date." In August 1966, after considerable oral and written communication about his prospective salary, he received a letter from President Dewey F. Barich terminating his employment on the ground that he had no contract.

The Wayne County circuit court held that he had no contract for academic year 1966-67 because no salary was specified. In the Michigan Court of Appeals, Presiding Judge T. M. Burns reversed this judgment, and held that in view of the past practices between the parties, and their obvious intent when they agreed to the two-year contract, that contract was valid for the academic year 1966-67 and made mandatory a salary of at least $7,500. He also directed the lower court to determine any damages in excess of one year's salary which the facts and the law might justify.[7]

### Board Rule Increasing Credit for Prior Teaching Experience on Salary Scale Need Not Be Retroactive

Donald B. Sayre was employed as a teacher by the Coalinga College

6. *Vandever* v. *State Board of Higher Education,* (Ore. App.), 491 P. 2d 1198 (1971).

7. *Bruno* v. *Detroit Institute of Technology,* (Mich. App.), 193 N.W. 2d 322 (1971).

District in California for the academic year 1963-64. He had 12 years of prior teaching experience. He was given five years' credit for this experience and placed on the sixth step of the district's salary schedule, because at that time five years was the maximum credit allowed for prior teaching experience. Thereafter, along with other teachers, he advanced one step each year, so that he was in the seventh step for the year 1964-65.

But in 1964 the board of trustees changed its rule and increased the maximum credit from five years to nine years. This was deemed desirable to facilitate the recruiting of experienced teachers. The change was not retroactive, and did not apply to teachers employed prior to the 1964-65 academic year. If it had been retroactive, it would have placed Sayre on the tenth step instead of the seventh step for that year.

He asked for a writ of mandate to compel the board to reclassify him and place him in the tenth step for 1964-65, and pay him the additional compensation he would have received if he had been properly classified. His petition was denied by Judge Kenneth Andreen of the superior court of Fresno County, and the judgment was affirmed by the court of appeal, in an opinion by Associate Justice Roy J. Gargano with Presiding Justice Frederick E. Stone concurring.[8]

### A Claim for Salary Is a "Property or Monetary Claim" Not Actionable in Federal Courts Under Civil Rights Act (28 U.S. Code 1343)

Man M. Kochhar, a native of the Punjab in India and an associate professor in the school of pharmacy at Auburn University, alleged "grave injustice" to himself and to a female laboratory assistant, saying that the University authorities, on the basis of unfounded and untrue rumors (apparently of misconduct), and without any hearing, decreased his salary from $14,352 for 1968-69 to $13,800 for 1969-70. He sued in the U.S. District Court as for deprivation of a civil right.

Chief District Judge Frank M. Johnson, Jr., responded: "Kochhar's complaint seeks protection of a 'property right' and not a 'civil right' within the meaning of 28 *U.S. Code*, sec. 1343, and thus fails to allege any basis for federal jurisdiction under that jurisdictional statute." Also,

---

8. *Sayre v. Board of Trustees of Coalinga College District*, (Cal. App.), 88 Cal. Rptr. 355 (1970).

the amount of money involved was apparently less than the $10,000 minimum required to invoke federal jurisdiction.[9]

A quotation from the Seventh Circuit U.S. Court of Appeals, by Chief Circuit Judge John S. Hastings sitting with Circuit Judges Thomas E. Fairchild and Roger J. Kiley, in a Wisconsin state income tax case involving payment by residents of other states, supports Judge Johnson's conclusion: "Thus far, at least, it is quite clear that the courts have generally treated this statute, (28 *U.S.C.* 1343) as applicable to personal liberty rather than to a property or monetary claim."[10]

### New York State's One-Year Moratorium on Sabbatical Leaves Caused Annoying Complications

At the City University of New York the recognized bargaining agency representing the senior faculties (named the Legislative Conference) was party to an agreement providing (Article XXVI) that the Board of Higher Education would designate $1 million to fund sabbatical leaves. The agreement (Article XIV) gave the right to *apply* for sabbatical leave, and stated that the granting of sabbatical leave should not be in any sense automatic. Final decision in each instance would lie with the Board of Higher Education.

Applications from faculty members were presented to the Board in April 1971. On May 3 the Board denied all applications because on April 12 the state legislature had enacted a measure stipulating that no leave of absence or sabbatical leave should be granted to any public officer or employee, for a period of one year commencing July 1, 1971. The applicants thereupon sued for an order staying the Board from refusing to grant the leaves in accord with their collective agreement.

Justice Isidore Dollinger of the New York County supreme court summarily dismissed the complaint. The contention that the applications had been collated, with other routine matters, in the "chancellor's report" during April for presentation to the Board, and that the Board's action on this bundle of routine was no more than *pro forma*, had no merit. A Board rule of April 26, 1965, specified that any Board member could have any item removed from the chancellor's report and placed on the policy calendar by a simple request to the chairman of the Board. This is a general practice in matters of this type.

---

9. *Kochhar* v. *Auburn University*, (U.S.D.C., Ala.), 304 F. Supp. 565 (1969).
10. (U.S.C.A., Wis.), 371 F. 2d 172 (1966).

Moreover, there was a failure to prove that approvals had actually been obtained from the presidents of the respective colleges of the university prior to April 12, the effective date of the moratorium act. Therefore the opinion of the state Director of the Budget that any approval of a sabbatical leave given by an authorized university officer prior to April 12 resulted in a contractual right, not within the scope of the prohibitory act, was of no weight in this case.

Justice Dollinger was empathetic: "The court is cognizant of the fact that many of the people involved had made plans and expended large sums of money on the basis of having been approved for such sabbaticals by their superiors. Nevertheless, the final approval had to be made by the board. The court is also mindful of the fact that these people may suffer severe economic hardship because of the board's denial. While the equities may favor the plaintiff, the board under said moratorium had no choice but to follow the law and deny said sabbaticals."[11]

A parallel case involving public school teachers below the college level was adjudicated by Justice Bertram Harnett of the Nassau County supreme court. Here the bargaining agreement between the Plainedge Federation of Teachers and the school board specified that "the Superintendent shall make every effort to approve not less than two per cent of the teaching staff," but nowhere was the board bound to grant any sabbaticals whatever. The agreement specifically reserved to the board the right to reject any or all applications.

The petitioner in this instance filed his application March 30, 1971. The superintendent recommended approval and transmitted it to the board (but apparently not before April 12). On June 14, mindful of the moratorium, the board rejected all applications. Said Justice Harnett: "Petitioner had no vested right on April 12, 1971 to a sabbatical leave. The board is barred from giving him a sabbatical leave this year. Accordingly, this proceeding must be dismissed on the merits."[12]

## "Return or Repay" Agreement on Sabbatical Leave Is Enforceable

Gerd W. Ehrlich, an assistant professor of social science at Essex

---

11. *Legislative Conference of the City University of New York. v. Board of Higher Education*, 324 N.Y.S. 2d 924 (1971).

12. *Ewen v. Board of Education of Union Free School District No. 18, Town of Oyster Bay*, 323 N.Y.S. 2d 789 (1971).

Community College in Maryland from 1957 to 1964, applied for a sabbatical leave for the academic year 1964-65. In the letter granting the request, President Moses Koch wrote: "Any person to whom sabbatical leave is granted shall be required to agree to return to the service of Essex Community College for at least one year following expiration of his leave. Should the teacher not return, he will be required to return the money granted for sabbatical leave." Ehrlich accepted by letter April 1.

He took graduate courses at Johns Hopkins University during his sabbatical, took another year of leave without pay for 1965-66, and in March 1966 wrote to the president that he would not be returning to Essex. President Koch responded that he could still return to the position he held when he departed. Meantime, it seems that Koch had appointed another political scientist to be head of the department of social science, and Ehrlich was disgruntled at this because there had been an oral understanding that he would return as acting head.

In the Baltimore County circuit court the college was given a summary judgment for $4,750 (the amount he had been paid while on leave) against Ehrlich, as for willful violation of contract. No accessory agreement was adequately alleged or proven (and even if it were, it would seem to be rendered ineffective by the well-known parol evidence rule). The judgment was affirmed by the Maryland Court of Appeals.[13]

### Compensation While on Maternity Leave Can Not Be Paid Retroactively In New York State

Christine Antonopoulou, a lecturer at Queens College of the City University of New York, was given maternity leave for the academic year 1969-70. In January 1970 she asked to be allowed to resume her work for the Spring semester, but by letter of February 17 the acting dean of faculty refused that request. On April 27 the United Federation of College Teachers filed a "Step Two Grievance" in her behalf, pursuant to its agreement with the Board of Higher Education. May 8 the second-step hearing was held before the chancellor of the City University, and on May 12 he directed that she be restored to employment with pay retroactive to February 1.

---

13. *Ehrlich* v. *Board of Education of Baltimore County*, (Md.), 263 A. 2d 853 (1970).

The City Comptroller rejected this direction and refused to approve payment, on the theory that this would constitute a gift of public funds and thus would violate Article VIII, Section 1, of the New York State Constitution, since no services had been performed. In the local supreme court, Justice Francis J. Bloustein conceded that the process by which the settlement was reached should be accorded dignity, but said, "If the arbitrator exceeds his power or if the award or grievance settlement contravenes public policy, it can not be enforced"; and "in essence, her right to compensation depends upon work performed and she can not recover except for services actually rendered."[14]

### University Regulation of "Outside Work" of Professors
### Can Not Be Capricious or Discriminatory

The Board of Trustees of State Institutions of Higher Learning in Mississippi adopted on November 17, 1966, a rule regarding faculty "moonlighting":

"Outside employment, or practice of profession, by members of faculty and staff of the several institutions of higher learning is authorized provided

(1) that it does not interfere with the regular work of the employee,

(2) that it is in reasonable amount,

(3) that it does not bring discredit to the institution and that it does not bring the employee into antagonism with his colleagues, community, or the State of Mississippi, including this Board,

(4) that the official connection of the employee with the institution of higher learning is not used in connection with such employment, and

(5) employees wishing to engage in such employment or practice shall submit applications to their respective executive heads of institutions for approval before beginning or continuing such activity."

The foregoing probably does not differ greatly from what good sense and ordinary courtesy would require, nor from the customs and practices in many universities and colleges; but litigation under it reached the Fifth Circuit Court of Appeals because it was alleged that it was being administered in a discriminatory manner against certain professors of law in the University of Mississippi Law School to prevent

---

14. *Antonopoulou* v. *Beame*, 67 Misc. 2d 851, 325 N.Y.S. 2d 12 (1971).

them from devoting small fractions of their time to legal services for the poor, in the North Mississippi Rural Legal Services Program, financed by the federal Office of Economic Opportunity.

The professors concerned were told they had the option of ceasing this type of legal aid work or of losing their places on the faculty. It appeared that other law professors in the same faculty were allowed to engage in a variety of part-time remunerative practice, none of which related to the OEO. The District Court held for the university, but was reversed in an opinion by Circuit Judge Bryan Simpson. With him on the Fifth Circuit panel were Circuit Judge Robert A. Ainsworth, Jr., and District Judge Lansing L. Mitchell.

"It appears clear that the only reason for making a decision adverse (to the professors) was that they wished to continue to represent clients who tended to be unpopular. This is a distinction that can not be constitutionally upheld." These were the words of Circuit Judge Simpson for the majority of the court.[15] District Judge Mitchell dissented.

### Part-Time Local Public Office Is Generally Compatible with Professorship in State College or University

An associate professor of education at Lamar State College of Technology in Texas was elected a member of the Council of the City of Beaumont. When his vote in the Council was responsible for the enactment of a hotly contested zoning ordinance, someone pointed to Article 16, paragraph 40, of the Constitution of Texas, which forbids any person to hold "two civil offices of emolument."

The court of civil appeals took the matter calmly and decided it correctly: "The office of City Councilman is a civil office of emolument. Hybarger is an employee of a state-supported school and paid with funds derived from taxation; however, a professorship is not a public office."[16] That a professorship, or an administrative post in a state college or university is not a civil office, has been the law in every state for many decades. All are employees of the institutional governing board.

---

15. *Trister* v. *University of Mississippi*, (U.S.C.A., Miss.), 420 F. 2d 499 (1969).
16. *Tilley* v. *Rogers*, (Tex. Civ. App.), 405 S.W. 2d 220 (1966).

## When a Professor Becomes a "Public Figure," the Chances of Maintaining a Libel Suit Against a Detractor Are Greatly Diminished

In the landmark case of *New York Times Company* v. *Sullivan* (1964), the U.S. Supreme Court held that a public official can not recover damages for defamatory statements against him unless he can prove that they were written with knowledge of their falsity or with reckless disregard of their truth or falsity.[17] Soon the principle was broadened to include not only public officials, but also other persons who could properly be called "public figures" by reason of being in the limelight and being widely known for one reason or another.

Thus in 1965 the Supreme Court decided that the head football coach at the University of Georgia was a "public figure" such that he fell under the *Sullivan* rule;[18] and in the same year a U.S. Circuit Court of Appeals applied the same doctrine to Dr. Linus Pauling, famous scientist, winner of both the Nobel Prize in chemistry and the Nobel Peace Prize, who was suing the Globe-Democrat newspaper in St. Louis for alleged libelous statements in an editorial opposing his views on nuclear testing.[19]

A more recent case terminated similarly in the supreme court of Minnesota, where Arnold Rose, an internationally known professor at the University of Minnesota and once a member of the Minnesota legislature, unsuccessfully sued a publisher who circulated untrue and defamatory accusations to the effect that Rose was a subversive person disloyal to the government of the United States.[20]

---

17. 388 U.S. 130. Discussed at pages 50 and 115 in *The Colleges and the Courts, 1962-66.*

18. *Curtis Publishing Company* v. *Butts*, 388 U.S. 130 (1965); reversing (U.S.C.A., Ga.), 351 F. 2d 702 (1965).

19. *Pauling* v. *Globe-Democrat Publishing Company*, (U.S.C.A., Mo.), 362 F. 2d 188 (1965).

20. *Arnold Rose* v. *Gerda Koch*, (Minn.), 154 N.W. 2d 409 (1967).

# CHAPTER 6

## DISCHARGE FOR CAUSE; SUSPENSION; RESIGNATION; RETIREMENT

The Second Circuit U.S. Court of Appeals held in 1966 that an employee of a municipal hospital in New York City was entitled under New York law to written notice of charges and a hearing thereon before being discharged for cause; and also that he had a cause of action under the federal Civil Rights Act (42 *U.S. Code,* Section 1983) because the public institution had summarily fired him without notice or hearing.

(This case, not discussed in chapters 2 and 3 of this volume because it did not involve a question of reappointment after the expiration of a contract term, is included in the simple tabulation at the end of Chapter 3, in which decisions by each of the 11 federal circuits are exhibited.)

Dr. Birnbaum, a staff physician at the Coney Island Hospital, a municipal institution in Brooklyn, sued for $25,000 damages and costs against the City Commissioner of Hospitals and his deputy, and the head of a local labor union, alleging that the three had conspired to have him discharged summarily. Although Section 1983 does not apply to private persons except when acting under color of governmental power, the court held, on the authority of earlier decisions, that an action for conspiracy may be brought when a private person is alleged to have conspired with public officers or employees to violate the act.

After failure of his suit in first complaint to the U.S. District Court, and on first appeal to the Second Circuit, and again in a second action in the District Court, Dr. Birnbaum obtained a favorable opinion in his second appeal to the U.S. Court of Appeals. The opinion was by Circuit Judge Robert P. Anderson, with Circuit Judge Paul R. Hays concurring specially, and Circuit Judge Sterry R. Waterman also participating.

Birnbaum's allegations were principally two: (1) that his dismissal was due to race prejudice against him because he was white, and on at least four occasions had reproved or reprimanded Negro employees of the hospital; and (2) that the Commissioner had refused to give him a statement of charges, and held a travesty of a hearing after Birnbaum had declined to attend it without an advance copy of the charges; and that the deputy had not only notified him that he was dismissed, but also sent a letter to all other New York City municipal hospitals with instruction not to put Dr. Birnbaum on their staffs.

The court did not regard the race prejudice as proved, although the labor leader defendant announced he had procured the dismissal and continued to accuse Birnbaum of abusing Negroes. The decision was based chiefly on the Commissioner's failure to afford Birnbaum a hearing:

"If (Birnbaum) had been given opportunity at a hearing prior to his discharge to contest charges of anti-Negro bias, he might have been able to dispel the rumors and charges immediately, before his reputation suffered 'material damage.' Furthermore, if he failed to do so, he could have had no complaint under federal law about his dismissal. . . . In either case, a full hearing was the only way his substantial interests could have been protected, and Section 1983 affords him a right of action for injuries suffered in consequence of the denial of such a hearing."[1]

*California Court Rejects Allegation of "Inefficiency,"*
*but Finds "Undue Discourtesy to Subordinates"*
*and Remands to Personnel Board for*
*Redetermination of Penalty*

At the Neuropsychiatric Institute at the University of California

---

1. *Birnbaum* v. *Trussell*, (U.S.C.A., N.Y.), 371 F. 2d 672 (1966).

at Los Angeles a doctor of medicine holding the position designated as Psychiatric Resident II was ordered dismissed by the State Personnel Board after a hearing on charges that he was (1) discourteous to fellow employees (*Government Code*, Section 19572 m), and (2) inefficient (*Government Code*, Section 19572 c).

The superior court of Los Angeles set aside the dismissal. The Court of Appeal found the evidence insufficient to support the charge of inefficiency, but sufficient to document the charge of discourtesy. Accordingly it reversed and remanded the judgment, with instruction that the Personnel Board be directed to redetermine the penalty in the light of these findings.

In support of the accusation of discourtesy, the record showed that Dr. Sidney Walker's immediate supervisor testified that at successive meetings with psychology interns (subordinate trainees without medical degrees) Dr. Walker had displayed hostility to the interns, spoken to them in abrasive tones, and treated them brusquely. A male student psychology fellow and a female psychology intern, both of whom had been assigned to work with Dr. Walker, testified to separate occasions on which he had grown angry over some trivial matter, shouted at them, gesticulated, grown red in the face, and had difficulty with his articulation. Another psychiatric resident confirmed one of these incidents, saying he had heard through the closed door of his office, which was ordinarily sound-proof, Dr. Walker angrily shouting at a woman intern.

Regarding the evidence as sufficient to support the charge of discourtesy, the Court of Appeal remarked: "We think those responsible for the orderly administration of public agencies would be neglectful of their duties if they failed to take steps to discipline a superior employee for discourtesy to inferior employees."

As to the charge of inefficiency, the evidence was found to be insubstantial. Dr. Walker differed from his colleagues on the emphasis to be placed on investigation of possible organic defects as the origin of symptoms commonly associated with mental illness. He would consider the possibility of an organic basis for mental illness in 30 to 40 per cent of his cases. One of his colleagues testified that in only one out of 30 cases could there be a legitimate suspicion of an organic basis for an emotional disorder; and this apparently was the prevailing doctrine at the Institute, and was a principal element in the written charges of inefficiency, which stressed "your inability to place physical organic aspects in a more appropriate perspective with the remainder of the patient's life situation."

Said the court: "We find it intolerable that Dr. Walker's dismissal should be upheld because his views failed to conform to current theoretical dogma on the causes of mental illness. . . . Some witnesses thought Dr. Walker failed to emphasize the "psychological dynamics" of his patients' illnesses. But there is no indication that he did not investigate these dynamics or did not understand them. Rather, the record suggests that he was interested in aspects of his patients' illnesses in addition to their psychological dynamics. . . . Given the never-ending changes in the medical arts and the continuous development of new methods of treatment for mental illness, we do not believe the evidence supports a finding that Dr. Walker was inefficient within the meaning of *Government Code*, Section 19572 c."

The conclusion was: "Since we can not tell what penalty the Board would have imposed for discourtesy alone, whether discharge, or temporary suspension, or reduction in rank, or reprimand, we return the cause to the Board for redetermination of the penalty."[2]

### Discharge for Vulgarity Amounting to Unfitness

William Hensey, a tenured junior college teacher in southern California, was discharged under the statutory "immorality and unfitness" stated cause on four charges:

1. In the new junior college building the electronic system intended to signal the beginning and end of class periods, to serve as a fire alarm, and to serve as an announcement system for the college, was malfunctioning and making disturbing noises. Hensey said it "sounded like a constipated elephant," and, in the presence of his class, physically tore the loudspeaker from the wall of his classroom, after saying it "sounded like a worn-out phonograph in a whorehouse."
2. He addressed the Chicano students in his class, in the presence of other members of both sexes, saying there was "super-syphilis" in San Luis (a village on the Mexican border), and advising them to be careful when visiting there.

---

2. *Walker v. State Personnel Board of California*, (Cal. App.), 94 Cal. Rptr. 132 (1971).

3. On one occasion he licked the chalkboard with his tongue while saying that the county superintendent of schools spent too much time "licking up the board of education."

4. On one occasion in the presence of his coeducational class he referred to the walls of the buildings as "looking as though someone had peed on them and then smeared them with baby crap."

The three judges of the California court of appeals were unanimous in deciding that while perhaps these types of conduct were not all "immoral," they were certainly vulgar and indicative of "evident unfitness to teach," within the meaning of the California statutes and decisions. As to any constitutional issue, the conclusion was that "It can not be questioned that (Hensey) had a right as a teacher and a citizen to differ with, to dissent from, and to criticize the superintendent. However, the means of expression used puts him far outside the protection of the First Amendment."[3]

## Discharge for Misbehavior: Sexual Misconduct

A tenured member of the faculty of the Compton Junior College in California was suspended for 30 days and dismissed permanently on the statutory charges of (1) immorality, and (2) evident unfitness for service. The male teacher was found by a policeman in a parked car in a state of undress with a female student. He assaulted the policeman and attempted to escape.

A California court of appeals, sustaining the dismissal, made some comments regarding the teaching profession after noting the facts of this case: "The integrity of the educational system under which teachers wield considerable power in the grading of students and the granting or withholding of certificates and diplomas is clearly threatened when teachers become involved in relationships with students such as indicated by the conduct here."[4] The opinion was by Justice Lynn D. Compton, sitting with Presiding Justice Lester William Roth and Justice Roy L. Herndon.

Also, "There are certain professions which impose upon persons

---

3. *Palo Verde Unified School District of Riverside County* v. *Hensey*, 9 Cal. App. 3d 967, 88 Cal. Rptr. 570 (1970).

4. *Board of Trustees of Compton Junior College District* v. *Stubblefield*, 16 Cal. App. 2d 120 (1971).

attracted to them responsibilities and limitations on freedom of action which do not exist in regard to other callings. Public officials such as judges, policemen and school teachers fall into such a category." One might remark that this doctrine of double or multiple standards of behavior may now be becoming somewhat outmoded; but that this purports no debasing of the ethics of the teaching profession, but rather an elevation of the general norms of conduct on a basis of equality.

In a case at the Mount San Antonio Junior College in California in 1963, the college authorities chose not to hold a hearing, but elected instead to file suit asking that the superior court inquire into the charges, determine whether or not they were true, and if true, whether they constituted sufficient grounds for dismissal. This was authorized under Section 13412, *Education Code.*

The trial court found that "the evidence in support of the charge as to the defendant's relationship with a woman, herein designated as Patricia, constituted cause for the defendant's dismissal on the grounds of immoral conduct and evident unfitness for service, under Section 13403, *Education Code.*" Patricia had been one of the defendant's students. One month after his wife had died in 1961, Patricia had left her husband and cohabited with the defendant during much of the year 1962, while she was still married to another man.

Another charge found true and sufficient cause for dismissal was that during the fall of 1960 the defendant had lived in an apartment with another woman designated Frances, "under the name of Mr. and Mrs. Hartman, while at that time he was married to Barbara Jean Hartman." The California Court of Appeal sustained the dismissal.[5]

### Discharge upon Evidence of Unsatisfactory Work or Incompetency

The head of the catalog department of the medical center library of the University of California, employed on a non-tenure basis, was dropped from her job (apparently at the expiration of her current one-year contract, and after notice and hearing), for the stated reason that her "supervisory relationship with subordinates made it impossible for this employee to be retained." The trial court found the termination

---

5. *Board of Trustees of Mount San Antonio Junior College District* v. *Hartman,* (Cal. App.), 55 Cal. Rptr. 144 (1966).

justified, and a California court of appeals affirmed, after reviewing the facts and the applicable university rules.[6] The court said, "She was discharged because she lacked supervisorial qualifications. She has not been deprived of the right to work as a librarian."

One Canty was a probationary junior high school teacher in New York City, dismissed after his first month of service on an emergency basis, on a long list of stated reasons. He carried the litigation to the Second Circuit U.S. Court of Appeals, where Circuit Judge Paul R. Hays wrote the opinion, sitting with Senior Circuit Judge J. Joseph Smith and District Judge Milton Pollack. The court said in effect that preponderant evidence of unsatisfactory work renders unnecessary any examination of the federal civil rights aspect alleged, and the case was not cognizable in federal court. It was adjudged not necessary for the school authorities to provide him with a full trial-type hearing. Though the teacher might find it more difficult to obtain employment, the impact on his reputation did not effectively destroy his ability to engage in his occupation.[7]

### Sovereign Immunity Bars Suit for Breach of Contract in West Virginia

Peter Kondos was notified in writing April 14, 1969, of his appointment as assistant football coach at Marshall University in West Virginia for a period of 12 months, beginning July 1, at a salary of $10,440. The notice was signed by the president of the univesity and was from the State Board of Education (predecessor of the Board of Regents as governing board).

By letter of August 1, 1969, the president informed Kondos that "the Athletic Committee and the University Council have recommended that I take steps which lead to your dismissal"; and "I am recommending to the Board of Regents that your contract for 1969-70 be terminated as of September 30, 1969. This recommendation is based on the judgment that you have performed your duties as assistant football coach in an incompetent manner." The same letter also enumerated specific shortcomings on which the judgment was based. These do not

---

6. *Ishimatsu* v. *Regents of University of California,* (Cal. App.), 72 Cal. Rptr. 756 (1968).

7. *Canty* v. *Board of Education of the City of New York,* (U.S.C.A., N.Y.), 448 F. 2d 428 (1971).

appear in the court record. It also informed Kondos that he could appeal, if he wished, to a faculty committee appointed by the Chairman of the University Council; and a channel of further appeal would be to the Board of Regents. Kondos spurned the proffered right to appear before the faculty committee, and the president notified him by letter on August 28 that his contract was terminated as of September 30, 1969. He then sought an appeal to the Board of Regents, and was informed by that body on February 4, 1970, that it had dismissed his appeal and confirmed the action of the president in his case.

Kondos then began an original action in the Supreme Court of Appeals of West Virginia, asking for a writ of mandamus to compel the Board of Regents and the president to reinstate him for the duration of his contract, with full pay and allowances. The writ was denied in an opinion by Judge Fred H. Caplan, showing that in no statute of West Virginia, nor any rule of the Board of Regents or its predecessor board, was there any provision relating to tenure of college or university faculty members and other employees, or to the manner in which they were to be suspended or discharged. Hence, thought the court, Kondos served at the pleasure of the Board of Regents, and that body was under no obligation to afford him a hearing prior to dismissing him for alleged incompetency, especially since he had at the outset waived his opportunity to be heard by a faculty committee.[8]

Being a citizen of another state, Kondos was able immediately to go into the United States District Court, suing the Board of Regents for breach of contract, and suing the president for libel and slander, asking monetary damages from both. In "diversity of citizenship" cases such as this, federal courts apply the substantive law of the state concerned; and U.S. District Judge Sidney L. Christie readily found that the doctrine of "sovereign immunity" prevailed in full force by virtue of a clause in the state constitution forbidding suits against the state or its agencies while engaged in governmental functions. Nor could the state or the Board of Regents be held responsible for libel or slander by the president while acting within the scope of his authority.

The president himself could not be held personally liable either for breach of contract or libel or slander because he, too, was protected by the doctrine of sovereign immunity unless it be proved that he acted

---

8. *State ex rel. Kondos* v. *West Virginia Board of Regents*, (W.Va.), 175 S.E. 2d 165 (1970).

maliciously or corruptly. The pleadings in this case did not even exhibit any words written or spoken by the president that were specifically alleged to be knowingly untrue or defamatory. Thus there was insufficient basis for an action against the president individually, and the suit was dismissed as to both defendants.[9]

At the conclusion of his opinion Judge Christie remarked that although the harsh doctrine of sovereign immunity prevailed in West Virginia, nevertheless *West Virginia Code*, 14-2-13, provided that the state's Court of Claims may hear and adjudicate claims against the state or any of its agencies, "which the state should in equity and good conscience satisfy and pay," and that the state's highest court had recently held that the jurisdiction of the Court of Claims extended to the Board of Regents. Although Kondos found his action for breach of contract barred by sovereign immunity, there was yet a chance that the Court of Claims might hear it, and if this court adjudged his claim meritorious, award a suitable indemnity.

*Penalties Lighter Than Discharge: Suspensions, Even
If with Pay, Must Be Made with
Regard to Due Process*

It is reported that university administrators and governing boards, in disciplining errant faculty members, are generally reluctant to employ penalties less than dismissal, though the American Association of University Professors in its efforts to facilitate practices that are fair and consistent with academic freedom sometimes suggests in particular cases that a lighter penalty might be a better solution.

Early in 1970 four professors of English at Wisconsin State University at Whitewater were said to have publicly criticized a decision of the president in the presence of many students, and to have participated actively in meetings, processions, and demonstrations in protest against the decision. The president summarily suspended them with pay, and ordered them to stay off the campus during the temporary suspension. In the words of District Judge James E. Doyle, "None had been notified of the nature of the charges against him, none had been given notice that he could be heard on the charges, and none had in

_____

9. *Kondos* v. *West Virginia Board of Regents*, (U.S.D.C., W.Va.), 318 F. Supp. 394 (1970).

fact been heard. Even the notice of suspension itself failed to state in any intelligible way the basis for the action. . . ."

Judge Doyle granted a temporary order of immediate reinstatement "with the same rights, privileges, and immunities which attached to their status as faculty members prior to their suspension." He made clear that there was nothing in the order to prevent the university from starting its own proceedings in accord with due process, to discipline or dismiss the professors. He granted the order for two reasons prescribed by the canons of federal practice in such cases: (1) The plaintiffs were likely to prevail in subsequent litigation, alleging that they had been suspended without due process; and (2) their abrupt expulsion from the campus, even if only of short duration, would result in irreparable harm to them. Both the immediate consequences to the professor, and the long-range consequences to him in terms of his career and his professional standing, are obviously not measurable in financial terms, thought Judge Doyle.

The same court has held, in cases of suspension of students, that summary action can only be justified by one of two conditions: (1) if danger to persons or property requires the immediate removal of the accused from the campus, or (2) if conditions are such that it is impracticable or impossible to give the accused an "emergency temporary hearing" prior to his temporary suspension. Neither of these conditions appeared to have been present here. Accordingly the injunctive order of reinstatement was issued and promptly complied with.[10]

Within a few months, however (in August 1970), while the academic disciplinary mill was grinding on this case, the president suddenly reassigned the four professors to full-time research instead of teaching, without prior notice to or consultation with them. (It might be conjectured that this may have been in anticipation of their probable dismissal early in the academic year 1970-71.) At any rate, the plaintiffs, alleging that this action was so unusual and contrary to academic usage as to amount to a violation of their order of reinstatement, asked Judge Doyle to hold the president in contempt of court. This he declined to do. It could not be said with certainty, he thought, that the president actually knowingly violated the order of the court.[11]

---

10. *Lafferty* v. *Carter*, (U.S.D.C., Wis.), 310 F. Supp. 465 (March 9, 1970).
11. This is the contempt action in *Lafferty* v. *Carter*, which was adjudicated September 14, 1970, some six months after the original action of March 9, 1970, which is cited in the immediately preceding footnote.

U.S. District Judge James E. Doyle of the Western District of Wisconsin is known for his devotion to enlightened and advancing concepts of due process in university disciplinary cases involving either students or faculty members. For a discussion of his judgments in several contemporary cases involving students, recourse may be had to pages 229-234 in the earlier companion volume, *The Colleges and the Courts: The Developing Law of the Student and the College*, published by The Interstate Printers & Publishers, Inc., of Danville, Illinois 61832.

### Termination by Resignation

At San Angelo State College in Texas in 1967 there was in effect a rule of the governing board (the Board of Regents, State Senior Colleges) providing that "employment contracts are for one year only and the president nominates faculty annually for employment and re-employment."

During his third year of service, a faculty member submitted his resignation in writing to the president April 19, effective at the end of the semester. (He had learned secondhand from his department head that the president had doubts about re-employing him, because of a supposed complaint of his past behavior at the University of Michigan, an alleged night of debauchery he had spent in Houston, and his unsatisfactory progress toward a doctoral degree.)

Then on May 1 he wrote the president asking for an interview and referring to his former letter as "resignation by intimidation." Meantime he had leaked to the local newspaper that he would not be at the college next year, and some of the students began demonstrating on his behalf.

May 19 at its regular meeting the governing board formally accepted his resignation (perfunctorily, with 14 others). Later in the same day it convened to give him an audience, which he had requested. Having already accepted the resignation, it refused to allow him to withdraw it, and declined to hear testimony. It told him he could reapply. He did so, but the president never acted on this application.

The U.S. District Court denied him any relief, and this judgment was affirmed by Circuit Judge David W. Dyer, sitting with Circuit Judges Homer Thornberry and Charles Clark: "The situation in this case does not involve either a refusal to recommend for the following year or a discharge. He resigned before either of these possibilities had an opportunity to come to fruition. . . . The District Court specifically found that his resignation was voluntary and there is more than ample support in the record for this finding.

"Therefore, the board did not deny him due process or equal protection in refusing to hear him."[12]

### Retirement Allowances Under North Carolina Retirement Act Were Deferred Compensation for Public Services, Unaffected by Post-Retirement Earnings

An acting dean retired (Harrill) and a former president (Hill) of Western Carolina University at Cullowhee asked the North Carolina supreme court for a declaratory judgment of their rights under the state retirement act for teachers and state employees in 1967. The legislature had delegated authority to administer the act to a Retirement Board, which had adopted a rule that in the case of retired academic employees who were allowed to continue teaching part-time and be remunerated from course-by-course fees, whenever earnings thus received exceeded $1,500 in any year, the retired teacher's regular retirement allowance under the act would be withheld.

Harrill and Hill earned about $1,700 each as temporary emergency employees, and their regular monthly retirement allowances for December 1966 were accordingly withheld. "Unless provided or authorized by statute," said the court, "we are of opinion, and so decide, that plaintiffs' acceptance of part-time re-employment did not suspend or otherwise affect their retirement allowances." They did not lose their retired status and rights.[13]

As to the reasoning, "The retirement payment provided for by this act constitutes delayed compensation in consideration of services rendered. It is compensation for public services." Hence it was not offensive to Article I, Section 7, of the state constitution specifying that "No person or set of persons are entitled to exclusive or separate emoluments or privileges from the community but in consideration of public services."

---

12. *Smith* v. *Board of Regents, State Senior Colleges*, (U.S.C.A., Tex.), 426 F. 2d 492 (1970).

13. *Harrill* v. *Teachers' and State Employees' Retirement System*, 271 N.C. 357, 156 S.E. 2d 702 (1967).

The court also enunciated a second well-recognized principle, but regarded it as unnecessary to the decision in this case: "The General Assembly can not delegate legislative power, and, where authority is conferred on a commission or board, the legislative body must declare the policy of the law, fix legal principles which are to control in given cases, and provide adequate standards for the guidance of the administrative body or officer empowered to execute the law." This had not been done in such manner as to authorize the Retirement Board's withholding of the allowances.

### Where University Rules Reserve to the Board the Option of Ordering Compulsory Retirement Between Specified Ages, the Motives of the Board Are Immaterial, Says Tennessee Court

The University of Tennessee employed Dr. Douglas H. Sprunt as professor and head of the department of pathology on its medical campus at Memphis from 1944 to August 31, 1968. His sixty-eighth birthday had occurred four weeks earlier, on August 3. Early in the same year the Board of Trustees had notified him of its forthcoming meeting February 2, at which it intended to consider retiring him as of August 31, on the recommendation of the central administrative officers of the medical unit. He appeared at the February 2 meeting with counsel and supported with oral and written statements his request that he be allowed to continue in his present position until he reached age 70. After deliberation, the Trustees voted to retire him August 31, 1968.

The University retirement regulations had been adopted pursuant to *Tennessee Public Acts* of 1941, Chapter 42. After having been amended by the Trustees in 1958, the regulations set the age of automatic retirement at 65, with the right of the Board of Trustees to extend employment on a year-to-year basis.

Dr. Sprunt asked the supreme court of Tennessee to review the action of the Trustees in his case. The court concluded that either under the retirement regulations of 1941, or as amended in 1958, the Board acted within its authority in retiring him, since he had already reached an age beyond 65. He asserted, however, that not his age, but differences between him and his immediate administrative superior, Dr. Rowland H. Alden, dean of the school of basic scientists, regarding the employment of personnel and the operation of the pathology department, were the real cause of Dr. Alden's recommendation that led to his retirement.

Assuming that Dr. Sprunt may have been wholly correct in that dispute, thought the court, would not affect the right of the Board of Trustees to retire any employee reaching the age of 65, whatever the motives of the Trustees for so doing. "The question of whether this situation should exist does not address itself to the judiciary."[14] In affirming the decree of the trial court and remanding the case, the supreme court intimated that there might be a possibility of a suit for damages for breach of contract available to the plaintiff, either on an alleged promise of 1944 that he could continue until age 70, or on the allegation that his retirement was actually an unjust dismissal without adequate cause, which might be an actionable breach of contract. Adjudication of these matters was left to the lower court.

---

14. *Sprunt* v. *Members of the Board of Trustees of the University of Tennessee*, (Tenn.), 443 S.W. 2d 464 (1969).

# CHAPTER 7

## DISCRIMINATION: RACE;
## RELIGION; SEX;
## IDEOLOGY

Discrimination on racial grounds against faculty members may occur (and no doubt has occurred at many times in many places) in initial appointments, in the fixing of salaries, in effecting the termination of contracts under various circumstances, and at many other points. The subject is large and complex. No great number of cases involving educational institutions above the secondary level appears to have reached the higher state and federal courts. A few landmark cases touching local public school districts, are, however, important as indicating progress.

At least as early as 1940 the Fourth Circuit U.S. Court of Appeals "struck down a practice of paying lesser salaries to Negro school teachers." The opinion was by Circuit Judge John J. Parker, sitting with Circuit Judges Morris A. Soper and Armistead M. Dobie. The complaint, coming from black teachers in the city of Norfolk, Virginia, asked for a declaratory judgment that fixing of salaries of Negro teachers at a lower rate than that paid to white teachers of equal qualifications and experience is violative of the due process and equal protection clauses of the Constitution. It also asked for an injunction restraining the Norfolk school board from making any distinctions on the ground of race or color in fixing salaries of public school teachers in Norfolk.

The action was dismissed in the U.S. District Court, but this judgment was reversed and remanded with directions by the Court of Appeals.[1] The U.S. Supreme Court declined to review.

### It Is Unconstitutional to Drop Teachers as a Penalty
### for Participation in Local Civil Rights Activities,
### Such as Voter Registration Drives

Mrs. Henry, a Negro school teacher in Coahoma County, Mississippi, for 11 consecutive years, was not recommended for employment for the academic year 1962-63 by the county superintendent, allegedly because she was an active member of the National Association for the Advancement of Colored People, and her husband was the state president of that organization, and he was also running for the office of state senator.

The county superintendent, when pressed by the U.S. District Court, testified that he did not recommend her because her husband had been convicted on a morals charge and was under an adverse judgment in a libel suit, and Mrs. Henry herself was about to be sued in respect of a fraudulent conveyance of property made to her by her husband.

Relief was denied in the District Court, and the judgment was affirmed in the Court of Appeals, *per curiam*, by Circuit Judges Joseph C. Hutcheson and John R. Brown, and Chief District Judge Lewis R. Morgan. Judge Brown wrote a short concurring opinion in which he emphasized that the county superintendent's discretionary power to recommend or not to recommend does not prevent judicial inquiry into the constitutional propriety of his motives; and stressed that the negative decision rested wholly on the inadequacy of the plaintiff's proofs:

"The Court affirms because the plaintiff failed to prove either that the superintendent's refusal to recommend her was based on the civil rights activities of her and her husband, or that her husband's criminal record . . . arose primarily from constitutionally protected assertions of civil rights."[2]

---

1. *Alston* v. *School Board of City of Norfolk*, (U.S.C.A., Va.), 112 F. 2d 992 (1940); certiorari denied, 311 U.S. 693, 61 S. Ct. 75, 85 L. Ed. 448 (1940).

2. *Henry* v. *Coahoma County Board of Education*, (U.S.C.A., Miss.), 353 F. 2d 648 (1966); affirming (U.S.D.C., Miss.), 246 F. Supp. 517 (1963).

### Teacher Can Not Lawfully Be Dropped Because of Civil Rights Activities

"The record discloses, the defendants concede, and the court found that the plaintiff (Willa Johnson), a Negro, was a well-qualified, conscientious and competent teacher of English at the T.S. Inborden High School in Enfield, North Carolina, for a period of nearly twelve years preceding the incidents involved here." Thus wrote Circuit Judge J. Spencer Bell, for the majority of the Fourth Circuit Court, composed of himself and Circuit Judges Clement F. Haynsworth, Simon E. Sobeloff and Herbert S. Boreman. (Circuit Judge Albert V. Bryan dissented.)

Mrs. Johnson had also done a great deal of "extracurricular work for the school and for student activities, which indicated her devotion to her professional work." Both the principal and the superintendent had officially given her "excellent" and "above average" ratings and testified she was doing very satisfactory work.

In 1963 Enfield became a center of active racial civil rights activities, including a voter registration drive, candidacies of black persons for public offices, and picketing of segregated places of public accommodation. A Negro high school student tried to use the public library; the local theater closed; and "mass convictions for restaurant picketing were finally reversed by the U.S. Supreme Court (*Blow* v. *North Carolina*, 379 U.S. 684, 85 S. Ct. 685, 13 L. Ed. 2d 608 (1965)."

Mrs. Johnson took a prominent part in voter registration, and in one of the demonstrations; both her husband and her father were candidates for public offices. At hiring time the school board summarily dropped her and allowed her twelfth one-year contract to expire without renewal. U.S. District Judge John D. Larkins dismissed her suit for recourse; but the Fourth Circuit reversed and remanded, with instructions to enter an order directing the school board to renew her contract for the next school year (1966-67) and to determine her damages.[3]

"We take it to be beyond cavil," wrote Circuit Judge J. Spencer Bell, "that the state may not force the plaintiff to choose between exercising her legitimate constitutional rights and her right of equality of opportunity to hold public employment." He quoted from the opinion in *Alston* (cited at footnote 1 in this chapter): "It is no answer to this

---

3. *Johnson* v. *Branch*, (U.S.C.A., N.C.), 364 F. 2d 177 (1966); certiorari denied, 385 U.S. 1003, 87 S. Ct. 706, 17 L. Ed. 2d 542 (1967).

to say that hiring of any teacher is a matter resting within the discretion of the school authorities. . . . If a state may compel the surrender of one constitutional right as a condition of its favor, it may, in like manner, compel a surrender of all. It is inconceivable that guarantees imbedded in the Constitution of the United States may thus be manipulated out of existence."

Sharpening the distinction between contract rights and constitutional rights, Judge Bell went on: "The law of North Carolina is clear on the procedure for hiring teachers. All contracts are for one year only, renewable at the discretion of the school authorities. A contract must be signed by the principal as an indication of his recommendation, and then transmitted to the district school committee, whose business it is to approve or disapprove in its discretion. There is no vested right to public employment. No one questions that the plaintiff had neither a contract nor a constitutional right to have her contract renewed. These questions are not involved in this case.

"It is the plaintiff's contention that her contract was not renewed for reasons which were either capricious or arbitrary, or in order to retaliate against her for exercising her constitutional right to protest racial discrimination. . . . However wide the discretion of school boards, it can not be exercised so as to arbitrarily deprive persons of their constitutional rights."

During the course of the lengthy opinion several of the decisions of the United States Supreme Court in the teachers' loyalty oath cases were cited and quoted; notably *Shelton* v. *Tucker*, 364 U.S. 479, 81 S. Ct. 247, 5 L. Ed. 2d 231 (1960), which invalidated the Arkansas oath law: "The vigilant protection of constitutional freedoms is nowhere more vital than in the community of American schools." And, "The classroom is peculiarly the 'marketplace of ideas.' The Nation's future depends upon leaders trained through wide exposure to that robust exchange of ideas which discovers truth 'out of a multitude of tongues' and not through any kind of authoritative selection."

*Retention and Discharge of Teachers upon Closing of*
*Skyway Campus of St. Petersburg Junior College in*
*Florida Was Held to be Non-discriminatory*

In Florida the St. Petersburg Junior College operated, in addition to and apart from its main campus, a Skyway Campus for a time prior to 1967, when this outlying branch was closed because of drastically declining attendance. It was merged into the two other campuses in the system.

At that time there were 31 black teachers and 8 white teachers at Skyway. Nineteen of the black teachers and four of the white teachers were reassigned to the remaining two campuses. Thus 12 blacks and 4 whites were not reassigned in the junior college because there were no places available. The blacks were on tenure; the whites were not.

Seven of the 12 blacks sued in the federal District Court, alleging that they had been denied reassignment within the junior college solely because of their race, and in violation of the Florida teacher tenure laws. Of these seven, all but one were offered related work, and three of them accepted it—one as a high school teacher, one as a teacher of shorthand and typing, and one as an instructor in education. Two who were offered jobs as teachers in the county system of elementary and secondary schools rejected them, and a third who was offered a place as a program planner rejected it. (Of the four white teachers left unassigned, two accepted jobs in the county school system, one found a position at another junior college, and one resigned for personal reasons.) Whether any of the persons shifted lost any time between jobs, and if so how much, does not appear in the record.

Section 231.36 (2) of *Florida Statutes Annotated* (a subsection of the Florida teacher tenure act) specified:

"Should the county board of public instruction have to choose from among its personnel who are on continuing contracts as to which should be retained, among the criteria to be considered shall be educational qualifications, efficiency, compatibility, character, and capacity to meet the educational needs of the community. Whenever a county board is required to or does consolidate its school program at any given school center by bringing together pupils theretofore assigned to separated schools, the county board may determine on the basis of the foregoing criteria from its own personnel, and any other certificated teachers, which teachers shall be employed for service at this school center, and any teacher no longer needed may be dismissed. The decision of the board shall not be controlled by any previous contractual relationship. In the evaluation of these factors the decision of the county board of public instruction shall be final."

U.S. District Judge Ben Krentzman entered judgment for the board of public instruction. On appeal by the teachers, the Fifth Circuit

Court of Appeals affirmed the judgment, in a *per curiam* opinion, with Circuit Judges Walter Pettus Gewin, James P. Coleman, and Robert A. Ainsworth, Jr. sitting: "We are of the opinion, from this record, that the trial judge did apply the plain words and the clear intent of the quoted statutes, and that he did not abdicate any duty imposed upon him by the doctrine of pendent jurisdiction.[4]

### Fourth Circuit Court of Appeals Ordered Equitable Treatment for Black Teachers Discharged in Giles County, Virginia, upon Abandonment of Two Negro Schools

A somewhat similar case in the public schools of Giles County, Virginia, came out with a different result. In the course of racial integration of the schools, two Negro schools were abandoned and their pupils transferred, and some of the teachers discharged. Seven Negro teachers sought recourse in the federal District Court. U.S. District Judge Thomas J. Michie held that the discharges were improper in violation of the Fourteenth Amendment, and ordered the county school board to notify the discharged teachers of any future vacancies for which they were qualified, and offer them opportunity to apply in competition with other applicants.

In the Fourth Circuit Court of Appeals, Circuit Judge J. Spencer Bell, sitting with Chief Circuit Judge Clement F. Haynsworth and Circuit Judges Simon E. Soboloff, Herbert S. Boremen, and Albert V. Bryan, decided that the remedy was insufficient: "We think the individual plaintiffs are entitled to re-employment in any vacancy which occurs for which they are qualified by certification and experience."[5] A modification was added: "If the board can objectively demonstrate to the court that two of the seven teachers about whom some question was raised, would not have been re-employed under any circumstances," then the District Court should take due cognizance of that.

Accordingly the judgment was reversed and remanded, "in order that the district court may amend its order to conform with this opinion."

---

4. *Smith* v. *Board of Public Instruction of Pinellas County, Florida,* (U.S.C.A., Fla.), 438 F. 2d 1209 (1971).

5. *Franklin* v. *County School Board of Giles County,* (U.S.C.A., Va.), 360 F. 2d 325 (1966).

## Court-ordered Desegregation of Cooperative
## Agricultural Extension Service in Alabama

The federal-state Cooperative Agricultural Extension Service has in every state a network of county agricultural agents, county home demonstration agents, and their staffs, as well as a division of agricultural extension at the land-grant university. Officers and employees of this far-flung service are regarded as members of the staffs of the land-grant universities in their respective states, and their salaries from both state and federal sources are paid through that channel.

A current suit against Auburn University in Alabama seeks to stimulate desegregation of the service in that state. Brought by a black man alleging that he has been the victim of racial discrimination in the filling of the position of director of information of the Alabama Cooperative Extension Service, he instituted a class action in the U.S. District Court for the Middle District of Alabama. He alleged further that the statewide services are provided on a discriminatory basis; that there was discrimination against Negroes in hiring and promotion and in conditions of employment; and that the 4-H and home demonstration clubs for boys and girls were racially segregated.

The court found the averments true, and entered a detailed decree:

1. Give Negro employees priority for all future promotions to county extension agent and associate extension agent, such promotions to be based on objective standards to be presented to the court within 30 days; and where a Negro is the best qualified employee and is not appointed, this must be justified with compelling reasons.

2. Offer certain named Negro employees positions of responsibility commensurate with their backgrounds; give others priority for openings in which they have had experience; and submit a report to the court indicating steps taken toward compliance.

3. Abandon the custom of recommending three names to county governing boards, in favor of recommending one name; report a plan for public announcement of all vacancies; refrain from ascertaining or considering in any degree whether the county boards would accept a Negro; and refrain from eliminating Negroes from consideration because they have no technical background from Auburn University.

4. Present a plan to equalize the salaries of Negroes and whites on the basis of stated objective criteria; have the county contributions paid not to the county staffs but to the statewide office at Auburn University, which is ordered to divide the total of all county contributions equitably between white and Negro employees.

5. Discontinue the assignment pattern of replacing whites with whites and blacks with blacks; fill approximately 50 per cent of all vacancies with Negroes until they represent the same percentage of the total as do Negroes of the state population; and present a plan within six months indicating steps taken toward compliance.

6. Submit a plan within 90 days for the complete elimination of segregation in 4-H and homemaker clubs, and in educational benefits.[6]

### Affirmative Duty to Dismantle Dual Discriminatory Systems of Higher Education Is Subject of U.S. District Court Decision in Tennessee

It will be recalled that in 1968 a special three-judge District Court in Alabama declined to interfere with the prospective build-up of a full-fledged four-year degree-granting campus of Auburn University (Auburn) at Montgomery, although the predominantly black Alabama State College (now University) had long been at that city, and despite the averment that this plan would produce one black university and one white university in Montgomery instead of advancing desegregation.[7]

Also in 1971 a similar court in Virginia made what has been called a directly contrary decision in the case of Richard Bland College, a two-year predominantly white branch of the College of William and Mary (Williamsburg) located at Petersburg, the long-time seat of the

---

6. This is the case of *Strain* v. *Philpott*, (U.S.D.C., Ala., 1972), as yet not officially reported. Synopsis of opinion adapted from the *Circular Letter* (mimeo) of the National Association of State Universities and Land-Grant Colleges, 1972.

7. *Alabama State Teachers Association* v. *Alabama Public School and College Authority*, (U.S.D.C., Ala.), 289 F. Supp. 784 (1968); affirmed in 393 U.S. 400 (1969), with Justice William O. Douglas and Justice John M. Harlan dissenting separately. Discussed at pp. 21-25 in *The Colleges and the Courts: The Developing Law of the Student and the College* (1972).

predominantly black Virginia State College. The court declared unconstitutional and void a state appropriation of funds to escalate Richard Bland to become a four-year institution, on the ground that this would frustrate the efforts of Virginia State College to desegregate, and would perpetuate the racially identifiable dual system.[8]

Observe that both of the foregoing decisions were summarily affirmed by the U.S. Supreme Court. Meantime in 1968, in a somewhat similar situation at Nashville, U.S. District Judge Frank Gray, Jr., had declined to enjoin the University of Tennessee (Knoxville) from enlarging its Nashville Center in the home city of the predominantly black Tennessee State University, because he took the intent of the University of Tennessee to be not to make its Center a degree-granting day institution, but only to "provide a quality continuing education and public service center for Nashville and Middle Tennessee with overwhelming emphasis being placed upon the provision of educational opportunity for employed persons of all races who must seek their education at night."[9]

Judge Gray went a step further and ordered the higher educational authorities of the state of Tennessee to prepare and submit to the court a plan for the eventual dismantling of the dual racially segregated system of higher education.

Came next in February 1972 another order from Judge Gray's court in response to another suit, in which he gave special attention to Tennessee State University, as had been requested in the prior litigation of 1968. He ordered that there be submitted a plan to be implemented at the beginning of the 1972 academic year that would provide, as a minimum, a substantial desegregation of the Tennessee State University faculty and the allocation to the campus of programs that would insure a "substantial white presence" on the campus. Furthermore, it was ordered that additional methods, such as possible merging of Tennessee State University into the multi-campus University of Tennessee system, be considered and reported upon to the court by August 1, 1972.

Judge Gray believed that the argument that "a good faith open door policy" satisfied the requirements of the Fourteenth Amendment

---

8. *Norris* v. *State Council of Higher Education*, (U.S.D.C., Va.), Eastern District, Richmond Division, Civ. Action No. 365-70-R (1971). Discussed at pp. 27-28 in *Ibid.*

9. *Sanders* v. *Ellington*, (U.S.D.C., Tenn.), 288 F. Supp. 937 (1968). Discussed at pp. 24-25 in *Ibid.*

was unpersuasive. From his study of all the desegregation cases, he set forth what seemed to him to be the state of the law in 1972:

1. There is an affirmative duty on a state to dismantle its dual system of education, when such system is a vestige of *de jure* segregation.
2. The means of eliminating discrimination in college necessarily differ from those of eliminating it in elementary and secondary schools, but the state's duty is equally exacting.
3. A federal District Court, in order to ensure that such duty is performed, is to proceed as a traditional court of equity.
4. In framing relief, the court must balance the interests involved and take into account the administrative feasibility of the proposed relief, and fashion the remedy to fit the scope of the violation.
5. In cases involving higher education, the interests of the state in setting its own educational policy are to be given especially great weight.[10]

In different states, the future of each public black college is a delicate question. Some of these colleges have already become racially integrated. Others, proud of their traditions and unique points of excellence, and conscious of a responsibility to Negro youth at least until interracial inhospitability has been further diminished, do not want to lose their distinctive identity as predominantly black institutions.

## Alleged Religious Discrimination Against Faculty Members at Queens College of the City University of New York Can Be Investigated by the State Division of Human Rights

Dating from the early 1960's is litigation in which it is averred that faculty promotion practices at Queens College involve discrimination against Catholics. In 1971 the five-judge Appellate Division unanimously reversed a judgment of the New York County supreme court which would have denied the jurisdiction of the State Division of Human Rights in this matter and prohibited it from holding a public hearing on a complaint by an individual.

The Board of Higher Education, governing Queens College, claims

---

10. *Geier v. Dunn*, (U.S.D.C., Tenn.), 337 F. Supp. 573 (1972).

exclusive jurisdiction over the colleges under its governance; while the State Division of Human Rights asserts limited investigative powers under its statutory mandate. The issue was decided against the Board in 1964 by a 4 to 3 vote of the seven-judge New York Court of Appeals (state tribunal of last resort); and that decision is now cited and followed.[11] The upshot is that while the Board of Higher Education has undoubted power to act against discrimination in the institutions under its control, the State Division of Human Rights has a concurrent limited authority to make investigations of the same subject. The current "second amended complaint" of one Professor Lombardo "contains matter, including charges of retaliation and ethnic discrimination, which were not before the courts in the proceeding initiated by him in 1962." The earlier litigation is discussed at some length at pages 78-83 in *The Colleges and the Courts, 1962-1966.*

### Religious Freedom Does Not Exculpate Disregard of Public Law

The rare litigated controversies involving the actions of faculty members allegedly based on their religious convictions are not really matters of discrimination. Rather they seem to stem from what some individuals regard as too rigidly uniform application of law, either statutory or judge-made, to all persons, with too little concern for freedom of conscience and of religious faith. There is something of the notion of "Equal justice under law" involved.

At the interface between private religious action and public law, the United States constitutional stance is neutral: "no law respecting an establishment of religion, or prohibiting the free exercise thereof"; but there is no doubt that allegedly religious practices that violate criminal statutes will be subject to the penalties of the law. There is, however, a misty area in which no one can be too sure of his opinions, as is evidenced by the 1972 decision of the U.S. Supreme Court granting some concession to members of the Old Order Amish faith who object strenuously to exact compliance with the compulsory schooling laws

---

11. *Board of Higher Education v. State Division of Human Rights and Josef Vincent Lombardo,* 36 A.D. 2d 764, 321 N.Y.S. 2d 229 (1971), citing and following *Board of Higher Education v. Carter and State Commission Against Discrimination,* 250 N.Y.S. 2d 33, 14 N.Y. 2d 138, 199 N.E. 2d 141 (1964).

of the states in which they live,[12] as well as by the decision of 1943 in *West Virginia State Board of Education* v. *Barnette* regarding the civil liberties of public school pupils belonging to the sect Jehovah's Witnesses.[13]

In the case of the Amish farmers, Mr. Chief Justice Warren Burger wrote: "In sum, the unchallenged testimony of acknowledged experts in education and religious history, almost 300 years of consistent practice, and strong evidence of a sustained faith pervading and regulating respondents' entire mode of life support the claim that enforcement of the State's requirement of compulsory formal education after the eighth grade would gravely endanger if not destroy the free exercise of respondents' religious beliefs."

The Chief Justice also asserted that the state's interest in universal education is by no means absolute to the exclusion or subordination of all other interests.

Another recent decision of the high tribunal (May 29, 1972) summarily affirmed a judgment of a special three-judge federal court in Albany, New York, that sustained the dismissal of a school teacher in Syracuse who refused to sign the simple "loyalty oath" which the state requires of all teachers. Sari K. Bicklen said she was a Quaker, and as such could not subscribe to any form of oath. She stood on her religious freedom, saying her religious scruples would not allow her to subscribe to any oath whatsoever.

She was unmoved when the school authorities offered to allow her to substitute such a phrase as "pledge and declare" to support the state and national constitutions. The oath approved by the New York courts and by the Supreme Court of the United States in 1968 requires only that pledge in simple words, plus "I will faithfully discharge, according to the best of my ability, the duties of the position. . . ."[14] It is not to be confused with the tangle of anti-subversive statutes that were invalidated by the high court in the famous case of *Keyishian* v. *Regents*, frequently cited elsewhere in this volume.

Circuit Judge William H. Mulligan, writing the opinion of the

---

12. *Wisconsin* v. *Yoder*, (U.S. S. Ct.), 92 S. Ct. 1526 (May 15, 1972).

13. *West Virginia State Board of Education* v. *Barnette*, 319 U.S. 624, 63 S. Ct. 1178, 87 L. Ed. 1628, 147 A.L.R. 674 (June 14, 1943); mentioned *supra* in Chapter 4.

14. The full text of the brief and simple oath appears in Chapter 9 herein, in connection with the case of *Knight* v. *Board of Regents of the University of the State of New York.*

three-judge court composed of himself and Chief District Judge James T. Foley and District Judge Edmund Port, said:

"The Supreme Court has consistently held that the religious freedom guarantee embraces 'freedom to believe and freedom to act. The first is absolute, but, in the nature of things, the second can not be.' *Cantwell* v. *Connecticut*, 310 U.S. 296, 60 S. Ct. 900, 84 L. Ed. 1213 (1940). . . .

"The extent to which one may act upon the dictates of his conscience is necessarily circumscribed by the serious needs of society. Yet, freedom of religion is a fundamental liberty and only a compelling societal interest can justify a state's intrusion upon one's religiously motivated activities."

Mr. Justice William O. Douglas dissented from the summary affirmance by the Supreme Court in the *Sari K. Bicklen* v. *Syracuse* case.[15]

A faculty member's religious orientation also played a large part in the case of *Jones* v. *Hopper,* in which the Tenth Circuit U.S. Court of Appeals affirmed the summary dismissal of the suit of George Jones, Jr., an associate professor of philosophy at Southern Colorado State College who alleged he was dropped from the faculty at the end of his second probationary year solely because of his religious convictions concerning pacifism and his spoken and written expressions on that issue. Both the majority and dissenting opinions are discussed herein in Chapter 3.[16]

## Expression of Individual Conscience Is Protected

Nancy L. Hanover, teacher of the seventh and eighth grades in Roxbury, Connecticut, did not lead the conventional "Pledge of Allegiance" each morning, but had one of her pupils lead it while she herself sat silent at her desk with her head bowed. When ordered by the superintendent to lead the pledge, she declined, whereupon he charged her with insubordination; and the board of education, after a hearing, voted to terminate her contract.

---

15. *Sari K. Bicklen* v. *Board of Education of Syracuse,* (U.S.D.C., N.Y.), 333 F. Supp. 902 (1971). Subsequently affirmed by the U.S. Supreme Court, with Mr. Justice William O. Douglas dissenting.

16. This case was decided by an unusually large panel of seven Circuit Judges, of whom two, Circuit Judges Oliver Seth and William J. Holloway, dissented cogently from the opinion of the majority.

Her refusal was not on any religious or sectarian belief, but on individual social conscience. She did not believe the words "with liberty and justice for all" were a true statement of present fact; and they were not an expression of an ideal to be striven for, because they did not say that. U.S. District Judge M. Joseph Blumenfeld held that there was no question but that her act was "a form of expression protected by the First Amendment which may not be forbidden at the risk of losing her job. . . ." He then enunciated a principle worthy of a Supreme Court Justice:

"First Amendment rights of expression are fundamental to the preservation of an open, democratic society, since restriction on their exercise inhibits the debate by which society's values are set and its laws reformed to reflect prevailing opinion."

He immediately issued a temporary injunction restraining the board from terminating Mrs. Hanover's contract, and ordered that she be reinstated until final disposition of the action.[17]

Subsequently the U.S. Supreme Court declined to review a similar decision by the Second Circuit U.S. Court of Appeals in a parallel case arising in Henrietta, New York. (*Central School District No. 1* v. *Susan Russo*, U.S. S. Ct. No. 72-1109, April 16, 1973.)

### Discrimination Against Women in Higher Education Is Only Now Coming to Be Seriously Recognized

So subtle that many of those who practice it are themselves scarcely aware of it, and hitherto almost always hushed and unmentioned, sex discrimination in university and college faculties and staffs has existed throughout the century and a half since women were first admitted as members of academic communities. That comparatively few appointments should go to women, that they should be paid less for similar work, and that they should seldom be promoted, have been widespread but unspoken customs.

Litigation on the point is in its infancy. Much federal administrative activity goes on since the inclusion of sex discrimination within the purview of the civil rights legislation; and the impending ratification

---

17. *Nancy L. Hanover* v. *Northrup, Superintendent of Schools*, (U.S.D.C., Conn.), 325 F. Supp. 171 (1971).

of the Twenty-Seventh Amendment (equal rights for women) may bring on a flood of lawsuits in this field. Meantime a decision of U.S. District Judge Halbert O. Woodward involving Texas Tech University at Lubbock casts a ray into a field as yet largely unexplored.

Lola Beth Green began as instructor in English at Texas Tech in 1946. She obtained an earned doctoral degree in 1955, and was promoted to assistant professor in the same year; and to associate professor in 1959. Beginning in 1962 she applied periodically for promotion to full professor and was denied each time, through 1969. She alleged that these denials were based solely on the fact that she is female and that such action on the part of Texas Tech University is exemplary of a long-standing pattern and policy of the university of discrimination against women.

She introduced evidence of her professional competence and achievements as well as those of her male colleagues in the English department who had been granted the rank of full professor. She submitted statistical evidence of a pattern of discrimination against women in the hiring, salary, and promotion practices of the English department. She contended that this showed a wide discrepancy in the salaries of men and women of the same rank, in the length of time each must spend in one rank before promotion, and in other related factors.

The fact that the suit was not cast in the guise of a class action, thought Judge Woodward, made it "unnecessary to reach a determination concerning the possibly discriminatory policies or practices of the University or department against women as a class." He added, "The statistical and comparative evidence has been considered by the court in determining whether the denial of plaintiff's promotion was the result of any such sex discrimination."

He was mindful of the recent U.S. Supreme Court decision declaring unconstitutional an Idaho statute that stipulated that as between persons equally entitled to administer an estate, males must be preferred to females. This was Reed v. Reed, U.S. S. Ct. No. 70-4, decided November 22, 1971; reversing 93 Idaho 511, 465 P. 2d 635 (1970). Judge Woodward made a significant positive statement: "Were this Court able to find that the denial of plaintiff's promotion was because of her sex, she would certainly be entitled to recover." He went on to say, "The overwhelming evidence, however, is that the decision not to promote plaintiff was based entirely on considerations other than that of her sex and was completely uninfluenced by the fact that she is a woman."

The university had mustered a phalanx of witnesses who had served in the chain of review of the application at various levels from the department through the Board of Regents, who unanimously testified that their recommendations would have been the same had the applicant been a man with the same qualifications. One woman, herself a full professor, who was on a reviewing committee, testified that the decision not to promote was based solely on the facts of plaintiff's record, with no thought being given to her sex.

The court's conclusion was: "The criteria for promotion to full professor are especially exacting . . . the court finds that these criteria are reasonable . . . and reasonably applied in this case. They call for careful evaluation of (a) teaching ability, (b) publications and scholarly activity, and (c) service to the community and to the University. It is undisputed that such evaluations are necessarily judgmental, and the Court will not substitute its views for the rational and well-considered judgment of those possessing expertise in the field." All relief was denied, and costs taxed against the plaintiff.[18]

On the point of judicial non-interference with university promotion practices, Judge Woodward cited the contemporary case of Lewis v. Chicago State College, discussed herein in Chapter 5.

Other suits similar to that of Lola Beth Green in the U.S. District Court in Texas were reported in the press as in early stages of pendency; but in 1972, the making of judge-made law of sex discrimination in higher education lay largely in the future.

Rather than recount the history of Title VII of the Civil Rights Act of 1964 (which inexplicably excludes educational institutions from its coverage), and of Presidential Executive Order 11246 as amended by Executive Order 11375 (32 Federal Register 14303, October 17, 1967), and of the well-publicized efforts of the Department of Health, Education and Welfare to obtain compliance by several leading universities, it seems preferable to look to the future and list some affirmative actions that are now proposed.

---

18. Lola Beth Green v. Board of Regents of Texas Tech University, (U.S.D.C., Tex.), 335 F. Supp. 249 (1971).

*The President of the American Council on Education*
*Suggests What Colleges and Universities Can*
*Do About Sex Discrimination*

In a *Special Report* dated April 20, 1972, President Roger W. Heyns, of the American Council on Education, included a listing of possible steps which is here quoted:[19]

"Because of the diversity among institutions, there are no prescriptions that will remove all impediments. Nonetheless, some—although not enough—colleges and universities have begun to reduce barriers to women by taking such steps as:

"Removing in coeducational institutions of different bases for the admission of women and men students; for example, quotas, cut-off levels on test scores, limited dormitory accommodations for women, conventions about what is 'man's work.'

"Revising advisory services that deal with the concerns of men but not with the problems encountered by women.

"Giving attention to the special needs of mature women seeking to return to college. Flexible admissions requirements and timing patterns for study and credit for work experience will encourage such women to use their talents.

"Modifying the curriculum to include subjects of special concern to women and to improve the understanding of the roles of women in our society.

"Equalizing, among both faculty and staff, the status of and rewards to men and women who have the same qualifications and perform the same duties.

"Adopting of positive steps to ensure that those involved in the employment of faculty and staff seek women candidates and consider them along with men candidates, applying the same qualification requirements to both.

"Encouraging of women whose preparation for academic positions was interrupted to return and complete their training.

"Nominating women staff members for internships and other extrainstitutional opportunities to qualify them for positions of greater responsibility.

---

19. Roger W. Heyns. "Sex Discrimination and Contract Compliance Beyond the Legal Requirements." *Educational Record* 53: 265-266 (Summer 1972).

"Cooperating with national organizations that are preparing rosters of professional women qualified for academic and advisory positions, and using these rosters (as they become available) in filling institutional vacancies.

"Actively pursuing and using governmental funds for training women professionals and, where possible, recommending changes in government funding patterns in order to give women the same advantages as men (for example, scholarship and fellowship funds for part-time students).

"Finding ways to protect the institution against the presumed evils of favoritism without perpetuating anti-nepotism regulations that almost invariably discriminate against the professional wife.

"Providing part-time employment for professional women and applying reward, fringe benefit, and tenure policies equitable with those of full-time faculty.

"Providing maternity leave without loss of employment rights.

"Providing child-care facilities for women students and staff."

Concluding the brief report, President Heyns added:

"There are enormous potentials of strength and performance in the women of the nation. Creating the conditions under which these potentials are likely to be realized is a necessary, honorable, and rewarding assignment."

Illustrating that unjust and inequitable sex discrimination can be rectified within a university's organization without going to court, the University of Michigan established in September 1971 an internal complaint procedure under which first resort is to the president, who then arranges for a hearing of the grievance by an internal faculty committee. He then reviews the committee's findings and recommendations, and makes the decision. Cheryl Clark, a female research associate in the Highway Safety Research Institute, brought the first case, saying her initial salary, as well as her present salary, was markedly below that of a male employee doing substantially the same work. After hearing the complaint, the internal committee recommended that her salary be brought up to an equitable basis, and that she be paid some $1,140 in back pay. President Robben W. Fleming approved the recommendation.

The committee found no evidence of "willful, deliberate, *ad hoc*" discrimination against Cheryl Clark as an individual, but decided that for her position at the time of her first appointment the University had no "salary structure or policy reflecting a consistent evaluation of factors not related to sex" on which it could support the practice of offering a female employee lower pay than a male employee for the same work.[20]

### The First and Fourteenth Amendments Interdict Automatic Disqualification of a Faculty Member for Membership in the Communist Party

A resolution of the Regents of the University of California dating from June 24, 1949, declared that membership in the Communist party was incompatible with teaching and the search for truth, and directed that the services of any faculty member found to be a member of the party be terminated. Twenty years later Angela Davis, brilliant young black teacher of philosophy at the University of California at Los Angeles, made no secret of her espousal of Communist ideology. Although a faculty committee and the chancellor of the institution recommended that her employment be continued, the Regents took the matter into their own hands and terminated her appointment.

Four taxpayers challenged this action of the Regents as unconstitutional under the First and Fourteenth Amendments to the United States Constitution and Article I, Sections 9 and 10, of the constitution of California. The Los Angeles Superior Court gave summary judgment for the plaintiffs, and this judgment was affirmed by the California Court of Appeals. The resolution of 1949 was unconstitutional and void, and any use of tax moneys to implement it was an impermissible use of public funds. Certain similar resolutions of the 1950's were likewise invalidated.[21] The judgment was sustained, in the opinion of both courts, by the reasoning in *Keyishian* v. *Regents*, 385 U.S. 589 (1967); *Elfbrandt* v. *Russell*, 384 U.S. 11 (1966); and *Vogel* v. *County of Los Angeles*, 68 Cal. 2d 18, 434 P. 2d 961 (1967). These decisions are cited in Chapter 9 and elsewhere in this present volume.

Although the decision was by an intermediate appellate court in

---

20. This account is condensed from press reports. It is not from the official record.

21. *Karst, and Davis, Intervenor* v. *Regents of the University of California,* (Cal. App.), 2 Civil No. 38410 (Jan. 26, 1972); affirming (Super. Ct. Los Angeles County), No. 962388 (October 1969).

California, it is unquestionably in accord with the prevailing law of the land. It affords another illustration of the sea-change in the climate of American law and public policy since the late 1940's and early 1950's, when hysterical cold-war anti-Communism was at a high stage.

The outcome speaks well for the intellectual integrity, level-headedness, and courage of the California trial court and appellate court involved, as well as of the faculty committee and the chancellor of the University of California at Los Angeles.

The suit, begun in 1969, pre-dated and had no connection whatever with the widely-publicized later events in which Angela Davis was indicted for serious crimes and held in prison until she was finally acquitted in 1972.

# CHAPTER 8

## FREEDOM OF SPEECH; EXPRESSION;
## ASSEMBLY; PETITION

Grouped in this chapter are the cases which most plainly appertain to the First Amendment rights mentioned in its title. Several other cases in which these same rights appear as a factor are included in other chapters, more or less throughout this volume, because their other major aspects make that seem appropriate. Here at the outset is an undoubted landmark decision of the United States Supreme Court of 1968.

*U.S. Supreme Court Holds Teacher Can Not Be*
*Discharged Because He Published Criticism*
*of School Board*

Probably the one decision most often cited and relied upon in the numerous recent cases touching the constitutional civil rights of faculty members is the 1968 opinion of the U.S. Supreme Court in which that tribunal declared: "In sum, we hold, . . . absent proof of false statements knowingly or recklessly made by him, a teacher's exercise of his right to speak on issues of public importance may not furnish the basis for his dismissal from public employment."

Marvin L. Pickering, a teacher in High School District 205, Will

County, Illinois, wrote and published in a local newspaper a letter critical of the school board's general fiscal management of the district. A pervading theme of the letter was that too much of the taxpayers' money was spent on athletic activities at the expense of educational programs. The letter also strongly inferred that the board did not live up to its promises made in its publicity in favor of bond issues and tax levies. Incensed, the board gave Pickering a full hearing and discharged him under its statutory authority to remove teachers "when the best interests of the schools require it."

Pickering did not go to the federal courts, but to the state courts of Illinois, where the trial court, the court of appeal, and the state supreme court successively upheld his discharge. The opinion of the Illinois supreme court was, however, subscribed to by only five of the seven Justices, headed by Justice Ray I. Klingbeil. A convincing dissent was written by Justice Walter V. Schaefer, joined by Chief Justice Roy J. Solfisburg.

Said Justices Schaefer and Solfisburg: "It is not clear to me that this language of the General Assembly (*Illinois Revised Statutes* 1965, Ch. 122, paragraphs 10-22.4) intended to authorize a school board to discharge a teacher for criticizing the policies and actions of the board. Such an authorization would tend to cut off a valuable source of information about the conduct of a most important public undertaking. And if the General Assembly did intend to authorize the imposition of the ultimate sanction of discharge against a teacher for exercising First Amendment rights, I think that the State and Federal constitutions require a more precise standard than "the interests of the schools.""

Moreover, "To be entitled to the protection of the First Amendment it is not necessary that the plaintiff's letter be a model of literary style, good taste, and sound judgment. . . . The letter is substantially accurate, and, more important, it has not been shown to be knowingly false. Teachers are not necessarily the best critics in matters of school finance and administration, but they are in closer touch with the actual operation of the schools than anyone else, and the public should not be deprived of their views."

These views of the minority justices were substantially adopted by the U.S. Supreme Court when it reviewed the case, and accordingly the judgment of the Illinois supreme court was reversed. The opinion of the high tribunal was by Mr. Justice Thurgood Marshall, with a brief special concurrence by Justices William O. Douglas and Hugo

L. Black, and a separate opinion by Mr. Justice Byron R. White concurring in part and dissenting in part.

The gist of the opinion of the court was that although some of the eight major statements made in Pickering's letter were incorrect in more or less negligible respects, the letter was a true statement in the main; and there was no evidence that any part of it was known by him to be false when he published it, and no evidence of any bad faith or intent to deceive the public. In a large school system his work as a teacher did not put him into such intimate daily contact with the board or the superintendent as to cause his views to be disruptive of personal relationships and thus damaging to the operation of the schools. His exercise of his constitutional right of freedom of expression was thus adjudged to outweigh any legitimate interest of the state in advancing good operation of its public schools, in this particular case.[1]

This decision has become something of a flagship in the growing fleet of federal court judgments directed at new concepts of balancing the constitutional rights of faculty members against the legitimate interests of the state in operating public schools, colleges, and universities.

## Professor's Averment of Administrative Discrimination Against Him Because of His Letter to the Editor of a Popular Magazine Is a Cause of Action in Federal District Court

U.S. District Judge Ted Dalton of the Western District of Virginia received the complaint of Dr. Edward D. Jervey, professor at Radford College, who alleged he was the victim of administrative discrimination solely because of a "letter to the editor" he had written and which had been published in *Redbook* magazine, in which Jervey had praised the author of an article on premarital sex in a previous issue of the magazine, and stated he intended to use the article in his teaching. The published letter had identified him as a professor at Radford College.

Professor Jervey averred that although the president, Charles K.

---

1. *Pickering v. Board of Education of High School District 205, Will County, Illinois*, 391 U.S. 563, 88 S. Ct. 1731, 20 L. Ed. 2d 811 (1968); reversing 36 Ill. 2d 568, 225 N.E. 2d 1 (1967).

Martin, had recommended and the Board of Visitors had voted that his salary for 1968-69 be raised from $11,500 to $12,700 a year, nonetheless the $1,200 raise had been denied him because the president and the board members became aware of the *Redbook* letter. He also alleged that for the same reason, he had subsequently been excluded from summer school teaching, and that President Martin had imposed other restrictions, academic and social, upon him and his wife. He claimed this was actionable infringement of his constitutional right of freedom of expression.

The college moved to dismiss the case for want of a cause of action. Judge Dalton overruled this motion and ordered the college to file an answer to the complaint within 20 days:

"This court realizes that the Board of Visitors of Radford College does and should have wide discretion in managing that educational institution. However, the court feels that the governing board of a state university should not administratively penalize the exercise by a faculty member of his First Amendment rights by use of the power granted by state statutes. (*Virginia Code*, Section 23-155.7.) This is not to say that such action was done in this case, for that is a question for the jury; however, this court feels that (Jervey's) complaint does set forth a cause of action which is cognizable in the federal courts."[2]

Thus, Professor Jervey would have his day in court.

In March 1973, the press reported that an out-of-court settlement of this case had been made, whereby Professor Jervey received an increase in salary and the sum of $9,000 as damages.

### Protection from Discharge for Assigning and Discussing in High School English Class a Scholarly Article Containing a Word Objectionable to Some Persons

When Robert J. Keefe, teacher of a high school senior English class in Ipswich, Massachusetts, began the school year early in September 1969, he found that his department head had supplied him with multiple copies of the current *Atlantic Monthly*. He gave out 27 copies to his class, and assigned the leading article for reading and discussion.

---

2. *Jervey v. Martin*, (U.S.D.C., Va.), 336 F. Supp. 1350 (1972).

The article, a scholarly sociological essay, contained the obscene word "motherfucker." Keefe discussed the word briefly along with the whole of the article in class, whereupon a storm arose among some of the parents of some members of his class.

Keefe was on tenure. Yielding to the importunities of the parents, the School Committee notified him that it would hold a forthcoming meeting to consider suspending him for 30 days for "conduct unbecoming a teacher and other good causes"; that another meeting would be held one month later to consider permanently dismissing him for the same causes; and that he was "entitled to a written charge or charges, and to a hearing before the School Committee at which you may be represented by counsel, present evidence, and call witnesses to testify in your behalf, and to examine them and to cross-examine other witnesses."

Keefe then asked U.S. District Judge Andrew A. Caffrey for a temporary injunction to prevent the second meeting of the School Committee. Judge Caffrey held that the injunction would not be justified, for the two reasons often invoked under federal court rules: (1) the plaintiff was unlikely ultimately to prevail on the merits, and (2) he would not be irreparably harmed if he lost, because he could bring suit for damages. This judgment was reversed and remanded by the First Circuit Court of Appeals (Chief Judge Bailey Aldrich and Circuit Judges Edward M. McEntee and Frank M. Coffin). Judge Aldrich wrote the opinion:

"We accept the conclusion of the court below that 'some measure of regulation of classroom speech is inherent in every provision of public education'. . . . But we find it difficult not to think that its application to the present case demeans any proper concept of education. The general chilling effect of permitting such rigorous censorship is even more serious." Here he quoted from the United States Supreme Court in the Oklahoma loyalty oath case of *Wieman* v. *Updegraff* 344 U.S. 183, 73 S. Ct. 215, 97 L. Ed. 216 (1952): "Such unwarranted inhibition upon the free spirit of teachers affects not only those who are immediately before this Court. It has an unmistakable tendency to chill that free play of the spirit which all teachers ought especially to cultivate and practice. . . ."

Judge Aldrich thought it probable that Keefe would prevail "on the issue of lack of any notice that a discussion of this article with the senior class was forbidden conduct." And he was "not persuaded by the district court's conclusion that no irreparable injury is involved because the plaintiff, if successful, may recover money damages. Academic freedom is not preserved by compulsory retirement, even if at full pay." He also pointed out that no fewer than five books by different authors, containing the allegedly obscene word in question, were in the school library. "It is hard to think that any student could walk into the library and receive a book, but that his teacher could not subject the content to serious discussion in class."[3]

Two years later a controversy closely paralleling the Ipswich case arose in Lawrence, Massachusetts. Roger A. Mailloux, a tenured teacher of eleventh graders in high school, took occasion to discuss the occurrence of "taboo words" in different times and places, as part of the current study of a novel in which that phenomenon was mentioned. He switched for a moment from historical instances to the present day and wrote the word "fuck" on the chalkboard as an example of a "taboo word" of today. Some of the parents of some of his pupils were outraged by the accounts they received of this incident. The school committee of the city of Lawrence suspended Mailloux for a few days and then discharged him for "conduct unbecoming a teacher." He asked for injunctive relief from U.S. District Judge Charles Edward Wyzanski.

Judge Wyzanski issued a judgment against the city of Lawrence and the individual members of the school committee, including a triple order: (1) Continue Mailloux in employment until the end of the academic year, (2) expunge from the records all references to his suspension and discharge, and (3) compensate him for salary loss (approximately $2,000).

The reasoning in the opinion of Judge Wyzanski was quoted at length by the First Circuit Court of Appeals when it subsequently affirmed his decision:

"I support a qualified right of a teacher, even at the secondary level, to use a teaching method which is relevant and in the opinion of experts of significant standing has a serious educational purpose. This is the central rationale of academic freedom. The Constitution recognizes that freedom in order to foster open minds, creative imaginations, and adventurous spirits. Our national belief is that the heterodox as

---

3. *Keefe* v. *Geanakos,* (U.S.C.A., Mass.), 418 F. 2d 359 (1969); reversing 305 F. Supp. 1091 (1969).

well as the orthodox are a source of individual and of social growth. We do not confine academic freedom to conventional teachers or to those who can get a majority vote from their colleagues. Our faith is that the teacher's freedom to choose among options for which there is any substantial support will increase his intellectual vitality and his moral strength. The teacher whose responsibility has been nourished by independence, enterprise, and free choice becomes for his student a better model of the democratic citizen. His examples of applying and adapting the values of the old order to the demands and opportunities of a constantly changing world are among the most important lessons he gives to youth."

Judges Aldrich, McEntee, and Coffin of the First Circuit, after thus quoting District Judge Wyzanski, then went on to say in their *per curiam* opinion:

"We find the ground relied on below as dispositive to be both sound and sufficient. . . . The district court found that the plaintiff's conduct was within standards responsibly, though not universally recognized, and that he acted in good faith and without notice that these defendants as his superiors, were not of that view. Sanctions in this circumstance would be a denial of due process."[4]

### A Plea That a Faculty Member Has Been Dropped for Exercise of Constitutionally Protected Free Speech in the Classroom Is a Cause of Action in Federal Court

At Eastern Kentucky University, Mrs. Phyllis B. Hetrick was dropped at the end of her first probationary year because she had allegedly discussed the Vietnam war and the military draft in one of her classes during the "Vietnam Moratorium" in mid-October 1969. She was notified in February 1970 that she would not be reappointed for the academic year 1970-71, but never formally given reasons or a hearing. She was told that she was "unsociable" and that her class assignments were "inconclusive."

Her complaint in the court of U.S. District Judge Mac Swinford was met by a motion to dismiss, which Judge Swinford testily denied:

---

4. *Mailloux* v. *Kiley*, (U.S.D.C., Mass.), 323 F. Supp 1387 (1971); affirmed in (U.S.C.A., Mass.), 448 F. 2d 1243 (1971).

"The principal questions raised by the pleadings are whether Mrs. Hetrick's activities came within the area of speech protected by the First Amendment and whether her dismissal was predicated on her engagement in these activities.

"It may be fairly stated that an employee of a state does not have a constitutional right to have his contract renewed, but does have a constitutional right not to be dismissed solely because he has exercised his constitutional rights in a manner displeasing to certain of his superiors."[5] Thus Judge Swinford ordered that the trial go on and the complaint be answered, not dismissed.

He quoted from the decision in *Ferguson* v. *Thomas*:[6] "While he (state college instructor) has no right to continued public employment, such a teacher may neither be dismissed or not re-hired for constitutionally impermissible reasons such as race, religion, or the assertion of rights guaranteed by law or the Constitution."

### Summary Discharge of College Teacher for Speech and Petition in Behalf of State Prison Improvement in Arkansas Is Redressed by Eighth Circuit Court of Appeals

H. Brent Davis, a citizen of Texas, was employed to teach language and literature at the Arkansas A & M College at College Heights in southeastern Arkansas from August 1, 1965, to May 31, 1966, at a salary of $6,000. The Board of Trustees summarily dismissed him on October 29, 1965, as of October 31, without ceremony and without explanation.

He sued in U.S. District Court for an injunction to restore him with back pay, and for $25,000 damages for the tort of wrongful deprivation of employment, under 42 *U.S.C.A.* 1983.[7] Diversity of

---

5 *Hetrick* v. *Martin*, (U.S.D.C., Ky.), 322 F. Supp. 545 (1971).

6. *Supra*, in Chapter 2.

7. 42 *U.S. Code Annotated*, Section 1983, provides:

"Every person who, under color of any statute, ordinance, regulation, custom, or usage, of any State or Territory, subjects, or causes to be subjected, any citizen of the United States or other person within the jurisdiction thereof, to the deprivation of any rights, privileges, or immunites secured by the Constitution and laws, shall be liable to the party injured in an action at law, suit in equity, or other proceeding for redress."

citizenship and the claim for damages in excess of $10,000 also made the case clearly one for federal cognizance.

Davis had spoken uncomplimentary words about the treatment of prisoners in the Arkansas state penitentiary, had advocated the abolition of corporal punishment in the prison, and had circulated a petition to that effect among students and others. The president of the college had warned him against this. He averred that this was the real and only reason for his sudden discharge; and that the Board had deprived him of his constitutional rights under the First and Fourteenth Amendments, and had unlawfully breached the contract of employment, to his irreparable loss, injury, and harm. Chief District Judge Oren Harris denied the Trustees' motion to dismiss the complaint and held there must be a trial on the merits. He said "Exemplary or punitive damages may be awarded." Meantime the Trustees took an appeal to the Eighth Circuit Court of Appeals, where the judgment of Judge Harris was affirmed, and the case sent back to him for trial and decision.

The Circuit opinion was by Circuit Judge M. C. Matthes, sitting with Chief Circuit Judge Martin D. Van Oosterhout and Circuit Judge Donald P. Lay. The Trustees could not interpose the defense of "sovereign immunity" (the Eleventh Amendment protects a state from suits by citizens of another state, except with its consent) because that defense is not available to state or federal officials who act beyond their authority or in violation of the U.S. Constitution. The conclusion was that here was a well-stated claim for relief under 42 *U.S. Code* 1983, against the individual members of the Board of Trustees and the college president, though not named. The court did not hold that a valid claim was stated against the college or the state.

As to the remedy: "If upon trial the District Court finds that the trustees and president did, in fact, subject Davis to a deprivation of his constitutional rights, we have confidence that the Court will formulate such relief as will be just and appropriate.[8]

---

8. *Board of Trustees of Arkansas A & M College* v. *Davis*, (U.S.C.A., Ark.), 396 F. 2d 730 (1968); affirming (U.S.D.C., Ark.), 270 F. Supp. 528 (1967). Certiorari denied, 393 U.S. 962, 89 S. Ct. 401, 21 L. Ed. 2d 375 (1968).

*College Professor Recovered Damages Against Board*
*Members and Administrators for Unjustified*
*Harassment and Prejudicial*
*Termination of Service*

An associate professor of history at Dixie Junior College in Utah, a public institution then governed by the State Board of Education, began his service in September 1965 and continued under four successive one-year contracts until his employment was terminated in May 1969. Near the end of his third year, in accord with the policies of the board and the practices of the college, he was recommended for permanent tenure status by his department head and by the faculty personnel committee. The president of the college, supported by the dean of academic affairs and the dean of applied arts, rejected those recommendations and advised the board that tenure should be denied in this case. The board acquiesced without giving the professor a hearing.

Near the end of his fourth year, it was alleged, the president and the dean of academic affairs had made statements to faculty members and students, allegedly untrue and defamatory, to the effect that he had been guilty of serious misconduct of an undisclosed nature, and that in order to protect him the details would not be made public. This created innuendoes of immoral or illegal conduct, and influenced the faculty personnel committee to recommend that he be denied tenure and that his employment be terminated. When the president and the dean carried this recommendation to the board, it was adopted without any investigation of the reasons that lay behind it. The members of the board felt that their duty was to support the president.

The court was convinced that the actions of the president and the dean in circulating the uncorroborated hints about misconduct were willful and malicious, and that they had seriously damaged the professor's reputation among faculty and students, and made it impossible for him to obtain another teaching position. Testimony caused the court to believe that the real reason for the hostility of these administrators was to punish him for having supported a particular candidate in a state political election, and for his activities as an officer of the local faculty association, including some statements in opposition to certain administrative policies while acting in that capacity.

Against all the board members and the two administrators, jointly and severally, the court awarded damages of $4,100 for loss of salary and attempts to mitigate damages (search for other work); and $40,000 in general compensatory damages for harassment, injury to reputation, and loss of opportunity to continue as a teacher. In addition, punitive damages were awarded in the amount of $2,500 each against the president and the dean of academic affairs.[9]

This condensation of the story is not from the official report, but from the reliable secondary source named in the footnote appended to this page.

The action was in the court of U.S. Chief District Judge Willis William Ritter of the District of Utah, and the adjudication was by him.

### Freedom of Speech Is Contingent upon Appropriateness of Time, Place, and Manner; All-Night Mass Sit-In in Campus Building May Not Be Appropriate

On the evening of May 4, 1970, and for a succeeding day or two, there was apparent likelihood of disorder on the campus of the University of Nebraska at Lincoln. On the afternoon of the fourth a crowd of students assembled to protest the Cambodian incursion and the Kent State tragedy which had occurred that day. They marched to the Military and Naval Science Building, entered it, and took seats in a large central first-floor assembly-room commonly known as "the pit." One of their principal aims seemed to be to obtain from the University administration a strong political statement condemning both Cambodia and Kent, and purporting to commit the University unanimously to that political position.

When administrators appeared in the evening to request the students to leave the building, the students locked arms in "civil disobedience" and refused to move. The president and a few of his administrative colleagues decided to take the path of peaceful negotiation rather than employ force. They opened a smaller side room and invited the students to send in about 20 of their number for discussion. The discussions went on all night without much result. The administrators,

---

9. *Smith* v. *Losee*, (U.S.D.C., Utah), Civ. No. C-283-69 (January 28, 1972). The synopsis recounted here is derived from *College Law Bulletin*, Vol. 4, Nos. 5-6 (January-February 1972), page 41.

reluctant to issue a public statement that would commit the university officially to a political position, prepared statements which the students rejected as unsatisfactory.

Early in the morning of the fifth, the president made another effort to persuade or direct the students to leave the building, but without much success, though some of them left. A regular class was scheduled for one of the smaller rooms, to begin at 7:30 a.m. There were some signs of disgruntlement among the students who had spent the night in "the pit," and some muttered threats were heard about possible violence to students who might enter the building to attend the class. In this circumstance the president ordered the class cancelled, and steps were set in motion to obtain as soon as possible from the local court a writ of injunction which would order the students out of the building on pain of being subject to arrest and punishment for contempt of court. The injunction was not used, because the document had not arrived before the last 100 of the students left the building shortly before 10 a.m., seemingly to attend another campus meeting for discussion of the events of the fourth, scheduled in another building.

Now back to the beginning. Stephen Rozman, an assistant professor of political science, was a part of the scenes as described, throughout. He accompanied the march to the building on the afternoon of the fourth because he was sympathetic with the views of the students, and he thought this demonstration would be a good way of communicating the views that he thought were right. He did not instigate the march, nor did he lead it. He participated with the students in defying the orders and requests to vacate the building. During the night of negotiation he was admitted to the negotiation room and took a prominent part, always denouncing the president's proposals as "too weak" and on one occasion addressing the president with the expression, "For crying out loud!," for which he immediately apologized when requested. He was among the last to leave the building on the following morning.

The Board of Regents, disturbed by the happenings, first directed the appointment of non-university persons to compose a Commission of Inquiry on Disruptive Actions (this came to be known as the Spelts Commission). It reported August 18. Among its findings was the statement that Professor Rozman's actions were improper, and very inappropriate for a faculty member. The Regents then referred to the "Faculty Committee on Academic Privilege and Tenure" the question of whether the actions were in fact improper, and if so, what sanctions should be applied. This committee muffed the question, and after weeks of delay the Regents then referred the same question to a Special Faculty Fact-Finding Committee (this came to be known as the Holtz-claw Committee). It heard the testimony of 45 witnesses, made a tran-script of 1,000 pages, and reported to the Regents February 2, 1971.

The Holtzclaw Committee was invited to meet with the Regents for discussion on the evening of February 5, immediately preceding the regularly scheduled meeting of the Board the following day; and February 6 the Board formally voted that Professor Rozman's contract would not be renewed after it expired in June 1971.

The case came into the court of U.S. Chief District Judge Warren K. Urbom. He contemplated it:

"The competing interests in the dispute are that of freedom of expression, assembly and petition on the one hand, and freedom to employ or not to employ on the other. Neither set of interests is absolute. Identifying the finely honed edge which cuts between the sets of interests is the labor of the court. . . . I conclude that the plaintiff professor passed beyond the perimeters of protected freedom of expression and therefore that the non-renewal of his contract by the university was permissible.

"I offer no view as to the wisdom of the university's action. . . . In no sense am I guided by the rights of private employers to hire or not to hire whom they choose. Private employers are not limited by the Fourteenth Amendment . . . but public employers are. That Amendment prohibits a university, as an arm of the state, from depriv-ing a citizen of life, liberty, or property without due process of law, which means that the university can not fail to reappoint a non-tenured faculty member arbitrarily or capriciously or for constitu-tionally impermissible reasons, such as race, religion, or the exercise of rights protected by the Constitution." Citing *Freeman* v. *Gould*, 405 F. 2d 1153 (1969).

"Two areas of activity of Dr. Rozman," said Judge Urbom, "were outside the scope of constitutionally protected speech: One was in the negotiating room when he intruded into the responsibilities of the administrators for negotiating an evacuation of the building; the other was in the "pit" when by his presence he contributed to a cancellation of a class and defied a directive of the administration to leave the building promptly.

"I am thoroughly persuaded that Professor Rozman had a right to present his views by voice and physical presence about the Cambodian incursion and the Kent State tragedy. A time came in the negotiating room, however, when he temporarily abandoned that role. . . .

"In no way am I suggesting that a faculty member must parrot on substantive issues the views of the administration. I do say, however, that a faculty member can not assume, under the protective umbrella of the federal Constitution, the role of or intrude into another's rightful role of conducting the workings of a university. His cooperativeness to that extent, at least, was a matter of proper concern of the Board of Regents, who had to decide whether he was the kind of faculty member who should be employed by the university."[10]

The opinion was embellished by a quotation from the 1859 book "On Liberty" by John Stuart Mill, English economic and political philosopher:

"The object of this essay is to assert one very simple principle, as entitled to govern absolutely the dealings of society with the individual in the way of compulsion and control, whether the means used be physical force in the form of legal penalties or the moral coercion of public opinion. That principle is that the sole end for which mankind are warranted, individually or collectively, in interfering with the liberty of action of any of their number is self-protection. That the only purpose for which power can be rightfully exercised over any member of a civilized community, against his will, is to prevent harm to others. His own good, either physical or moral, is not a sufficient warrant. He can not rightfully be compelled to do or forbear because it will be better for him to do so, because it will make him happier, or because, in the opinions of others, to do so would be wise or even right. These are good reasons for remonstrating with him, or reasoning with him, or persuading him, or entreating him, but not for compelling him or visiting him with any evil in case he do otherwise. To justify that, the conduct from which it is desired to deter him must be calculated to produce evil to someone else. The only part of the conduct of anyone for which he is amenable to society is that which concerns others. In the part which merely concerns himself, his inde-

---

10. *Rozman* v. *Elliott*, (U.S.D.C., Nebr.), 335 F. Supp. 1086 (1971).

pendence is, of right, absolute. Over himself, over his own body and mind, the individual is sovereign."

Believing that Professor Rozman's activities as described were intrusive upon the rights of others, the court entered judgment for the Board of Regents.

### The Right to Petition Is Not to Be Lightly Impeded

"Where, as here, government is the desired audience, the First Amendment provides a specific constitutionally protected means for communicating effectively: the petition for redress of grievances."

Thus wrote Justice Raymond E. Peters of the supreme court of California, with Chief Justice Roger J. Traynor and Justices Marshall F. McComb, Mathew O. Tobriner, Stanley Mosk, Louis H. Burke, and Raymond L. Sullivan concurring. The court held unconstitutional and void an order of the Los Angeles Board of Education which prohibited teachers from circulating a petition relating to the financing of public education, during duty-free lunch periods on school premises.

The petition was addressed to the governor, the state superintendent of public instruction, and the Los Angeles city board of education. It was described by the court as "brief and respectful." The words of the petition:

"We, the undersigned certificated employees of the Los Angeles City School District, do hereby protest the threatened cutback in funds for higher education and imposition of tuition at college and university campuses.

"We further petition you to increase, not cut the revenues for public education at all levels to meet our soaring enrollments and big city problems—by overhauling our tax structure now, not by violating California's proud claim to free public education for all."

(Space for names and addresses)

On behalf of the board of education it was argued that the proposed circulation during the duty-free lunch period would diminish the harmony of the teaching staff, cause arguments, interrupt the work of many teachers because the duty-free periods were usually staggered and consequently at any given time the teachers' rooms would be occupied partly by those working on their lesson-planning or other duties, and partly by those relaxing; and unavoidably disrupt the work of the school.

The court responded: "The government has no valid interest in restricting or prohibiting speech or speech-related activity simply in order to avert the sort of disturbance, argument or unrest which is inevitably generated by the expression of ideas which are controversial and invite dispute. The danger justifying restriction or prohibition must be one which 'rises far above public inconvenience, annoyance, or unrest,' as was declared by the U.S. Supreme Court in *Terminiello v. City of Chicago*, 337 U.S. 1, 69 S. Ct. 894, 93 L. Ed. 1131 (1949). This is so because the free expression of ideas concerning controversial matters is essential to our system of government."

At another point: "The petition for redress of grievances epitomizes the uses of freedom of expression to keep elected officials responsive to the electorate, thereby forestalling the violence which may be practiced by desperate and disillusioned citizens. This is undoubtedly why it receives explicit First Amendment protection in addition to the protection afforded to freedom of expression generally. . . .

"Tolerance of the unrest intrinsic to the expression of controversial ideas is constitutionally required even in the schools." The superior court of Los Angeles County was directed to issue a writ of mandamus commanding the board to desist from interfering with the circulation of the petition.[11]

Another passage from the same opinion of the California supreme court, by Justice Raymond E. Peters for the unanimous court:

"The rights of students and teachers to express their views on school policies and governmental actions relating to schools, and the power of school authorities to regulate political activities of students and faculty, are of peculiar concern to our state and nation today. Education is in a state of ferment, if not turmoil. When controversies arising from or contributing to the turbulence are brought before the courts, it is imperative that the courts carefully differentiate in treatment of those who are violent and heedless of the rights of others as they assert their cause and those whose concerns are no less burning but who seek to express themselves through peaceful, orderly means.

---

11. *Los Angeles Teachers' Union, Local 1021 American Federation of Teachers* v. *Los Angeles City Board of Education*, 71 A.C. 572, 78 Cal. Rptr. 723, 455 P. 2d 827 (1969).

In order to discourage persons from engaging in the former type of activity, the courts must take pains to assure that the channels of peaceful communication remain open and that peaceful activity is fully protected."

# CHAPTER 9

## THE LOYALTY OATH FUROR

For a quarter of a century state statutes of the "anti-subversive" variety, including elaborate sworn declarations of allegiance for public employees or designated groups thereof, have been meeting the fate of total or partial invalidation at the hands of the U.S. Supreme Court. Often, but not always, these statutes owed their origin to wartime and postwar "witch-hunting" syndromes; especially to the years of "McCarthyism" in the early 1950's and the long-drawn "cold war" hysteria.

The high court struck down such statutes in Oklahoma (1952), Arkansas (1960), Florida (1961), Washington (1964), Arizona (1966), and New York (1967).[1] In this present chapter we find the trend continuing with a decision by the U.S. Supreme Court invalidating a Maryland act (1967), and the U.S. District Courts carrying the progression further in Georgia (1965), Oregon (1966), Colorado (1967), the District of Columbia (1968), Illinois (1969), again Florida (1969), and Mississippi (1970). State courts of last resort have invalidated oath laws in Oregon (1966), New Hampshire (1967), Massachusetts (1967), and California (1967). It appears that in at least one-third of the states, including 5 of the most populous 10, such statutes have been judicially

---

1. The first two of these decisions are discussed at pages 95-103 in *The Colleges and the Courts Since 1950* (415 pp., 1964); the next four at pages 91-102 in *The Colleges and the Courts, 1962-66* (326 pp., 1967); both published by The Interstate Printers & Publishers, Inc., Danville, Illinois 61832.

invalidated by federal or state court decisions. The issue is largely settled.

### California's "Levering Oath" for State Employees Survived Only About 15 Years

In California an unusual case decided in 1971 carries back to 1950. Albert E. Monroe was in 1950 a tenured full professor and chairman of the language arts department at San Francisco State College. In November he was discharged from his employment solely on the ground of his refusal to sign the "Levering Oath," a loyalty oath for state employees prescribed in Section 3103 of the *California Government Code* (transferred in 1953 to the state constitution, Article XX, section 3).

Monroe's dismissal was eventually sustained by the State Personnel Board on September 11, 1953; meantime the state supreme court had upheld the constitutionality of the Levering Oath in the case of *Pockman* v. *Leonard*, 39 Cal. 2d 676, 249 P. 2d 267 (1952).[2] (It is noteworthy that the redoubtable Justice Jesse W. Carter dissented outspokenly and prophetically from that decision.) In this situation Professor Monroe deemed it futile to resort to the courts. Fourteen years later, however, on December 21, 1967, the state supreme court concluded that the Levering Oath was unconstitutional in *Vogel* v. *County of Los Angeles*, 68 Cal. 2d 18, 64 Cal. Rptr. 409, 434 P. 2d 961 (1967); and expressly overruled its 1952 decision in *Pockman*.

The *Vogel* decision became final March 20, 1968, and within a week Monroe wrote to the Trustees of the California State Colleges requesting that (1) he be reinstated, (2) his pension rights be restored upon his payment of the requisite contribution to the pension fund, and (3) he be reimbursed for the difference between the salary he would have earned if he had not been dismissed and the salary he actually earned in other employment. The Trustees refused these requests; and on May 7 he filed with the State Board of Control his claim for some $79,000 differential in back pay, and his claim for the restoration of pension benefits. These claims were rejected and within the year he filed his petition for a writ of mandate to compel the Trustees of State Colleges to reinstate him with pension benefits and differential

---

2. Discussed at page 98 in *The Colleges and the Courts Since 1950.*

back pay. Judge Richard Schauer of the superior court of Los Angeles County dismissed the petition; but the state supreme court, in an opinion by Justice Mathew O. Tobriner, with Chief Justice Donald R. Wright and Justices Raymond E. Peters, Stanley Mosk, Louis H. Burke, and Raymond L. Sullivan concurring, reversed this judgment and held that the statute of limitations precluded an attack on his initial discharge in 1960, and that accordingly he was entitled only to reinstatement and back pay and pension benefits accruing since the refusal to reinstate him in 1968. (Justice Marshall F. McComb dissented.)

Justice Tobriner observed: "This 'right to reinstatement' in no way precludes the Trustees from inquiring into petitioner's present qualifications for his professorship status or from reordering his dismissal if it is determined, after notice and hearing, that there are grounds to justify discharge from his tenured position. His past refusal to sign the Levering Oath, however, can not properly be viewed as having any rational relation to his present fitness to teach, or as otherwise constituting 'cause' for his dismissal." Concluding, Justice Tobriner added: "Petitioner, a victim of the repressive political climate of the postwar era, has now remained forcibly separated by the state from his chosen profession of college teaching for more than 20 years. In holding that this court's ultimate vindication of Professor Monroe's long-held First Amendment rights in *Vogel* entitles him to reinstatement, we do no more than recognize that there now remain no constitutionally permissible grounds for continuing petitioner's exile from the state college system. . . . In light of *Vogel*, the state can no longer justify continued exclusion from the public university community of all those who chose to rebel against this form of 'guilt by association.' "[3]

## Maryland Oath Act Unconstitutionally Vague

Persons familiar with the recent history of loyalty oaths for employees of schools and colleges will remember that the Supreme Court of the United States invalidated two statutes of the state of Washington in a 1964 opinion by Mr. Justice Byron R. White, with six other Justices concurring in his judgment that both of the statutes violated due process of law because each was "forbidding or requiring conduct

---

3. *Albert E. Monroe* v. *Trustees of the California State Colleges*, 99 Cal. Rptr. 129, 491 P. 2d 1105 (1971); reversing 18 Cal. App. 3d 112, 95 Cal. Rptr. 704 (1971).

in terms so vague that men of common intelligence must necessarily guess at its meaning and differ as to its application."

Mr. Justice Tom Clark, with Mr. Justice John M. Harlan joining him, had dissented from this decision because he thought it was an overruling of a decision by the same court only 13 years earlier, in which the Maryland *Ober Act*, which was said to have been copied by the Washington legislature and some other state legislatures, had been held constitutional in a case involving requirements for getting a candidate's name on an election ballot.[4] The two dissenters apparently chose not to give much notice to the marked change in the tenor of public opinion from 1951 to 1964, shifting from postwar and cold war hysteria to a considerably more rational tone. The case is of interest at this point because in 1967 the Supreme Court declared Section 1 and 13 of the *Ober Act* were unconstitutional and void because they were too vague and overbroad in failing to delineate distinctly between permissible and impermissible conduct in the sensitive and important area of academic freedom. Thus one Whitehill, who was denied employment at the University of Maryland because he refused to subscribe to the required oath, won his case.[5] This time the majority opinion was by Mr. Justice William O. Douglas, with five other Justices concurring.

### District of Columbia Oath Invalidated

For the academic year 1968-69, the inaugural year of the new Federal City College of the District of Columbia (chartered by Congress in 1966), four persons who accepted appointments to the faculty, confirmed by vote of the Board of Higher Education, in due course moved to Washington to take up their duties. Some time thereafter they were advised that as a condition of receiving salaries, they would be required to execute the standard appointment affidavit for employees of the District Government:

"I do not advocate nor am I knowingly a member of any organization that advocates the overthrow of our constitutional form of government. I do further swear (or affirm) that I will not so advocate, nor will I knowingly become a member of such an organization during the

---

4. *Gerende* v. *Board of Supervisors of Elections*, 341 U.S. 56, 71 S. Ct. 565, 95 L. Ed. 745 (1951).

5. *Whitehill* v. *Elkins*, 389 U.S. 54, 88 S. Ct. 184, 19 L. Ed. 2d 228 (1967).

period that I am an employee of the District of Columbia Government."

This wording had been suggested by the Corporation Counsel in an opinion of August 23, 1968. Such an affidavit was required of all District employees by Title 5, *United States Code*, Section 3333. Its statutory base was another section of the same Title (Section 7311) enacted in 1964 but having a legislative history tracing back to the Hatch Act of 1939, relating to political activities of governmental employees.

Section 7311: "An individual may not accept or hold a position in the Government of the United States or the government of the District of Columbia, if he—

(1) advocates the overthrow of our constitutional form of government;

(2) is a member of an organization that he knows advocates the overthrow of our constitutional form of government;

(3) participates in a strike, or asserts the right to strike, against the Government of the United States or the government of the District of Columbia; or

(4) is a member of an organization of employees of the government of the United States or of individuals employed by the government of the District of Columbia that he knows asserts the right to strike (repeating)."

Claiming that the statutory provisions underlying the oath were unconstitutional, the four faculty appointees sued to enjoin their enforcement. A special three-judge federal court was convened, composed of Circuit Judges J. Skelly Wright and Harold Leventhal, and District Judge June L. Green. Their *per curiam* decision, referring directly to the wording of the statutes and of the oath, bluntly said, "Such a requirement has more than once been held unconstitutional by the Supreme Court," and cited the two most recent instances.[6]

In the *Keyishian* decision of 1967, said these three judges, "The Supreme Court makes clear that the language in the oaths presented to these plaintiffs suffers from impermissible overbreadth—as covering passive and inert members of an organization as well as leaders and active members, and as covering members indifferent or even opposed to this objective of the organization as well as those specifically intend-

---

6. *Keyishian* v. *Board of Regents (New York)*, 385 U.S. 589, 87 S. Ct. 675, 17 L. Ed. 2d 629 (1967); and *Elfbrandt* v. *Russell (Arizona)*, 384 U.S. 11, 86 S. Ct. 1238, 16 L. Ed. 2d 321 (1966).

ing its furtherance." Then in direct quotation of the words of the
Supreme Court: "mere knowing membership without a specific intent
to further the unlawful aims of an organization is not a constitutionally
adequate basis for exclusion from such positions as those held by
appellants (college professors)."

Proceeding from this point with moderation, the three-judge
court then declared: "It is clear that the Constitution precludes the use
of the appointment affidavit that the District officials require plaintiffs
to sign. We decide only the litigation before us, and rule only on the
statute as applied to these college instructors—through the insistence
on execution of the affidavit previously set forth. The plaintiffs are
entitled to an injunction restraining enforcement of the statute as applied to them through the use of this affidavit."[7]

Here the court footnoted another quotation from the Supreme
Court in *Keyishian*: "Academic freedom is therefore a special concern
of the First Amendment, which does not tolerate laws that cast a pall
of orthodoxy over the classroom." Later in the opinion there was pass-
ing mention of "a variant contention that would particularly condemn
the application of the oath to that unique government employee who is
a university professor, because he is a member of a class entitled to that
particular freedom of inquiry crystallized in the concept of 'academic
freedom' which may not be curtailed or trammeled unless both substantive standards and procedural techniques are demonstrated to be
necessary in the light of some paramount governmental interest." The
decision, however, was expressly not based on these considerations; nor
did it discuss that part of the statute bearing on the right to strike.

Circuit Judge J. Skelly Wright, joining in the unanimous opinion
of his three-judge court, also wrote a lengthy concurrence in which he
argued that the statute was unconstitutional on several other grounds.

### Illinois Loyalty Oath Act of 1969 Declared
### Unconstitutional by U.S. District Court

Suzanne McCormick Thalberg, a lecturer at the Chicago Circle
Campus of the University of Illinois, asked a special three-judge U.S.
District Court to declare void the Illinois act of 1969 which would re-
quire compensation to be withheld from any employee of the state or

---

7. *Haskett* v. *Washington*, (U.S.D.C., D.C.), 294 F. Supp. 912 (1968).

of its public school districts and universities who failed to sign a prescribed affidavit:

"I . . . do swear (or affirm) that I am not a member of or affiliated with the communist party and that I am not knowingly a member or knowingly affiliated with any organization which advocates the overthrow or destruction of the constitutional form of government of the United States or of the State of Illinois, by force, violence, or other unlawful means."

The Thalberg case was heard in conjunction with that of Ernestine Krehbiel, a kindergarten teacher in a public school district in Morgan County, Illinois, involving the same issue. The statute and the oath must fall, said the unanimous court (Senior Circuit Judge John S. Hastings and District Judges James B. Parsons and Bernard M. Decker), because it would penalize knowing membership without intent to participate in the unlawful activities or aims of an organization.

"The Supreme Court's rejection of the 'knowledge' standard in favor of the test of 'specific intent' is an affirmation that the First Amendment protects the right to knowingly associate with proscribed organizations absent some participation in the organization's illegal activities. Any lesser test runs the risk of punishing for 'knowing but guiltless behavior,' thereby chilling the right to free association."

Further in the opinion: "Clearly, it is too late in the day to resurrect the premise that public employment, or compensation therefor, may be conditioned on the surrender of constitutional rights that could not be abridged by direct governmental action. . . .

"In sum, the constitutional issues raised in these actions have been fully and finally determined by the Supreme Court in *Keyishian*,[8] *Elfbrandt*,[9] and *Whitehill*.[10] We are, therefore, left with no alternative but to conclude that the Illinois oath and underlying statute must fall as being in derogation of the First and Fourteenth Amendment rights of the plaintiffs."[11]

Besides declaring the statute void and enjoining its enforcement,

---

8. *Keyishian* v. *Board of Regents of University of the State of New York*, discussed at pages 98-101 in *The Colleges and the Courts, 1962-66*.

9. *Elfbrandt* v. *Russell*, discussed at pages 96-98 in *The Colleges and the Courts, 1962-66*.

10. Cited in footnote 2 in this chapter.

11. *Thalberg* v. *Board of Trustees of University of Illinois*, (U.S.D.C., Ill.), 309 F. Supp. 630 (1969).

the court also ordered that the plaintiffs be granted such "compensation, interest, damages and costs" as might be awarded by U.S. District Judge James B. Parsons, in whose court the actions originated.

### Florida Oath Act Receives Second Blow

Stella Connell, a teacher in the public school system of Orange County, Florida, brought a class action to have Section 876.05, *Florida Statutes Annotated*, declared unconstitutional; and asked a permanent injunction against its enforcement, as violative of her rights under the First, Fifth, and Fourteenth Amendments. The statute had already been previously judicially amended by the Florida supreme court in 137 So. 2d 828 (1962), pursuant to the judgment of the U.S. Supreme Court in *Cramp* v. *Board of Public Instruction*, 368 U.S. 278, 82 S. Ct. 275, 7 L. Ed. 2d 285 (1961).

Circuit Judge Bryan Simpson and District Judges George C. Young and Charles R. Scott sat as the special three-judge federal court. Judge Scott wrote the lengthy and meticulous opinion, reviewing each of the several recent loyalty oath cases from other states, and concluding the following declarations must be stricken from the oath as unconstitutionally infringing political and civil rights: "that I am not a member of the Communist Party," and "that I am not a member of any organization or party which believes in or teaches, directly or indirectly, the overthrow of the Government of the United States or of Florida by force or violence."

Circuit Judge Simpson dissented in small part, because he would have extended the pruning by also striking the declaration, "I do not believe in the overthrow of the Government . . ."; and for this his argument was convincing: "This provision deals solely with *belief*, with what is in the mind and may remain there forever unexpressed by word or deed. It does not deal with action. It does not even deal with spoken or written words advocating overthrow of government. Surely a teacher is entitled to his or her private, secret thoughts and beliefs."[12]

Judge Simpson's view was vindicated by the U.S. Supreme Court when in 1971 it affirmed in part and reversed in part the judgment of

---

12. *Connell* v. *Higginbotham*, (U.S.D.C., Fla.), 305 F. Supp. 445, 18 A.L.R. 2d 268 (1969). Affirmed in part and reversed in part, 403 U.S. 207, 91 S. Ct. 1772, 29 L. Ed. 2d 418 (1971).

the three-judge District Court, in an unsigned *per curiam* opinion holding that the last-quoted clauses must fall. Mr. Justice Thurgood Marshall, joined by Justices William O. Douglas and William J. Brennan, wrote an opinion concurring in the result. Mr. Justice Potter Stewart wrote a short opinion concurring in part and dissenting in part, because it seemed to him that the Florida courts should be given an opportunity to construe the clause before the federal courts passed on its constitutionality.

### Mississippi Oath Act Falls, on Authority of U.S. Supreme Court's Baggett v. Bullitt

Walton D. Haining, an oxygen technician at the University of Mississippi Medical Center, was severed from his employment because he refused to subscribe to the "Loyalty Questionnaire to Be Completed Under Subversive Activities Act of 1950 by Applicants for Positions in Institutions of Higher Learning." The document contained three queries: (1) Are you a subversive person . . . ? (2) Are you a member of a subversive organization . . . ? (3) Are you a member of a foreign subversive organization . . . ? Each ran on toward 200 words of the redundancies and repetitions common to such efforts; and were followed by an affirmation that the respondent understood that his answers were subject to the penalties of perjury, and were deemed to have been made under oath.

Haining asked a special three-judge federal court to declare the act of 1950 unconstitutional. It applied to all employees of the state, but he predicated a class action covering himself and all other employees of the Board of Trustees of State Institutions of Higher Learning. The court was composed of Circuit Judge Charles Clark and District Judges William Harold Cox and Walter L. Nixon. Judge Nixon wrote the opinion, declaring the act unconstitutional and permanently enjoining its enforcement.[13] The language of the statute and of the oath was "unduly vague, uncertain, and broad," the rationale as in the U.S. Supreme Court decision (written by Mr. Justice Byron R. White) in *Baggett* v. *Bullitt*, 377 U.S. 360, 84 S. Ct. 1316, 12 L. Ed. 2d 377 (1964), in which, at the petition of some 60 professors and other employees

---

13. *Haining* v. *Roberts*, (U.S.D.C., Miss.), 320 F. Supp. 1054 (1970).

of the University of Washington, two separate "loyalty oath acts" of
the Washington legislature were invalidated.

### Additional Federal and State Courts Follow U.S.
### Supreme Court in Holding Oath
### Acts Unconstitutional

*Baggett* v. *Bullitt, Elfbrandt* v. *Russell,* and *Keyishian* v. *Board of
Regents,* all decisions of the U.S. Supreme Court cited earlier in this
chapter, have provided the basis of reasoning for U.S. District Court
decisions elsewhere. A special three-judge federal court in Colorado,
composed of Circuit Judge John J. Hickey and District Judges Olin
Hatfield Chilson and William E. Doyle, invalidated the Colorado oath
act and enjoined its enforcement, at the petition of Alan C. Gallagher,
a member of the faculty of the University of Colorado.[14]

In Oregon, the state supreme court declared the oath statute unconstitutional at the petition of Florence Brush, an assistant professor
at Portland State College who refused to take the prescribed oath.[15]

In Georgia a three-judge federal court composed of Circuit Judge
Griffin B. Bell and District Judges Frank A. Hooper and Lewis R.
Morgan held unconstitutional two Georgia enactments of 1935 and
1949 which together prohibited all teachers in public schools, colleges,
and universities from subscribing to or teaching "any theory of government or of economics or of social relations inconsistent with the
fundamental principles of patriotism and high ideals of Americanism,"
and carried a penal provision that any violation of the oath to that
effect would constitute a misdemeanor and subject the violator to immediate summary discharge from his teaching position. Another provision required every person on the payroll of the state to swear "that
he has no sympathy for the doctrines of Communism and will lend
neither aid, support, advice, counsel, nor influence to the Communist
Party nor to the teaching of Communism."

The anti-Communist oath was void for vagueness. The penal provision was a denial of due process under the Fourteenth Amendment.
The prohibition of discussion of "any theory of government . . ." was
a denial of the First Amendment right of freedom of speech. "The

---

14. *Gallagher* v. *Smiley,* (U.S.D.C., Colo.), 270 F. Supp. 86 (1967).
15. *Brush* v. *State Board of Higher Education,* (Ore.), 422 P. 2d 268 (1966).

sum of our holding is that the plaintiffs may be required to uphold, support and defend the Constitution and laws of Georgia and of the United States and that they are not members of the Communist Party. They have not objected to doing so. The balance of the oaths described in these statutes are void."[16]

In New Hampshire the state supreme court, in an advisory opinion responding to a query from the governor and council, held the oath provided in the anti-subversive activities act unconstitutional for vagueness.[17]

In Massachusetts a statute providing for a very brief and simple oath was applied to employees of private colleges as well as to state employees. Joseph Pedlosky, an assistant professor of mathematics at the Massachusetts Institute of Technology, a private institution, challenged it. The text of the oath: "I do solemnly swear that I will support the Constitution of the United States and the Constitution of the Commonwealth of Massachusetts, and that I will faithfully discharge the duties of the position of _____ according to the best of my ability."

The Supreme Judicial Court of Massachusetts held that the second half of the statement might involve the courts in an evaluation process (deciding whether a teacher was performing up to the best of his ability) which "is altogether too vague a standard to enforce judicially," and declared: "It is not a reasonable regulation in the public interest." Accordingly the statutory provision underlying this oath was declared invalid.[18]

*A Simple Affirmation of Allegiance to the State and to the United States, with No Elaborate "Disclaimer" Features, Is Not Unconstitutional*

It is important to be aware that the type of "loyalty oath" which has been declared unconstitutional by the U.S. Supreme Court several times and by other federal and state courts is not the brief and simple

---

16. *Georgia Conference of American Association of University Professors* v. *Board of Regents of the University System of Georgia*, (U.S.D.C., Ga.), 246 F. Supp. 553 (1965); discussed at pages 95-96 in *The Colleges and the Courts, 1962-66.*

17. *Opinion of the Justices*, (N.H.), 228 A. 2d 165 (1967).

18. *Pedlosky* v. *Massachusetts Institute of Technology*, (Mass.), 224 N.E. 2d 414 (1967).

affirmation of allegiance resembling the constitutional oath of office for the president of the United States, and the oaths traditionally administered to high officers of the federal and state governments.

Instead it is the more elaborate "disclaimer" type of oath in which the oath-taker forswears past, present, or future beliefs or associations having any color of subversiveness, that the courts have repeatedly rendered void: "I am not now, never have been, and will not in the future become, a member or agent of the Communist party or of any subversive organization. . . ." It has been repeatedly held that mere membership, without knowledge of any unlawful aims of an organization, or without intent to participate in any such unlawful aims, can not be penalized or prohibited. Overbroad oaths of the type indicated are invalid on the ground of vagueness because they leave the oath-taker uncertain as to what is permissible and what is not as to his actions in relation to so-called "subversive organizations" and "subversive activities," and thus reach farther than intended to silence and inhibit freedom of speech and association, and violate the First Amendment.

The distinction between the two types of oath is illustrated by the experience of the State of Colorado. A statute (*Colorado Revised Statutes, 1963*, Article 17, sections 6, 7, 8) provided that any teacher employed at a university in Colorado should take a "disclaimer-type" oath which was prescribed in the statute. As already noticed herein (footnote 14), this was challenged by Alan C. Gallagher, a lecturer in physics at the University of Colorado, who asked a three-judge federal court to declare it unconstitutional. In an opinion by District Judge William E. Doyle, a three-judge court composed of Circuit Judge John J. Hickey, District Judge Olin Hatfield Chilson, and himself declared the pertinent statute invalid and issued a permanent injunction against its enforcement.[19]

The Regents of the University of Colorado then adopted a much simpler type of oath: "I solemnly swear that I will support the Constitution of the State of Colorado and of the United States of America and the laws of the State of Colorado and of the United States." When this was challenged by a group of faculty members, a three-judge federal court composed of Circuit Judge David T. Lewis, Chief District Judge Edwin Langley, and again District Judge William E. Doyle writing the opinion, decided that the oath was not unduly vague, but

---

19. *Gallagher* v. *Smiley*, (U.S.D.C., Colo.), 270 F. Supp. 86 (1967).

is "plain, straightforward and unequivocal. A person taking it is not left in doubt as to his undertaking. The obligation assumed is one of simple recognition that ours is a government of laws and not of men." The court specified, however, that the oath requirement must apply to all members of the faculty, and not merely prospectively to new members; and retained jurisdiction for 30 days to assure effectuation of that order.[20] The judgment was later affirmed without opinion by the United States Supreme Court.

The legislature of Colorado also labored to enact an oath law that would stand the test of constitutionality, and produced a simple oath: "I solemnly swear that I will uphold the constitution of the United States and the constitution of the state of Colorado, and I will faithfully perform the duties of the position on which I am about to enter." (The wording is almost, but not quite, identical with that of the Regents' oath which was sustained in *Hosack*.)

When this was challenged before a three-judge federal court in 1969 by a statewide group of state university and college faculty members, the constitutionality of the oath was upheld, and the complaint dismissed. Here again the opinion was written by District Judge William E. Doyle, sitting with Circuit Judge Jean S. Breitenstein and District Judge Frank G. Theis. The panel agreed that the case was controlled by *Hosack*.[21]

*For New York as Well as for Colorado, the U.S. Supreme
Court Has Sustained a Simple Affirmation of
Allegiance to the Laws of the
State and the Nation*

Although the U.S. Supreme Court mowed down a tangled thicket of anti-subversive statutes in New York in the famous case of *Keyishian* v. *Regents*, already cited in this chapter, the same high tribunal has also affirmed the judgment of a three-judge federal court in New York which upheld a state statute of 1934 requiring teachers in public and private tax-exempt schools, including universities and colleges, to sub-

---

20. *Hosack* v. *Smiley*, (U.S.D.C., Colo.), 276 F. Supp. 876 (1967); affirmed without opinion in 390 U.S. 744, 88 S. Ct. 1442, 20 L. Ed. 2d 275 (1968).
21. *Ohlson* v. *Phillips*, (U.S.D.C., Colo.), 304 F. Supp. 1152 (1969). Affirmed *per curiam* without opinion in (U.S. S. Ct.), 397 U.S. 317, 90 S. Ct. 1124, 25 L. Ed. 2d 337 (1970); and rehearing denied, 397 U.S. 1081 (1970).

scribe to a simple affirmation: "I do solemnly swear that I will support the constitution of the United States of America and the constitution of the State of New York, and that I will faithfully discharge, according to the best of my ability, the duties of the position of _____, to which I am now assigned." The opinion by District Judge Harold R. Tyler, Jr., sitting with Circuit Judge Leonard P. Moore and District Judge Sylvester J. Ryan, dismissed the complaint of 27 faculty members of Adelphi University, a private tax-exempt institution.

Speaking of the oath, the judges said: "The language . . . is simple and clear in its import. . . . The statutory language of support for the constitutional governments can be substantially equated to that allegiance which, by the common law, every citizen was understood to owe his sovereign." (Citing Blackstone.) With respect to the last 25 words of the oath, the court noted that the nearly contemporaneous decision of the Massachusetts Supreme Judicial Court in the *Pedlosky* case had "voided a strikingly similar portion of a Massachusetts statute" (on the ground that it might involve the courts in the inappropriate task of appraising the performance of faculty members); but remarked, "We are not persuaded by its reasoning. In our view, a state can reasonably ask teachers in public or tax-exempted institutions to subscribe to professional competence and dedication."[22] This judgment was summarily affirmed by the U.S. Supreme Court.

A lay commentator on this decision pithily said: "Thus it now seems clear that affirmative oaths are constitutional, disclaimers are not." There are other recent examples of federal court judgments striking down state loyalty oaths characterized by negativism and overbroad wordings.

### In Kansas and Massachusetts Federal Courts Struck Down Oaths Characterized by Negativism and Overbroad Wordings

*Kansas Statutes Annotated* section 21-305 was enacted as a part of Chapter 246, *Laws 1949*. It is a typical cold-war "witch-hunting" type.

---

22. *Knight* v. *Board of Regents of the University of the State of New York,* (U.S.D.C., N.Y.), 269 F. Supp. 339 (1967); affirmed without opinion in 390 U.S. 36, 88 S. Ct. 816, 19 L. Ed. 2d 812 (1968), with Mr. Justice Potter Stewart believing that probable jurisdiction should be noted (and presumably arguments heard).

It embodied the following oath for public employees, including teachers in public and private schools and universities and college professors and instructors, all of whom were required to subscribe to it on pain of immediate dismissal: "I swear that I do not advocate, nor am I a member of any political party or organization that advocates the overthrow of the government of the United States or of the state by force or violence; and that during such time as I am an officer or employee of the _____, I will not advocate nor become a member of any political party or organization that advocates the overthrow of the government of the United States or of this state by force or violence."

Gerald A. Ehrenreich, a clinical associate professor of psychiatry at the University of Kansas Medical Center, at Kansas City, Kansas, was joined by certain professors at the state universities at Lawrence, Wichita, and Manhattan, in asking a federal district court to declare the oath statute unconstitutional and enjoin its enforcement. A strong point in their pleadings was their showing that the act mandated instant discharge of non-compliant faculty members, with no provision for any hearing or judicial or administrative determination of the individual's reasons, and therefore was contrary to the requirements of due process of law.

The case came before U.S. Circuit Judge Delmas C. Hill and District Judges Wesley E. Brown and Arthur J. Stanley, Jr., constituted as a special three-judge court. Judge Stanley wrote the opinion, declaring the oath statute unconstitutional and enjoining its enforcement.[23]

In Massachusetts, Lucretia P. Richardson was employed as a research sociologist at the Boston State Hospital. After she had been on the job six weeks she was told she would have to sign the oath: "I do solemnly swear that I will uphold and defend the Constitution of the United States of America and the Constitution of the Commonwealth of Massachusetts and that I will oppose the overthrow of the government of the United States of America or of this Commonwealth by force, violence, or by any illegal or unconstitutional method."

Upon her refusal to sign, she was immediately paid for her services to date and told her employment was at an end. The three-judge federal court convened to hear her suit was composed of Chief Circuit Judge Bailey Aldrich and District Judges Anthony Julian and W. Arthur

---

23. *Ehrenreich v. Londerholm*, (U.S.D.C., Kas.), 273 F. Supp. 178 (1967).

Garrity, Jr. The opinion was written by Judge Aldrich. The court declared the oath unconstitutional, chiefly on the grounds that the word "oppose" was hopelessly vague, leaving a wide range of uncertainty as to what means or methods might be intended, so that an intelligent person could only guess at what might be expected of him, and persons of good judgment would differ as to its meaning. Its enforcement was enjoined.[24]

Approximately three years later, however, this judgment was reversed and remanded by the U.S. Supreme Court, sustaining the constitutionality of the Massachusetts oath act just quoted.[25] Mr. Chief Justice Warren Burger wrote the opinion of the high court, in the course of which he expressed some pointed strictures about what seemed to him to be mere semantic hair-splitting, and said bluntly, "We view the second clause of the oath as essentially the same as the first." Justices Potter Stewart, Byron R. White, and Harry A. Blackmun joined him in this opinion. Justices Lewis Franklin Powell and William H. Rehnquist took no part in the consideration or decision of this case. It was decided by a vote of four Justices against three.

Separate dissents were entered by Justices William O. Douglas and Thurgood Marshall, the latter being joined by Mr. Justice William J. Brennan. Mr. Justice Douglas said: "The 'oppose' clause is plainly unconstitutional by our prior decisions."

### Provision for Automatic Discharge in a "Disclaimer-Type" Oath Statute Makes It Unconstitutional as in Violation of Due Process

Federal courts have not invariably relied on vagueness and overbreadth as grounds for invalidating disclaimer-type oath statutes. In 1965 Circuit Judge M. Oliver Koelsch, Chief District Judge Fred M. Taylor, and Senior District Judge William C. Mathes, sitting as a special three-judge court in Idaho, had to pass upon the constitutionality of Chapter 210 of the Idaho legislative acts of 1963, which prescribed

---

24. *Lucretia P. Richardson* v. *Cole, Superintendent of Boston State Hospital,* (U.S.D.C., Mass.), 300 F. Supp. 132 (1969). Reversed and remanded in *Cole* v. *Richardson,* (U.S. S. Ct.), No. 70-14 (April 18, 1972).

25. *Cole* v. *Richardson,* (U.S. S. Ct.), remanded to determine mootness, 397 U.S. 240 (1970); and decided, No. 70-14 (April 18, 1972); reversing (U.S.D.C., Mass.), 300 F. Supp. 132 (1969).

a lengthy and elaborate "disclaimer-type" oath, and mandated automatic disqualification and discharge for any public employee who refused to subscribe to it.

The automatic discharge provision went against the grain of these three federal jurists. The law was obviously invalid, they said, because it made no provision for a hearing prior to a public employee's discharge, in order to determine the nature and quality of his membership, present or past, in an organization proscribed by the statute. Without this, it plainly failed to meet the requirements of due process.

To make their position clear, the judges said explicitly that the statute was not "void for vagueness," and not a bill of attainder or an *ex post facto* law. "But no discharge of a public employee, which operates to bestow a 'badge of disloyalty' or to create a 'built-in inference of guilt,' will be permitted without according the right to such hearing as is requisite to due process of law. . . ."[26]

The plaintiffs were more than 100 faculty members and other employees of the two Idaho state universities—the University of Idaho and Idaho State University, as well as certain public school teachers in Pocatello and elsewhere.

The late Mr. Justice Hugo L. Black was not a believer in elaborate disclaimer-type loyalty oaths. Here is a quotation from his concurring opinion in the 1958 case of *Speiser* v. *Randall*, 357 U.S. 513:

"I am convinced that this whole business of penalizing people because of their views and expressions concerning government is hopelessly repugnant to the principles of freedom on which this Nation was founded and which have helped to make it the greatest in the world. As stated in prior cases, I believe 'that the First Amendment grants an absolute right to believe in any governmental system, to discuss all governmental affairs, and to argue for desired changes in the existing order. This freedom is too dangerous for bad, tyrannical governments to permit. But those who wrote and adopted our First Amendment weighed these dangers against the dangers of censorship and deliberately chose the First Amendment's unequivocal command that freedom of assembly, petition, speech and press shall not be abridged. I happen to believe this was a wise choice and that our free way of life enlists such respect and love that our Nation can not be imperiled by mere talk. . . .'

"Loyalty oaths . . . tend to stifle all forms of unorthodox or un-

---

26. *Heckler* v. *Shepard*, (U.S.D.C., Idaho), 243 F. Supp. 841 (1965).

popular thinking or expression—the kind of thought and expression which has played such a vital and beneficial role in the history of this Nation. The result is a stultifying conformity which in the end may well turn out to be more destructive to our free society than foreign agents could ever hope to be. . . . I am certain that loyalty to the United States can never be secured by the endless proliferation of 'loyalty oaths'; loyalty must arise spontaneously from the hearts of people who love their country and respect their government."

For an instance of alleged conflict between religious scruples and the taking of a simple non-disclaimer type of loyalty pledge, or indeed any type of oath-taking whatsoever, see the case of *Biklen* v. *Board of Education of Syracuse*, which is discussed *supra* in Chapter 7, "Discrimination: Race; Religion; Sex; Ideology."

# CHAPTER 10

## FREEDOM OF ASSOCIATION: FACULTY ORGANIZATIONS; COLLECTIVE NEGOTIATIONS

The great Justice Benjamin N. Cardozo, serving in his earlier years as a judge of the court of appeals of the State of New York, wrote:

"The governing body of a university makes no attempt to control its professors and instructors as if they were its servants. *By practice and tradition,* the members of the faculty are masters and not servants. . . . They have the independence appropriate to a company of scholars."[1]

Forty-five years later, a New York lawyer expertly experienced in the law of collective negotiations in higher education commented: "While governing boards do not exercise the same type of managerial control over the internal decision-making process as is customary in a business enterprise, they are nevertheless vested with controlling legal authority and represent the interest and support of the larger community. The governing board acts as a check on myopic university decision-making. In times of stress this braking function becomes increasingly apparent in public institutions where not only the governing board but other levels of public managerial authority in the Execu-

---

1. In *Hamburger* v. *Cornell University,* 240 N.Y. 328, 148 N.E. 539 (1925).

161

tive branch become involved in education issues and major budgetary considerations."[2]

There is no conflict between the two foregoing statements. The later one hints at the long push, extending over half a century and intermittently felt in every state, toward ultimate total centralization of the management of public higher education in the executive department of the state, under the thumb of the governor, in the name of "efficiency, economy, and planning."

To say that this yearning is an effort to copy the administrative strategies of large business corporations would be to defame them, for they have long since recognized the values of decentralization. But their tendency toward bigness, bureaucracy, and impersonality (recently subject to some attempts at melioration), together with their formerly callous "master and servant" attitudes toward their employees and their often bitter opposition to labor organizations, have brought about a considerable degree of federal and state regulation of labor relations, so that collective bargaining in the domain of private employment has become a commonplace and increasingly respected device.

"Collective negotiations" in higher education has become in very recent years a healthy and rapidly growing infant, perhaps destined to encompass the whole field. It is not too much to suggest that unless the durable press to centralize the governance of public colleges and universities in the statehouses is moderated, it can only be a powerful impetus toward adversary organizations of the faculties and staffs, precisely as has already taken place in the industrial world. Irrespective of that point, it would be probably futile to lament the oncoming of collective bargaining in universities and colleges, because it already appears to be inevitable. It is an idea whose time has come.

*First Amendment Confers Right to Join Teachers'*
*Union, Held Seventh Circuit U.S.*
*Court of Appeals*

John Steele and James McLaughlin, probationary teachers in Cook County, Illinois, School District 149, were separated from their em-

---

2. William F. McHugh, in "Collective Bargaining with Professionals in Higher Education: Problems in Unit Determinations." *Wisconsin Law Review* (1971), 44-90.

ployment allegedly because of their connection with the local union of the American Federation of Teachers. Steele was not offered a second-year contract, and McLaughlin was dismissed before the end of his second year. Each sued in federal District Court for damages of $100,000 under 42 *U.S. Code*, Section 1983. District Judge James B. Parsons dismissed the suit on the ground that the plaintiffs had no First Amendment right to join or form a labor union, so that there was no jurisdiction under the Civil Rights Act.

Horrified at the idea of a union of public school teachers, Judge Parsons was emphatic in his hands-off statement: "The union may decide to engage in strikes, to set up machinery to bargain with the governmental employer, to provide machinery for arbitration, or may seek to establish working conditions. Overriding community interests are involved. The very ability of the governmental entity to function may be affected. The judiciary, and particularly this Court, can not interfere with the power or discretion of the state in handling these matters."

The judgment of dismissal was reversed and the case remanded for trial by the Seventh Circuit Court of Appeals. Circuit Judge Walter J. Cummings, sitting with Chief Circuit Judge Latham Castle and Circuit Judge Thomas E. Fairchild, spoke to the point:

"Concluding that the First Amendment confers the right to form and join a union, we reverse on the ground that the complaint does state a claim under Section 1983." Moreover, "It is settled that teachers have the right of free association, and unjustified interference with teachers' associational freedom violates the Due Process clause of the Fourteenth Amendment." He cited at this point *Shelton* v. *Tucker*, 364 U.S. 479, 81 S. Ct. 247, 5 L. Ed. 2d 231 (1960), and continued:

"Public employment may not be subjected to unreasonable conditions, and the assertion of First Amendment rights by teachers will usually not warrant their dismissal." Here he cited *Keyishian*, *Pickering*, and other recent Supreme Court decisions. "Unless there is some illegal intent, the individual's right to form and join a union is protected by the First Amendment." Citing several Supreme Court decisions and quoting from the opinion in *NAACP* v. *State of Alabama*, 357 U.S. 449, 79 S. Ct. 1163, 2 L. Ed. 2d 1488 (1964):

"It is beyond debate that freedom to engage in association for the advancement of beliefs and ideas is an inseparable aspect of the 'liberty' assured by the Due Process clause of the Fourteenth Amendment, which embraces freedom of speech."

In direct response to the qualms of the District Court: "Illinois has not prohibited membership in a teachers' union. No claim is made that either of the plaintiffs ever engaged in any illegal strike or picketing." Even the board had no rule against union membership. An Illinois statute permitted check-off of union dues from salaries of employees of local governmental agencies. "Collective bargaining contracts are not against the public policy of Illinois. *Chicago Education Association* v. *Board of Education of City of Chicago,* 76 Ill. App. 456, 22 N.E. 2d 243 (1966)."

"The superintendent and board members can prevail in this case only if they show the plaintiffs were discharged on justifiable grounds." Therefore the case was remanded to the District Court for trial of the facts.[3]

*Fifth Circuit U.S. Court of Appeals Held Palm Beach County Teachers Alleging Discrimination Against Them Because of Their Membership in an Organization of Their Choice Had Cause of Action in Federal Courts*

As an aftermath of the memorable and bitter statewide controversy in Florida in 1968 between teachers and the State Board of Education, the school system of Palm Beach County was alleged to be practicing unconscionably discriminatory treatment of its teachers who were members or officers of the County Teachers' Association (CTA), in an effort to destroy that organization. When the complaint reached the Fifth Circuit Court of Appeals, there was forthcoming a ringing judicial pronouncement that the constitutional right of association could not thus be infringed, and the case must go back to the District Court and be tried on the facts, and not summarily dismissed.

This judgment was in the concise and lucid prose of Circuit Judge John Minor Wisdom, of which but little can be deleted without damage to the meaning. Sitting with Judge Wisdom were Circuit Judges Walter Pettus Gewin and Robert A. Ainsworth. The allegations as described by Judge Wisdom:

"From 1949 until early 1968, the Palm Beach County Board of Public Instruction recognized and dealt with the Palm Beach County

---

3. *McLaughlin* v. *Tilendis,* (U.S.C.A., Ill.), 398 F. 2d 287 (1968).

Teachers Association as the representative of the classroom teachers in Palm Beach County. But during the early part of 1968, a bitter controversy erupted throughout Florida. . . . In Palm Beach the controversy between CTA and the school board produced a work stoppage and attempted mass resignations. At that point the Palm Beach school board began to develop its 'Professional Affairs Policy, Number 8342.2.' In the words of the complaint, the Policy's purpose was 'to eliminate Plaintiff CTA and to create an organization of all employees over which the Defendant Board of Public Instruction would have complete control.' The Policy carried out this purpose by providing that the school board would hear representations only by individual teachers or by the committees set up by the Policy, not by organizations such as CTA. The complaint alleges instances where school board members acknowledged that the purpose of the Policy was to destroy CTA.

"Moreover, no longer can CTA members obtain leave, with or without pay, to attend meetings of CTA, the Florida Education Association, or the National Education Association. Before the implementation of the Policy, CTA members received such permission and, according to the complaint, non-CTA members still receive that permission. The schoolboard has now forbidden CTA its customary 'in-processing' function of welcoming newly hired teachers, informing them of benefit programs (health insurance, retirement plans, and a credit union), and inviting them to join CTA. Finally, agents of the school board have threatened CTA members with discriminatory treatment and in one case have fulfilled their predictions. The Superintendent allegedly told plaintiff Orr when the latter's name was on the promotion agenda that Orr could not be promoted because he was 'a leader of an antagonistic organization.' The allegation continued that when racial unrest was threatened Orr eventually received a position at a lower level than originally contemplated."

Now for the Circuit Court's disposition of the complaint, again in the words of Judge Wisdom:

"Under *Conley* v. *Gibson*,[4] 355 U.S. 41, S. Ct. 99, 2 L. Ed. 2d 80

---

4. This was a case in which Negro members of a railway labor union were suing the union to compel it to represent them without discrimination. Mr. Justice Hugo L. Black cut through the jungle of verbose and far-fetched pleadings that had frustrated these plaintiffs in lower federal courts; and concluded:

"The Federal Rules reject the approach that pleading is a game of skill in which one misstep by counsel may be decisive to the outcome, and accept the

(1957)," said Judge Wisdom, "we can not escape the conclusion that the plaintiffs have alleged discrimination that could significantly deter freedom of association. It may be that there is adequate explanation and justification for each of these alleged actions, but in this posture of the case we can not tell. It is equally possible that CTA members are being unnecessarily penalized for their choice of organization. We have no doubt that teachers possess constitutionally protected rights of free association and that Section 1983[5] provides a remedy against state interference. In *McLaughlin* v. *Tilendis* (7 Cir. 1968)[6] 398 F. 2d 287, for example, . . . the Seventh Circuit held that teachers have a right to free association without unjustified interference and the right to form and join a union unless there is illegal intent. That court concluded that Section 1983 provided a remedy. . . . The fact that here the discrimination has not extended to actual discharge does not preclude a remedy for the discrimination that has occurred.

"We expressly preclude discussion of what remedy is appropriate if the plaintiffs prove their case. The remedy will vary with what they prove, and we consider it unwise to speculate about appropriate action on such a sparse record.

"The defendants argue that the members of the school board acting in their official capacities are not within the coverage of Section 1983; that the plaintiffs' true remedy is in the Florida courts under Florida statutes and the federal courts should therefore abstain. We reject each of these contentions. . . . The plaintiffs have stated a federal cause of action and do not seek to interpret or attack Florida statutes. Finally, the defendants have shown no good reason why this action should not be sustained as a proper class action.

"We repeat, as always, 'that this case is recommitted to the supervision of the trial judge (U.S. District Court) without the slightest murmur of a suggestion as to how it should or will come out when the real facts, not what the lawyer says the facts are, are developed or the lack of them demonstrated to a certainty warranting summary judgment, directed verdict or the like.' "[7]

This is in refreshing contrast to the monotonous procession of

---

principle that the purpose of pleading is to facilitate a proper decision on the merits."

5. The Section is quoted in full in footnote 8 of Chapter 4, *supra*.
6. Discussed previously in this chapter.
7. *Orr* v. *Thorpe*, (U.S.C.A., Fla.), 427 F. 2d 1129 (1970).

negative summary judgments coming too frequently from some U.S. district courts. Compare the words of Circuit Judge Wisdom with the colorful strictures of Chief Circuit Judge John R. Brown of the Fifth Circuit in the case of *Pred* v. *Board of Public Instruction* (1969), discussed in the early part of Chapter 3 herein, in which he characterized some summary judgments as "too quick, too soon, too enigmatic."

### Dropping of Teachers Because of Their Lawful Activities in Behalf of Faculty Unionization Is Not Acceptable

Donald E. Leon, an assistant professor at New York's State University College at Cortland, after some five years of probationary service was informed his contract would not be renewed for 1968-69. Convinced that the sole reason was that he had been vocal in faculty union advocacy, he asked the local supreme court to declare the notice void. Dismissing his petition, the court said: "Since the petitioner had not attained tenure or near-tenure status, he had acquired no vested or property rights to have his contract renewed on its terminal date. . . . Further, when no right to re-employment exists, the decision not to re-employ is essentially administrative and thus not otherwise subject to review on the facts here.[8] Leon then took his case to the New York Public Employment Relations Board, whose hearing officer investigated and decided that his allegation was true, and recommended that he be given another two-year contract. Although not concurring with this finding, the college administration agreed to follow the recommendation.

At the Northern Virginia Community College at Alexandria, one Haubner, professor of police science, alleged his contract was not renewed because of his efforts to organize the Northern Virginia Community College Faculty Association, a chapter of the National Faculty Association of Community and Junior Colleges, and an affiliate of the National Education Association. He asked for $100,000 compensatory damages and $50,000 punitive damages, and was awarded a judgment for $20,000 against Rushton, acting president, and Hamel, chairman of

---

8. *Leon* v. *Rogers*, Cortland County supreme court, Index No. 13516 (April 23, 1968).

the governing board,[9] by the United States District Court, according to press reports.

Allegations that a faculty member has been dropped because of union activity are not always successfully proved to the satisfaction of a court. At Chicago State College, when the Cook County College Teachers' Union made the allegation as joint plaintiff with two members of the department of psychology faculty who had been dropped, U.S. District Judge Richard B. Austin held a four-and-a-half-day hearing in which the testimony of four top-echelon administrators of the college convinced him that the college rules had been carefully followed in this case, and that there was no substance in the averment that union activity was the cause, but in fact the college had other good reasons for terminating the service of the two plaintiffs. Stressed was the fact that the vote of the members of the psychology faculty was split 6 to 5 in each case; that this vote was only a recommendation to the department head, who was required to make an *independent* recommendation, which he did, adverse to the plaintiffs.

The Seventh Circuit Court of Appeals affirmed Judge Austin's conclusions, in an opinion by Circuit Judge Wilbur F. Pell, sitting with Circuit Judges Thomas E. Fairchild and Robert A. Sprecher: "It is not our function to evaluate a professor's competence nor to determine whether he any longer fits the needs of a school that is expanding its programs and attempting to upgrade the quality of its faculty. We can not so far involve this court in the discretionary decisions made by state-controlled colleges." It was also mentioned that the suit, brought as a class action, did not meet any of the requisites of the federal rules for class actions: only nine teachers were dropped in that year, and hence joinder of all as plaintiffs was not impracticable; at that time the union had only a minority of the faculty as members, and had not been recognized as a bargaining unit; and though the court agreed it was true that the outcome might conceivably affect the interests of the whole faculty, and indeed possibly of the whole public, the specific requisites for a class action were unmet.[10]

During the preceding year the same court had decided a somewhat similar case arising in Indiana, and involving one teacher in a public

9. *Haubner* v. *Rushton and Hamel*, (U.S.D.C., E.D. Va., Alexandria Div.), Civil Action No. 4885-A (December 5, 1969).

10. *Cook County College Teachers Union, Local 1600* v. *Byrd*, (U.S.C.A., Ill.), 456 F. 2d 882 (1972).

school district who was denied tenure, allegedly on account of anti-union bias in the board. The court saw no evidence of anti-union bias, and concluded that there had been a non-prejudicial appraisal of the teacher's performance, including evidence of several instances of personal conduct verging on disqualifying misbehavior: the teacher habitually came late and left his classes early; he admitted having made improper statements in the classroom, including some abusive and inappropriate comments; he encouraged students to violate school rules; during a teachers' party at a public restaurant he was under the influence of alcohol and acted in an obnoxious manner, much to the embarrassment of other teachers present.[11]

In 1969 a U.S. District Court in Louisiana found no substance in averments by a teacher at Delgado College (a state-subsidized institution formerly operated and supported by the city of New Orleans) of anti-union bias and discrimination in the decision not to renew the teacher's contract.[12]

### The Euphemistic Phrase "Shared Governance" Is Broad Enough to Include Many Forms of Faculty Organizations, with Diverse Purposes and Methods

The governance of colleges and universities varies from instances wherein there is almost no organized faculty participation, to cases where the elected "faculty senate" or equivalent body by some other name is an efficiently organized, industrious, respected, and influential body. A recent tendency is to combine representatives of the faculty (constituting a majority) with representatives of the student body and of the college administration in a single organization bearing some such name as "University Senate." Altogether there is an almost infinite variety of structures, all intended to advance participatory democracy. However, under existing law in all states, the conclusions of any and all such bodies are no more than recommendations to the president and

---

11. *Knarr* v. *Board of School Trustees of Griffith*, (U.S.C.A., Ind.), 452 F. 2d 40 (1971).

12. *Beauboeuf* v. *Delgado College*, (U.S.D.C., La.), 303 F. Supp. 861 (1969). Affirmed in (U.S.C.A., La.), 428 F. 2d 471 (1970).

through him to the lay governing board, in which plenary power to manage the institution is vested by state statutes.[13]

This statement scarcely needs documentation, but it is illustrated by a decision of a California court of appeal in 1972. The Regents of the University of California govern that nine-campus institution by virtue of the California Constitution of 1879 which vests plenary power in them as an autonomous corporation. They have a standing rule delegating to the academic senate power to "authorize and supervise courses and curricula." On September 9, 1968, the "board of educational development," an organ of the Berkeley division of the academic senate, approved the organization and structure of a course for the fall quarter entitled "Dehumanization and Regeneration in the American Social Order" and designated as Social Analysis 139X. There were to be 20 lectures, of which 10 were to be given by Eldridge Cleaver, the black activist, who was not a member of the faculty.

The majority of the Regents were somewhat aroused and much inclined to disapprove the plan. At a meeting of the Board of Regents on September 30, before the opening of the fall quarter, the Board resolved: (1) "effective immediately . . . no one may lecture . . . for more than one occasion during a given academic quarter on a campus in courses for University credit, unless he holds an appointment with the appropriate instructional title . . ."; and (2) "if Social Analysis 139X can not be restructured to satisfy this policy     it shall not be offered for credit. . . ."

The course was given as originally planned and approved by the board of educational development. On November 17 the Board of Regents resolved that it "not be given academic credit, directly or indirectly." Some students and some faculty members contested this determination in the local trial court, but were defeated by a demurrer (plea of no cause of action); and eventually this disposition of the case was affirmed by the intermediate appellate court in an opinion by Presiding Justice Murray Draper, in which Justices Harold C. Brown and Thomas W. Caldecott concurred without opinion:

"In any event, the power delegated to the senate is neither exclusive nor irrevocable. . . ." To accept the contrary argument "would be to hold that a delegation of authority . . . amounts to a surrender of

13. Exception: In many instances the applicable state statutes provide that the governing board may *confer degrees* only upon the recommendation of the faculty, and not otherwise.

authority." It was of no consequence that the Board of Regents did not in this instance follow their own bylaw as to procedure for formally amending their standing rules.

"The dispute here is essentially whether the regents or the faculty shall control university policy in determining whether credit is to be given for courses conducted by non-members of the faculty." This power is unmistakably vested in the Regents.[14]

The resolution of the Regents of November 17 added, "The Regents censure those within the academic senate and its board of educational development who were responsible for this action." Four members of the faculty alleged that this would subject them to punishment without due process; but the court gave this no countenance, noting that the censure named no one, and did not require any notation to be made on any faculty member's record. Thus there was no substantial evidence that it would have any adverse effects on possible future promotions or anyone's opportunities to advance in his profession or obtain other employment.

Whatever their form, internal institutional faculty organizations in general have a reputation for elaborate gentility, much time-consuming debate, and ultimate ineffectiveness. If not vetoed or sidetracked by the president of the institution, their recommendations are often disapproved or ignored by the governing board, though sometimes adopted by it and made a part of its ordinances and rules.

This is not to deny that a great many determinations of faculty bodies (senates and committees of various types, as well as the faculties of instructional departments and divisions) actually are made effective with only the tacit consent of the governing board, and in many instances even without its knowledge, when they pertain to matters of detailed operation deemed to be below the level of generality to which the governing board ought to confine its attention. But any of these lesser-level decisions may be instantly rendered void by the governing board, if and when it so decides. Any authority exercised by faculty bodies is by delegation from the governing board; and delegated authority may be withdrawn. Though literally millions of decisions in the detailed operation of universities and colleges are made by faculty bodies and individual faculty members, all this is subject to the express

---

14. *Searle* v. *Regents of University of California* (and *Celinda Tabucchi* v. *Regents*), 23 Cal. App. 3d 448, 100 Cal. Rptr. 194 (1972).

or tacit approval of the governing board which is the receptacle of legal power. In general, but by no means always, governing boards have tended to exercise a commendable restraint in abstaining from interfering in the detailed academic administration.

A starkly different relationship between faculty and governing board is introduced by the advent of collective bargaining. Here the two deal as equals "at arm's length" across the negotiating table to reach mutually satisfactory agreements regarding specified matters for limited periods of time. At law the board's power is the same as it was before, because to negotiate does not mean to capitulate; but the board's representatives come face to face with the faculty's representatives for sustained and serious discussion of matters of importance to the continued successful operation of the institution and the welfare of its students and faculty, knowing full well that an impasse in the process may have damaging consequences for the whole enterprise and all persons connected with it; whereas the making of successive contracts covering crucial issues may pay large dividends in "job satisfaction" for all employees and in lifting the morale of students and faculty and all the other institutional constituencies.

### Brief Synopsis of the Legal Aspects, in Mid-1972, of Collective Negotiations in Higher Education

Although it was said early in 1972 that already one-third of the faculty members in universities, colleges, and junior colleges in the 50 states were working in institutions where collective bargaining between board and faculty prevailed, the volume of judge-made laws on the subject was as yet scanty, and few precedents had been firmly established. The "nuts and bolts" of the process were in a formative stage, being initially developed by such quasi-judicial administrative agencies as the National Labor Relations Board and the state labor relations commissions in the several states having such agencies.

The National Labor Relations Act, in its earlier forms at least up to 1973, expressly excluded employees of states and their local subdivisions from its coverage. In 1972 the National Education Association was urging the Congress to amend the Act to include public universities, colleges, and junior colleges, because, the Association argued, state regulation of collective bargaining was spotty and diverse, presenting a chaotic picture where at least some degree of nationwide uniformity was needed.

In its earlier years the National Labor Relations Board abstained from taking jurisdiction over non-profit educational and charitable institutions, thus excluding private non-profit universities and colleges.[15] It deviated from that policy in a few later cases involving employees in certain defense-related research projects conducted by private universities; but as recently as 1965 it declined to take jurisdiction in a matter concerning employees of a computer center operated by the Massachusetts Institute of Technology.[16]

In 1970 the Board took jurisdiction in cases concerning Cornell University and Yale University, and adopted a rule asserting its jurisdiction over any private non-profit college or university having an annual gross revenue of at least $1 million from all sources, excluding gifts by their own terms not available for operating expenses.[17] This embraces a large majority of all private institutions of higher education.

### What Is an Appropriate Bargaining Unit?

In *Cornell University*[18] the Board rejected a plea for a separate unit for employees of the New York City Office of the State School of Labor and Industrial Relations (which is a state-supported college adjacent to the Cornell campus at Ithaca, and administered by Cornell's Board of Trustees, a private corporation); and in *Yale University*[19] it rejected a request for a separate unit for the employees of the Epidemiology and Public Health Department. But in 1971 the Board yielded to the persuasiveness of the law professors and determined in *Fordham University*[20] that the members of the Fordham Law School Faculty would constitute an appropriate unit for collective bargaining separate from the other faculty members of the university. Despite this break,

---

15. *Trustees of Columbia University*, 97 N.L.R.B. 424 (1951).

16. *Massachusetts Institute of Technology*, 152 N.L.R.B. 64 (1965).

17. N.L.R.B. *Rules and Regulations*, Section 103.1. 35 *Federal Register* 18370 (1970).

18. *Cornell University*, 183 N.L.R.B. 41 (1970).

19. *Yale University*, 184 N.L.R.B. 101 (1970).

20. *Fordham University*, 193 N.L.R.B. 23. Also see article by Rock: "The Appropriate Unit Question in the Public Service: The Problem of Proliferation." 67 *Michigan Law Review* 1001-1016 (1969).

the trend will undoubtedly be toward recognition of university-wide and statewide units.

*Which Faculty Members, If Any, Are Supervisory or Administrative, and Hence Excluded from the Bargaining Unit?* Although Cardozo said "faculty members are masters, not servants," he undoubtedly meant that they are masters of independent scholarship and not straw bosses of hordes of subordinates; and he would never have inferred that they are more nor less than servants of the public in a very broad and elevated sense. He was speaking in the narrower context of the traditional master-servant relationship as it has existed from time immemorial in private affairs.

The National Labor Relations Board has been generally realistic about this, and in more than one decision has held that the quasi-supervisory and policy-recommending authority which adheres to faculty status (and is exercised in part through internal faculty organizations) does not make faculty members supervisory or managerial employees.[21] Part-time or "adjunct" members of the faculty are includable if they are employed as teachers one-fourth time or more. The decisions are not uniform as to the inclusion or exclusion of the heads of instructional departments. Usually they are at once teachers (often full-load) and part-time administrators. The volume of administrative work and the amount of authority exercised vary widely in different institutions. Some departments have only a handful of professors, while some have hundreds, partly organized in sub-departments. In some colleges authority is in practice nearly all centralized in the president and the deans, while in others it is largely decentralized to the departments. By and large, department heads are probably generally better classified as faculty members than as administrators, though there are important exceptions.

There will always be "fringe problems" requiring case-by-case decisions. In looking at librarians and counselors (academic, vocational, and other), it is sometimes difficult to draw the line accurately between those whose academic qualifications and performance clearly merit faculty status, and those who are too junior in rank or qualifications. Military personnel assigned to teach in a unit of the Reserve Officers'

---

21. *Long Island University* (*C.W. Post Campus*), 189 N.L.R.B. 109; and *Long Island University* (*Brooklyn Center*), 189 N.L.R.B. 110.

Training Corps on the campus were excluded in one recent decision.[22] Another has decided that graduate assistants be excluded, because, although they perform faculty-related functions, they are primarily students, and have none of the prerogatives of faculty status.[23]

Confronted with a somewhat similar issue in a public university, a Michigan appellate court reversed a decision of the Michigan Employment Relations Commission which had held that the interns, residents, and post-graduate fellows at the Medical Center of the University of Michigan were eligible to form a unit of their own for collective bargaining. By a vote of 2 to 1, the court of appeals said that the university is a public employer, but its medical interns, residents, and fellows have more the status of students than employees. It added: "We would also note that in New York interns and residents may organize for purposes of collective bargaining; however, such bargaining units are specifically provided for by statute. The legislature of that state has spoken to the question; the legislature of Michigan has not."[24]

The foregoing rundown of detailed determinations is only fragmentary and incomplete, because this present discourse focuses generally on broader philosophical issues that have reached the higher courts.[25]

### Faculty Strikes: Concerted Withholding of Services by Public Employees Has Been Held Unlawful, Under Statutes and at Common Law

A few examples will serve to illustrate that faculty members who knowingly violate a court injunction against a strike may be fined and imprisoned for contempt of court. In late 1966 and early 1967, when there was disagreement between the governing board of the Chicago

---

22. *Manhattan College*, 195 N.L.R.B. 23.

23. *Adelphi University*, 195 N.L.R.B. 107.

24. *Michigan Interns-Residents Association*, (Mich. App.), 195 N.W. 2d 875 (1972).

25. There is a growing number of young lawyers who have acquired experience and expertise in this field, and who monitor the decisions of the federal and state labor relations agencies, and produce articles in the law reviews and other publications. One might say the current dean of this group is William F. McHugh, presently associate professor of law at the American University in Washington, D.C. Four of his recent articles are noted in the bibliography near the end of this volume.

City Colleges (a system of eight junior college campuses) and the Cook County College Teachers Union, Local 1600, a local court issued a temporary injunction restraining the union or any college teacher from "participating in, or causing, inducing or encouraging, any strike or other concerted withholding of service, by any employee . . . , or picketing, parading or patrolling at or in the vicinity of the junior college campuses. . . ."

Upon evidence that between 66 per cent and 85 per cent of the teaching staff did not report for work on December 1 and 2, 1966, and that Norman G. Swenson, the union's president, had led picketing at the board's offices and at some of the campuses, and circulated six letters stating the union's position and its determination to strike against the board, the court found the local and its president guilty of criminal contempt, fined the Local $5,000, and sentenced the president to $1,000 fine and 30 days in jail.[26]

Likewise, in New Jersey, after a work-stoppage in the public schools of Passaic, the local court imposed a fine of $500 on the Education Association of Passaic and sentences of from 30 to 90 days in the county jail for individual teachers convicted of contempt of court for violating an injunction against a teachers' strike. The Appellate Division modified the judgment somewhat by setting aside the conviction of William J. Flynn, field agent for the New Jersey Education Association and negotiator, and by giving Thane Emerson Bowen, local union president and teacher, one year's probation in lieu of imprisonment, on the ground that he had not personally violated the injunction and that his conduct had been exemplary under the circumstances.

The court remarked: "Were we to condemn on the basis of guilt by association we would be effectively destroying the concept of negotiation. It occurs to us that if the law requires a professional negotiator to disassociate himself entirely from his principals in the event of their illegal activity, we may be denying them and our society help when they need it most."[27]

---

26. *Board of Junior College District No. 508* v. *Cook County College Teachers Union,* Local 1600, 126 Ill. App. 2d 418, 262 N.E. 2d 125 (1970).

27. *In re Education Association of Passaic,* 117 N.J. Super. 255, 284 A. 2d 374 (1971).

*Strikes by Public Employees Are Generally Held Illegal;*
*but Concerted Submission of Bona Fide Resignations*
*Is Not Unlawful and Can Not be Penalized*

In Lee County, Florida, in the vicinity of Fort Myers, several hundred public school teachers handed in formal written resignations in February 1968 on account of the erratic antics of the incredible Governor Kirk. By March 8 it appeared that the governor would not veto the appropriation act of the recent special session of the legislature, as he had threatened to do; and the teachers were willing to negotiate with the school board, with a number of prominent local citizens acting as mediators. On March 15 an agreement was reached that the teachers be restored to their former status, but that each teacher make a payment of $100 to the board as a fine or penalty. Some of the teachers refused to pay the $100 and asked U.S. District Judge Ben Krentzman to take jurisdiction and adjudicate the matter. He said simply and forthrightly: "It is enough to say, as the board concedes, that the teachers had effectively resigned and were legally free not to return to the classroom. Given this fact, the School Board was not free to condition that return on the payment of a fine."

The court ordered the board to (1) pay $100 to each teacher who had paid the fine; (2) reinstate five teachers who had refused to pay the fine and had not returned; and (3) pay each of these five in damages the full amounts of salary and benefits each would have received from March 18, 1968, until the time of their reinstatement. (These amounts ranged from about $2,000 to about $5,000 each.)[28]

## What Constitutes a Faculty Strike?

In September 1971 the administration of Nassau Community College in New York asked for an injunction to restrain the faculty members from continuing their refusal to teach more than 12 hours per week. The contract between the faculty senate and the administration for the preceding year had provided for the 12-hour load. It expired on August 31, and efforts to negotiate a new contract had not yet been successful.

---

28. *National Education Association* v. *Lee County Board of Public Instruction,* (U.S.D.C., Fla.), 299 F. Supp. 834 (1969).

The administration had ordered a program of 15-hours-a-week teaching, in anticipation of enactment by the legislature of the 15-hour requirement (which had indeed been passed by the legislature, but vetoed by Governor Nelson A. Rockefeller July 6, 1971). Meanwhile additional students had been admitted to the community college, so that the additional teaching time must somehow be provided for.

Justice Joseph Liff of the local supreme court granted the injunction. The current impasse, he held, was a strike, forbidden by New York's Taylor Law (Article 14 of *Civil Service Law*, Section 211).[29] "Strikes by public employees," said the Justice, "may be prohibited without violating either the federal or state constitutions" (citing *City of New York* v. *De Lury*, 23 N.Y. 2d 175, 295 N.Y.S. 2d 901, 243 N.E. 2d 128 (1968). "The strike by public employees is illegal even in the absence of a statute prohibiting it" (citing *Board of Education of the City of New York* v. *Shanker*, 54 Misc. 2d 641, 283 N.Y.S. 2d 432; affirmed in 29 A.D. 2d 634, 286 N.Y.S. 2d 543 (1967).

### State Statute Requiring Collective Bargaining with Public Employees Is Valid Against Constitutionally Independent Universities

The Board of Regents of the University of Michigan is a constitutionally independent corporation, having had that status since 1850. The Constitution of 1963 extended similar powers to all other state universities in Michigan: "Each board shall have general supervision of its institution and the control and direction of all expenditures from the institution's funds" (Art. 8, Sec. 5).

Questioning whether general statutes applicable to public employers and employees and requiring collective bargaining were in contravention of Art. 8, Sec. 5 of the Constitution, if applied to the constitutionally independent state university, the Regents sought a declaratory judgment. The Washtenaw County circuit court held that the Regents were subject to such statutes, and the Michigan court of appeals affirmed.

Michigan Public Act No. 379 of 1965 conferred upon public employees the right to join a labor organization, to engage in certain activities for the purpose of collective bargaining through representa-

---

29. *Caso* v. *Katz*, 67 Misc. 2d 793, 324 N.Y.S. 2d 712 (1971).

tives of their own choice, to have an election to ascertain the collective bargaining unit and the bargaining representatives, and to have this election conducted by the State Labor Mediation Board.

It was the court's opinion that "in none of these activities, either by the employees, or in the administration of the act conducted by the Labor Mediation Board, do we find any interference with the general supervision of the university." Although the act required that the public employer bargain collectively with its employees' representatives at reasonable times and places relative to wages, hours, and other terms and conditions of employment, it also expressly provided: "but such obligation does not compel either party to agree to a proposal or require the making of a concession."[30] Negotiation does not necessarily mean capitulation; and when a governing board negotiates or bargains, it does not thereby surrender any of its constitutional or statutory powers.

Also, constitutionally independent state universities are not immune from the application of general state statutes designed to exercise the state's police powers in behalf of the public safety, health, and convenience. It was pointed out that the Michigan supreme court had a similar decision a generation ago, when in 1948 it held that the state workmen's compensation act applied to the Michigan State College (now Michigan State University), which also had constitutionally independent status.[31]

## Overcentralization: The Governor of New Jersey, No Less, Is the Public Employer in Higher Education Negotiations

When the Association of New Jersey State College Faculties sought an order commanding the State Board of Higher Education to meet and negotiate in good faith, it met with defeat, at least in the court of first instance. Judge Milton A. Fellar rested his decision on the law (which indeed has long exemplified an uncontrollable penchant for centralization in New Jersey state government), and also left no doubt as to what he considered to be the model:

"This court takes judicial notice that the custom and practice in

---

30. *Regents of the University of Michigan* v. *Labor Mediation Board,* (Mich. App.), 171 N.W. 2d 477 (1969).
31. *Peters* v. *Michigan State College,* 320 Mich. 243, 30 N.W. 2d 854 (1948).

industry and other business organizations is that a department or a department head within an organization is not an employer. The organization itself is the employer. . . . Apparently the intention of the Legislature in designating a school district as such is due to the fact that a school district is a legal entity separate and apart from the county or municipality where it is located. The Board of Higher Education is *not* a legal entity, but one of the principal departments of the Executive Branch of State Government."

The decision also declared lawful all the actions of Governor Cahill in creating by executive order of April 2, 1970, an Employee Relations Advisory Council and an Office of Employee Relations, and designating the latter to be the bargaining agent for the state as employer. It also upheld the constitutionality of Chapter 96, *Laws of 1970*, which appropriated funds for the implementation of a report by a management consultant (Hay Associates), and placed the state employees on the salary scales and ranges recommended in that report.[32]

### The Outlook from 1972 Forward for Collective Negotiations in Higher Education

Central Michigan University at Mount Pleasant, said to have been the first autonomous four-year state institution to execute a contract with its faculty represented by a collective bargaining agent, made such a contract covering fiscal year 1970-71. Its president, William B. Boyd, was quoted as saying: "The provisions will help retain and recruit excellent faculty. The result will clearly be a stronger university." In May 1971 a new contract, covering the four years 1971-1974 (a 40-page document listed as number 3 in the bibliography near the end of this volume), was signed.

In May 1972 it was reported that collectively negotiated agreements were in existence affecting about 250 campuses. Approximately 60 per cent were at two-year junior or community colleges. Three national organizations were competing for designation of their locals as exclusive bargaining agents. Units of the National Education Association were so designated on about 155 campuses; the American Federation of Teachers on about 50. (At an additional 20 institutions these two had forms of shared representation.) On 12 campuses the desig-

32. *Association of New Jersey State College Faculties, Inc.* v. *Board of Higher Education*, 112 N.J. Super. 237, 270 A. 2d 744 (1970).

nated representative was the local chapter of the American Association of University Professors, a large, old, and well-established society, but a newcomer in this field. Its annual meeting in 1972 voted 373 to 54 to "pursue collective bargaining as a major additional way of realizing the association's goals." A delegate said: "Collective bargaining is here to stay and it is the wave of the future."

At the large multi-campus City University of New York, two well-organized and competing faculty organizations merged in 1972 under the presidency of the intelligent activist Belle Zeller, professor of political science in Hunter College. In 1972 an agreement was adopted between the faculty of Boston State College and the trustees of the Massachusetts state college system embodying the entire faculty governance system, plus provisions for student participation, but not including a salary scale. Donald E. Walters, associate director of the state college system, and negotiator for "management," was quoted as saying: "Colleges should stop being panicked by the fact that collective bargaining has hit their campus. The attitude that 'My God, the union is on the campus' leads to the administration becoming very defensive, stuffy, and formal with the faculty. We ought to take the position that this is an opportunity."

A contract between the multi-campus State University of New York and the Senate Professional Association representing the 15,000 teaching and non-teaching employees was ratified in August 1971.

After a contest of some 20 months with the incoming "austerity" administration of Governor William Cahill, a collectively negotiated agreement between the state and the Association of New Jersey College and University Professors was ratified in February 1971, to be retroactive to July 1, 1970, and to cover two fiscal years. It brought substantial salary increases. On April 11, 1972, Carnegie Corporation of New York announced a grant of $102,000 to Rutgers, the State University of New Jersey, to support a study of collective bargaining in New Jersey's public colleges and universities.

The Association of Pennsylvania State College and University Faculties won the right to represent the 4,000 faculty members of the 14 state-owned institutions in an election October 6, 1971. Gabriel P. Betz, president of the California (Pennsylvania) State College, said: "The real winners are the students and citizens of Pennsylvania who stand to benefit from the educational improvements sought for their state-owned institutions."

# CHAPTER 11

## NON-ACADEMIC STAFF MEMBERS

The recent decisions quickly reveal that several institutions in some of the states are wholly outside the bureaucratic thicket of state civil service statutes and regulations. Among these are the University of California (nine campuses) and similarly constitutionally independent institutions in Michigan, Minnesota, and half a dozen other states. It also appears that the county community colleges in New Jersey are not under state civil service.

In some other states, where the somewhat anomalous state of affairs prevails in which university and college non-academic employees work under rules which are the product of an uneasy partnership between the state personnel board and the governing boards of the educational institutions, various litigated controversies, often rather petty, occur. Sometimes employees who feel themselves protected by state civil service laws and rules seriously question the right and power of a university president to appoint a director of personnel and to delegate to him full authority to make appointments and terminate individual contracts within the limitations established by law. This delegation is generally found to be within the intent of the state statutes and of the regulations of the university or college governing board.

*California Civil Service Laws Are Irrelevant to*
*the University of California, Which Is*
*Constitutionally Independent*

The California State Employees' Association and two of its members who were employees of the University of California sought a declaration that University employees were entitled to require the University to make salary deductions to pay membership dues of the Association.

There were indeed statutes (Government Code, Sec. 1150-1157.5) providing for salary deductions for employees of the state and for employees of "public agencies," the authorized deductions to provide for such purposes as purchase of savings bonds, contributions to charity, and employee association dues.

The Court of Appeal, by Associate Justice Winslow Christian, sitting with Presiding Justice Preston Devine and Justice Joseph A. Rattigan, correctly decided that these statutes were not intended to apply to the university, because under Article IX, Section 9, of the California Constitution the Regents of the University of California have "full powers of organization and government" of the university, and this is properly interpreted to include the determination of such matters as personnel policy in general and specifically policy regarding honoring of requests for payroll deductions.[1] The constitutional independence of the Regents as a fourth coordinate arm of the state government has been repeatedly sustained in a series of judicial decisions extending over a century.

The court here pointed out that the State Controller or Board of Control does not regulate the activities or policies of the university, and also cited *Newmarker* v. *Regents,* 160 Cal. App. 2d 640, 325 P. 2d 558 (1958), in which it was held that any and all rulings of the State Personnel Board are irrelevant to the university.

*County Community Colleges in New Jersey Are*
*Not Under State Civil Service*

Nonprofessional and noninstructional employees of county com-

---

1. *California State Employees' Association* v. *Regents of University of California,* (Cal. App.), 73 Cal. Rptr. 449 (1968).

munity colleges in New Jersey are not subject to the state civil service laws, even in counties whose boards of freeholders have adopted state civil service for their own county employees. This was a decision of the state supreme court in 1971, by Justice Proctor with all the other six Justices concurring.

By mid-1971 15 county colleges had been established under New Jersey Statutes Annotated 18A: 64A-1 *et seq.*, which authorized county boards of freeholders to petition the State Board of Higher Education for permission to create a county college.

On September 9, 1970, the State Civil Service Commission, acting in accord with a three-year-old opinion of the attorney general, issued a ruling that county college non-academic employees were under the state civil service system as adopted by their respective counties. Twelve of the colleges joined in appealing this ruling to the courts. The ruling was reversed.

Said the court: "We are not persuaded that county colleges are agencies of county government. Rather, we believe that they are separate political subdivisions which serve a separate purpose and operate apart from the governing bodies of the counties in which they are situated. Examination of the statutory scheme is demonstrative of this conclusion."

The county board of freeholders appoints the board of trustees of the county college, which has the usual powers of a college governing board, including authority to appoint and fix the compensation and terms of employment of members of the administrative and teaching staffs and "to appoint or employ such other officers, agents and employees as may be required . . . and to fix and determine their qualifications, duties, compensation, terms of office and all other conditions and terms of employment and retention."

The court reasoned that the fact that the county colleges were financed to the extent of about 43 per cent by state-appropriated funds, and approximately 26 per cent by county funds, did not make the members of their staffs employees of the state or of the county. Nor were they made county employees by the fact that the annual college budget request for county funds is fixed by a "board of school estimate" composed of the chairman of the county board of freeholders and two members of that board, plus two members of the county college board of trustees, and and that the county board of freeholders votes the sum thus fixed and certified.

The Civil Service Commission argued that since the statutes are silent as to whether employees of the county colleges shall be under civil service, it ought to be assumed that the legislative intent was that they should be. Weak on its face, this contention was vigorously rejected by the court, holding that it is impossible to reconcile the statutory powers of the Civil Service Commission with the powers granted to county college boards of trustees in the County College Law. Since the County College Law was the later of the two conflicting enactments, "we can only conclude that the Legislature meant to exclude county college employees from Civil Service."[2]

## Maryland Civil Service Laws Do Not Prevent State College from Discontinuing College-operated Food Service and Contracting with Private Concessionaire

Morgan State College in Baltimore decided to terminate its college-operated food service, and make an agreement with a private contractor for this service. Its governing board, the Board of Trustees of State Colleges, approved this policy and prepared to enter into a contract with a private corporation to provide food service at the college.

This entailed the abolition of the jobs of a number of state civil service employees in 10 classifications, including the food service manager and assistants, dining room supervisors, cashiers, and clerks. The contract with the concessionaire provided that employees who had been with the college five years or more would be retained in their jobs for at least one year after the change. The displaced employees sought an injunction to restrain the Board from entering into the contract. Their petition was dismissed.

The Maryland Merit System statutes made the usual provision for discontinuance of positions because of departmental reorganization or lack of work, and the usual protections for employees thus laid off, as indicated in the words of the Maryland Court of Appeals:

"The College, after contacting the Commissioner of Personnel for advice was specifically directed by the Commissioner to absorb the

---

2. *Atlantic Community College* v. *Civil Service Commission,* 59 N.J. 102, 279 A. 2d 820 (1971).

appellants in any vacant positions at the College which called for any of the appellants' classifications, and to notify other State agencies of the availability of these employees for placement with those agencies having vacant positions in similar classifications." In short, the Board followed the "layoff" procedure established by the statute, and that was all that was necessary.

"We think that the *Code*, Article 77, Section 165 (a) gives the Board authority to abolish positions in a department under its supervision and control by the language which invests it with 'all the powers, rights and privileges attending the responsibility of their management.'"

It was true that certain employees of the state colleges, including the classes concerned here, were covered by the merit system statutes; and under a section thereof only the Commissioner of Personnel, with the approval of the governor, was authorized to abolish "existing classes"; but it was a misapprehension to equate "existing classes" with "existing positions." The Commissioner's concurrence was not necessary in the abolition of *positions*, as distinguished from *classes*. In accord with the policy of merit system legislation in general, the governing board of the employing institution or agency has power to abolish positions for *bona fide* reasons related to the improvement of the service or to unavoidable financial stringency, but not as a subterfuge to accomplish the dismissal of any employee or employees for partisan or other unworthy reasons.

This is a point of tension in civil service administration. If a college or university governing board is required to have its non-academic employees under the state "merit system," constant vigilance must be exercised to see that the scope and meaning of the "merit system" statutes and rules are not unwarrantedly interpreted in a manner to deprive the governing board of its proper authority to manage the employment policies of its institution in the public interest.[3]

### Washington Statute Protects Employees When Change Is Made from College-operated Food Service to Private Contractor

The State Higher Education Personnel Law of 1969 (*Revised Code of Washington*, 28 B. 16.010 *et seq.*) provides that specified classes of

---

3. Ball v. *Board of Trustees of State Colleges*, (Md.), 248 A. 2d 650 (1968).

employees are civil service employees, under rules of tenure, probationary service, and other usual regulations of appointment, compensation, and termination, and includes provisions permitting some employees to be lawfully designated as exempted from civil service regulations.

Olympic College, a public junior college, operated a food service for several years with eight employees. This service was open only about six hours per day and served only breakfasts, luncheons, and snacks. In mid-1969 the Board of Trustees decided it would be necessary to build a residence hall to house some 200 students (total enrollment was about 2,500). The students living in the residence hall would require full food service, including dinners; and the trustees thought it not feasible to provide this additional service with its present organization, but better to discontinue its own food service and contract for it with a concessionaire. It made such a contract with Slater, Inc., a Delaware corporation, and instructed the college president to notify the eight food-service employees that their employment would be terminated June 12, 1970, because their positions would not exist after that date.

Their petition for reinstatement went first to the State Higher Education Personnel Board, which decided that the college's action was in actuality an unauthorized exemption of these employees from civil service status; and ordered their reinstatement. Next the Superior Court of Kitsap County reversed this decision, but did not disturb the finding that the eight employees were in the non-exempt civil service; the order was reversed, the court said, because it was based on a misconception of law, *viz.*, that the college trustees had no authority to engage an independent contractor to provide food service. In fact, in 1969 the legislature had amended the Junior College Act to authorize junior colleges to either rent or lease dormitories and food services; but, as was made clear when this case reached the state supreme court, this did not in any way avoid or supersede the provisions of the Higher Education Personnel Act.

The supreme court of Washington vacated the judgment of the lower court, in an opinion by Justice Morell E. Sharp, with the other eight Justices concurring, and ordered the eight employees reinstated.[4]

The rationale was that, although an existing statute specified that

---

4. *Cunningham* v. *Olympic Community College*, 79 Wash. 891 (1971).

"an appointing authority may separate an employee without prejudice because of lack of funds or curtailment of work," the college offered no solid evidence of either of these conditions. As to "lack of funds," neither the president, nor the chairman of the Board of Trustees, nor the business manager could cite any figures regarding projected costs of continuing the college-operated food service in sufficiently increased volume, or how much money might be available for the purpose. They only had a general feeling that "the money isn't there." As to curtailment of work, "all the evidence indicated that instead of curtailment there was contemplated expansion."

A feature of the Washington higher education personnel act which supports the foregoing decision also evidences the legislative intent to minimize the confusion and harassment of college and university administrators which can result from heavy-handed and undiscriminating imposition of civil service rules:

28 B. 16.040 (5) "The governing board of each institution . . . may also exempt from this chapter . . . classifications involving research activities, counseling of students, extension or continuing education activities, graphic arts or publication activities requiring prescribed academic preparation or special training, and principal assistants to executive heads of major administrative or academic divisions, as determined by the higher education personnel board: *Provided*, that *no* non-academic employee engaged in office, clerical, maintenance, or *food* and trade services may be exempted by the higher educational personnel board under this provision."

## Discharge of Non-academic Employees for Cause, in Varying Circumstances

An equipment operator at the university power plant at the University of Oregon (a civil service employee under Oregon law) was dismissed by the university personnel director for alleged insubordination. The Oregon Public Employee Relations Board accepted the complaint and upheld the dismissal; but the local district court in Lane County set aside this decision and ordered reinstatement with back pay. Next, in the Oregon Court of Appeals the judgment was reversed. Regarding the allegation that the university personnel director was without authority to discharge employees, but that this authority resided in the State Board of Higher Education (governing board of nine institutions) and could not be delegated, at least not to an employee below the rank of university or college president, the court decided that the law allowed a university president to designate a personnel director to exercise this authority.

The court added a bit of reasoning, perhaps of somewhat doubtful weight: In this case the aggrieved employee could show no documentation of his appointment other than a paper signed by the personnel director. If the personnel director lacked authority to discharge him, intimated the court, then he lacked authority to appoint him, and there had been no effective appointment in the first place.[5]

Harold Gordon was appointed an assistant purchasing agent at the State University of New York at Buffalo March 18, 1968. Subsequently the university informed him that his performance was not considered satisfactory and that his services would be terminated at the end of his probationary term. Immediately upon termination he started a grievance procedure, and on April 14, 1969, the grievance appeals board recommended that he be reinstated to a similar position in the state university, but preferably at a new location. It did not recommend back pay; but held that he had not been given sufficient opportunity to learn the job and demonstrate his competence, though recognizing that he had to some extent contributed to his own difficulties. He began an Article 78 action in the Albany County supreme court. The court ordered his reinstatement with back pay, and further ordered the Trustees of the State University of New York to investigate the truth of an affidavit of Harvey Randall, University personnel director, as to the availability of positions as assistant purchasing agent at Buffalo.

The five-judge Appellate Division reversed the judgment and dismissed the petition. Said the memorandum opinion: "There is evidence as to (Gordon's) performance being less than satisfactory, that his attitude was defensive when criticized or corrected, and that he refused to follow prescribed procedures." This court did not find that he was not given ample opportunity to show his ability, or that any bad faith or regional discrimination was involved in his dismissal. Nor did it find any reason to doubt the truth of Mr. Randall's affidavit.[6]

---

5. Beistel v. Public Employee Relations Board and University of Oregon, (Ore. App.), 486 P. 2d 1305 (1971).
6. Gordon v. State University of New York at Buffalo, (App. Div.), 315 N.Y.S. 2d 366 (1970).

*Termination of Service of Probationary Library Clerk by*
*President of Public Community College in New York*
*State Is Not for a Jury Unless Bad Faith Is Present*

George F. Chambers, president of Nassau Community College, terminated the employment of Rita Smith, a senior library clerk. The trial court put the matter to a jury, and the verdict annulled the termination and directed reinstatement. The five-judge Appellate Division reversed the judgment based on the verdict, and held that the issue should not have been submitted to a jury, because the pleadings and affidavits demonstrated that the termination of the probationary employee was not arbitrary or capricious but was in good faith. The court record contains no inkling of the facts in detail.[7]

Christopher Hays Clancy began work as a project director in the Center on Social Welfare Policy and Law at Columbia University January 1, 1970. He was dismissed January 21, 1971, after about four months of investigations, evaluations, and documentary complaints indicated to his employer that he was unsuitable for the job. He was not presented with any formal charges nor afforded a hearing prior to his discharge. Nor was the consent or approval of the U.S. Office of Economic Opportunity, which subsidized the Center, obtained.

Alleging denial of due process under New York's well-known "Article 78," he asked for judicial review of his dismissal, and also averred that it was in violation of Section 226 (8) of the Education Law, which provided that a dismissal of an employee of a university must be "on examination and due proof of the truth of a written complaint."

Justice Jacob Markowitz of the New York County supreme court dismissed the petition, denying each contention. Article 78 is not applicable to contracts of employment with a private university. The consent of the Office of Economic Opportunity was not necessary, according to its own rules. Section 226 (8) of the Education Law is by its own terms limited to institutions chartered by the Regents of the University of the State of New York, whereas Columbia University was chartered by the legislature in 1810, and is not subject to that

---

7. *Smith* v. *Chambers, President of Nassau Community College,* (N.Y. App. Div.), 303 N.Y.S. 2d 723 (1969).

enactment. Finally, there was no evidence that in this instance the university acted on whim or caprice.[8]

### Discharges for Inability to Perform, and for Neglect of Duty

A female domestic service helper in a cafeteria in the division of residence halls at the University of Wisconsin was employed November 1, 1963. At that time she had a back ailment which she had sustained previously while working for a different employer. She went to the hospital for surgery January 27, 1964, and was unable to return to work until April 6, 1964. She was not absent without leave, and became a permanent employee June 12, 1964; but was again off work from November 7 until she was discharged January 18, 1965, "in order to meet the operational needs of the division of residence halls." The State Board of Personnel sustained the discharge, and it was affirmed successively by the circuit court and the state supreme court.[9]

At Western Illinois University a female non-academic employee was suspended January 2, 1965, on charges of unauthorized absences, refusal to perform assigned work, failure to follow work schedules, insolence, carelessness, and loafing. She requested a hearing, and the Merit Board appointed a three-man hearing board to make findings of fact as provided in *Illinois Revised Statutes*, Chapter 24 1/2, Section 38b (14). By a 2 to 1 vote, this hearing board found her not guilty as charged. Nevertheless the Merit Board, after reviewing the transcript of the findings of fact, declared her guilty and ordered her discharge. She contended the Merit Board had no authority to overrule the findings of its hearing board. An Illinois Court of Appeals, affirming the judgment of the trial court, said: "The hearing board is merely a fact-finding arm of the Merit Board—an employee is not demoted or discharged until so ordered by the Merit Board—and judicial review is provided only from the decision of the Merit Board, not the findings of fact by the hearing board."[10]

---

8. *Clancy v. Trustees of Columbia University*, (Misc. 2d), 320 N.Y.S., 2d 592 (1971).

9. *Jabs v. State Board of Personnel*, 34 Wis. 2d 245, 148 N.W. 2d 853 (1967).

10. *Heap v. University Civil Service Merit Board*, 83 Ill. App. 2d 350, 227 N.E. 2d 560 (1967).

## U.S. Supreme Court Held in 1968 That Federal Fair Labor
## Standards Act Is Applicable to Universities,
## Colleges, Schools, and Hospitals

Over the objections of Maryland and 27 other states, in 1968 the U.S. Supreme Court declared that the wage-hour provisions of the amended Fair Labor Standards Act cover employees of state schools and hospitals. A *Headnote* said: "Congress, when acting within its delegated power to regulate interstate commerce, may override counter-vailing state interests by regulating wages and hours of state employees. When a state employs people to operate schools and hospitals it is subject to the same restrictions as other employers whose activities affect commerce, including privately operated schools and hospitals. . . . Since schools and hospitals are major users of imported goods, their labor conditions have a substantial effect on the flow of goods in interstate commerce." Mr. Justice John M. Harlan delivered the opinion for the court. Mr. Justice Thurgood Marshall took no part in this case. Mr. Justice William O. Douglas wrote a dissenting opinion protesting what seemed to him to be an unwarranted federal invasion of state sovereignty. In this he was joined by Mr. Justice Potter Stewart.[11]

## State Labor Legislation May Sometimes Be Hampered by
## Sovereign Immunity or Abstention:
## Arkansas and Massachusetts

On behalf of 68 women employed in the food services of the University of Arkansas at Fayetteville, the Arkansas Commissioner of Labor reached the state supreme court in 1966 with a complaint that these women habitually worked more than eight hours per day without overtime pay, in violation of the state wage and hour laws (*Arkansas Statutes Annotated*, Sections 81-613 *et seq.*); and sought an injunction to restrain the Board of Trustees from continuing this practice. The court, through Justice McFaddin, simply noted that this was a suit against the state, and as such could not be maintained; invoking *Arkan-*

---

11. *Maryland* v. *W. Willard Wirtz, Secretary of Labor*, 392 U.S. 183, 88 S. Ct. 2017, 20 L. Ed. 2d 1020 (1968).

*sas Constitution,* Article 5, Section 20: "The State of Arkansas shall never be made defendant in any of her courts."[12]

In Massachusetts, in 1967, certain employees in the food services at Wheaton College, a private liberal arts college, filed a petition for certification of their union as exclusive bargaining representative of the dining-room employees. Wheaton College, and the private concessionaire which it employed to operate the food services "jointly," joined in asking the state courts for a writ of prohibition to prevent the State Labor Relations Commission from hearing and determining the issue, claiming the Commission had no jurisdiction over the private college. Justice Reardon of the Supreme Judicial Court directed that the writ be issued.

He said Massachusetts labor laws and the National Labor Relations Act were consistent in excluding educational and charitable enterprises from their purview. This was true at that time (1967). "In furtherance of its educational purposes, Wheaton provides food and dining facilities for its resident students. Almost 20 per cent of Wheaton's student body earn part of their college expenses working in the dining rooms.

"Wheaton's dining facilities are not open to the public and do not make a profit. . . . That Wheaton has engaged a professional food management service to make more efficient the operation of its dining facilities and to provide its students with better food at lower cost does not compel the conclusion that Wheaton is thereby engaging in 'industry and trade.' "[13]


### Applicability of State Workmens' Compensation Acts

C. Jane Davis, a woman of 50, was a "visual consultant" in the "physical efficiency research program" of the University of Delaware. She had had experience in testing the vision of members of various major league baseball teams, and had worked for Bausch and Lomb, the internationally-known firm of optical manufacturers. She was contracted at the university for eleven months, from October 1, 1963, through August 31, 1964. Her pay was $1,100 a year, plus free tuition,

---

12. *State of Arkansas Commissioner of Labor* v. *University of Arkansas Board of Trustees,* (*Ark.*), 407 S.W. 2d 916 (1966).

13. *Wheaton College* v. *Massachusetts Labor Relations Commission.* (Mass.), 227 N.E. 2d 735 (1967).

room, and board—the latter items being paid for out of a grant from the Friends' Foundation. "Her employment by the University was primary. Her schooling was secondary. It was supplied by the University as part of the consideration for her services in its research program. This method of employment was used so as to obtain her services at a lower cost to the University."

August 3, 1964, at 11 p.m., she responded to a fire alarm in the dormitory in which she had a room by stepping out into the corridor with intent to leave the building as required in fire drills. A horde of students came running down the hall at the sound of the alarm, some of whom collided with her and caused her to lose her balance, fall, and sustain substantial injuries. She sued the university for damages. President Judge Stiftel of the Superior Court decided that she must seek her remedy under the Delaware Workmen's Compensation Act, because she was an employee of the University, on the University premises at the time of the injury, and not on any personal mission, but proceeding as required by university rules.[14] It could be said that she was injured while about her duties in the course of her employment—the classic definition of eligibility for a workmen's compensation award.

In Pennsylvania, Geneva College had an arrangement with the chief of police of the city of Beaver Falls whereby off-duty policemen patrolled the campus (never more than one at a time) and received $2 per man-hour from the college. One such patrolman was directing traffic immediately after an athletic contest, when he was struck by an automobile and injured. On this special occasion there were also three on-duty city patrolmen assigned to the vicinity, and three civil defense men; but this particular off-duty patrolman was acting in accord with a plan of assignments and requirements for off-duty men while in the employ of the college, which had been agreed upon by the college and the chief of police. It followed that he was an employee of the college when injured. Therefore the college and its insurance carrier would be responsible for his compensatory award, if any—not the city of Beaver Falls.[15]

---

14. Davis v. *University of Delaware*, (Del. Super.), 233 A. 2d 159 (1967).

15. Smakoscz v. *City of Beaver Falls and Geneva College*, 209 Pa. Super. 115 224 A. 2d 785 (1966).

# CHAPTER 12

## THE PRESIDENT; ADMINISTRATIVE
## STAFF; BOARD MEMBERS

The president and associated high-level administrators, a century or more ago, were usually also active professors. Sometimes, in very small colleges, the president also personally acted as registrar, librarian, and academic dean. (There was a time when the college library was customarily a padlocked storage place, opened only a half-day each week for students to check out and return books.)

Most administrators no longer do any classroom teaching. In large institutions each of them has a large lower-echelon administrative and clerical staff. There is a widespread custom, however, of appointing an individual to serve in a dual capacity—in the administrative post and with an appropriate academic title in one of the instructional departments. The latter can carry tenure, while the former does not. Thus, at the option of either party, an administrator can leave his post and function instead as a full-time teacher or researcher.

To round out the picture of all individuals having direct responsibilities for the operation and management of the institution, the members of the governing board (though usually laymen, unpaid, and serving only part time) must be included. They are the official link between the college and its constituency. Plenary legal power to manage the college or university rests with them in their corporate capacity.

There are some recent judicial decisions regarding the appointment, election, and succession of these individuals.

## The College President Has Less Employment Security
## Than Members of the Teaching Faculty

The president of Prairie State College (a public junior college in Illinois) was dropped allegedly because his memorandum to the board, intended to be confidential, recommending changes in the ethnic studies program, became public without his knowledge and caused heated controversy. Aware of recent interpretations of the First and Fourteenth Amendments in cases involving teachers, he sought a remedy in federal district court, claiming his memorandum was an exercise of free speech and he had been denied due process because he had not been given a formal hearing.

"This court does not think that there need be the same 'vigilant protection' when an administrator is involved as may be necessary when a teacher is," decided District Judge Richard B. Austin. "The need for teachers to have freedom in what they teach arises from the very heart of the First Amendment. The workshop of the administrator, however, is not the classroom but the office and the conference room. His primary duties are to coordinate, delegate, and regulate, not to educate. The fact that he is the 'executive officer of the board' . . . illustrates the need for . . . a close working relationship between him and the board. The public retains control of the school system by electing the board . . . , which in turn must manage and govern the college. . . . It does this through the chief administrative officer. . . . The board must therefore have wide discretion in deciding whether to hire or fire a person who will be or has been in essence its agent."

Accordingly, "This court finds that as a matter of law the plaintiff (president) has raised no constitutional issue and therefore the complaint is dismissed for failure to state a claim."

This decision was reversed and remanded by the Seventh Circuit U.S. Court of Appeals December 21, 1972 (Circuit Judges Luther M. Swygert, Latham Castle, and Wilbur F. Pell, with opinion written by Judge Castle), holding that in this case the president had stated valid causes of action showing that he was deprived of his First Amendment right to free expression and his Fourteenth Amendment right to due process of law, when he was denied a formal hearing by the board.[1]

At Kingsborough Community College in Brooklyn (a two-year college unit of the City University of New York), Dr. Theodore Powell was appointed president in March 1970 and removed from the presidency by the Board of Higher Education July 15, 1971, because the members of the board had lost confidence in his management, partly on account of complaints received from some of the department heads. He was also a professor of political science, and was retained in that capacity. His removal from the presidency was summary, with no charges and no formal hearing. He contended that under the bylaws of the Board of Higher Education the college presidents were "members of the instructional staff" and entitled to due process. On that ground Justice Francis J. Bloustein of the local supreme court ordered his reinstatement.

This judgment was subsequently reversed by a vote of 4 to 1 by the five-judge Appellate Division. The majority said the Education Law and the bylaws of the board "make it abundantly clear that the petitioner, in his capacity as president of the college, did not have tenure and consequently the Board of Higher Education had the power to remove him without preferring charges and without holding a hearing. . . . There being no term nor tenure provided for the position of president, he was employed 'at will,' and having been so employed, he was removable from his post as president at any time."[2] This is in accord with the law in New York, and also consonant with the tradition and practice in academic institutions everywhere. (Sometimes presidents are employed for a definite term specified in the contract, and then have rights under the contract if it is breached prior to its specified date of termination.)

The Contra Costa Junior College governing board recently adopted the unusual expedient of asking four statewide associations (relating respectively to teachers, school boards, school administrators, and junior colleges) to establish an investigative panel to report on the professional competency and performance of its chief executive agent

---

1. *Hostrop* v. *Board of Junior College District 515*, (U.S.D.C., Ill.), 337 F. Supp. 977 (1972). Reversed and remanded by Seventh Circuit, No. 72-1285 (1972).
2. *Powell* v. *Board of Higher Education of the City of New York*, (N.Y. App. Div.) Citation unavailable at this writing, (1971).

(superintendent). The panel was formed, met for four days, interviewed 130 persons who voluntarily appeared and testified, and issued a report embodying many findings derogatory to the superintendent's performance, and recommended that he be asked to resign.

The superintendent sued the four organizations and the members of the panel for damages, alleging that the report was libelous and defamatory. His case was dismissed because both the trial court and the Court of Appeal found no evidence that the report was "knowingly false" or published in reckless disregard of its truth or falsity, or that its preparation and publication were actuated by malice.[3]

The gist of a case arising at one of the California state colleges was: "The statute relating to reassignment of administrative employees of state colleges does not restrict reassignment of an administrator only to another administrative position, but authorizes reassignment of a college dean who had attained tenure as a teacher, to a position as professor of education, even though he was fully qualified as an administrator."[4]

### An Administrative Officer in a Public Junior College in Arizona Was Not Protected by the State Teachers' Tenure Act

Charles Kaufman was employed as dean of administration at the Pima Junior College in Arizona for the fiscal year 1968-69, and reappointed for 1969-70, with a tentative commitment for 1970-71. On September 16, 1969, the provost of the college transmitted to him a written request that he resign. He did not comply, and was subsequently locked out of his office and his pay stopped.

On November 4 he asked the local court for a writ of *mandamus* to reinstate him for the remainder of the fiscal year. He also asked the court to order the governing board of the college to recognize the existence of a contract with him for the following fiscal year (1970-71), and to give him a written statement of reasons for dismissal under that contract, and upon timely demand to grant him a hearing on such dismissal. His petition was dismissed by the trial court, whereupon he filed in the same court an action for damages, and at the same time

---

3. *McCunn* v. *California Teachers Association*, 3 Cal. App. 3d 956 (1970).
4. *Gilbaugh* v. *Bautzer*, 3 Cal. App. 3d 793, 83 Cal. Rptr. 806 (1970).

appealed the *mandamus* judgment to the intermediate appellate court of Arizona.

The court of appeals affirmed the judgment of dismissal. Not being employed as a teacher in an elementary school district or a high school district, and, indeed, not as a teacher in any school or college, Kaufman was not protected by the Arizona Teachers' Tenure Act.

The local governing board of the junior college contended that a resolution regarding tenure, adopted December 11, 1961, by the State Board of Directors for Junior Colleges, could not apply because it exceeded the powers of the State Board. The resolution directed:

"A. The County Board of Governors shall establish and implement a policy which protects the staff members from unreasonable dismissal and the college from the necessity to retain incompetent teachers.

"B. The policy shall employ such procedures as are found in continuing contract laws; reasonable period of probation, early notification of contract renewal or termination, written statement of reasons for dismissal for both probationary and established faculty members, and assurance of continuing equitable treatment and reasonable security after the probationary period."

The local governing board also contended that under *Arizona Revised Statutes*, section 15-679, subsec. A, paragraph 7, authorizing it to "remove any officer or employee when in its judgment the interests of education in the state so require," it had absolute power to discharge any employee without any reason whatsoever.

The court rejected both of these contentions. As to the latter, the statute gave authority only to exercise judgment, not arbitrarily or willfully, but with regard to what is right and equitable under the circumstances and the law.

As to the State Board resolution, it was applicable because it was authorized by *Arizona Revised Statutes*, sec. 15-600, which gave the State Board sweeping powers, including power to "Enact ordinances for the government of the institutions under its jurisdiction."

The court concluded, however, that Kaufman was premature in asking a writ to compel the local board to give him written reasons and a hearing, because he had not himself first demanded these procedures from the local board, and therefore had not yet exhausted his administrative remedies.[5]

---

5. *Kaufman* v. *Pima Junior College Governing Board*, (Ariz. App.), 484 P. 2d 244 (1971).

*Salary of an Administrative Officer at Marshall*
*University Is at Discretion of the Governing*
*Board, Not the Governor*

In West Virginia, the president of Marshall University recommended to the State Board of Education (then governing the institution) that a new position of Director of Finance be created, with an annual salary of $18,504, beginning March 25, 1969. The president proposed to provide the salary for the remaining three and one-quarter months of the current fiscal year by a transfer of $5,008 from the budget category of "extra help," leaving a balance of $995 in that item.

The Board approved the recommendation and forwarded an amended expenditure schedule to the State Commissioner of Administration and Finance, who refused to consent to it, maintaining that he had the power and duty of discretionary decision in such matters; that the proposed salary was higher than those of comparable positions in the other state institutions of higher education; and that in view of a slump in state revenue receipts his decision was sound fiscal policy.

Moreover, he said the governor had recently issued an executive order freezing all salaries except for such changes as the governor might personally approve; that he had conferred with the governor in this case, and the governor had supported his refusal, but had told him he would not object to the new position at a salary of $15,000. This amounted to the view that the governor had discretionary authority to fix the salary of an employee of the Board of Education. Not so, said the West Virginia supreme court of appeals. Existing statutes exempted the employees of the State Board of Education and the institutions under its governance from the authority of the governor and the commissioner of administration and finance to classify and fix salaries (until July 1, 1969, when the Board was superseded by the new State Board of Regents).

Therefore the governor's executive order could not extend to the position in question. The money at issue was within the total appropriated to Marshall University by the legislature for fiscal year 1968-69, and was not subject to the governor's order. Though the court conceded that the statutes gave the commissioner of administration and finance some discretionary latitude in the approval of expenditure schedules, it held that in this case the commissioner's interference was arbitrary and capricious and an abuse of his discretion, and issued a writ of mandamus to compel him to authorize the expenditure.[6]

The case is a classic example of a governor and a state fiscal officer (gubernatorial appointee) overstepping their lawful authority by attempting to interfere in the detailed fiscal management of an institution or agency exempted by law from such control. A governor can not nullify the terms of a legislative appropriation act; nor can his appointed fiscal officer take over the detailed management of an institution of higher education from its lawfully constituted governing board. Many illustrations of this type of abuse may be found in recent history of almost every state, as a result of the headlong stampede toward over-centralized state fiscal control. This trend is already far along toward robbing legislatures of their proper authority and aggrandizing the governorship to the point of potential executive tyranny.

## As to Administrative Salaries, the Board of Higher Education of the City of New York Is Entangled in the Toils of the City Fiscal Authorities, Though It Is an Autonomous State Agency

On February 28, 1966, the Board of Higher Education of the City of New York recommended that the salary of its "Legal Assistant, Grade 4" (legal counsel) be raised from $17,500 to $19,350. The City Budget Director submitted this to the mayor with his negative recommendation. The mayor did not approve it. The incumbent of the position began an Article 78 action to compel the budget director to certify the change, contending that for this position the mayor's approval was not necessary. Justice Sidney A. Fine of the New York County supreme court granted the application; but his judgment was reversed by a divided Appellate Division, holding that Section 6214 of the Education Law, containing an elaborate inventory of positions under the Board, must have been intended to include the law assistant (legal counsel), though the position is not specifically mentioned therein.

That conclusion would put it in Group IV of the inventory, which

---

6. *State ex rel. West Virginia Board of Education* v. *Miller*, (W.Va.), 168 S.E. 2d 820 (1969).

was a catchbasket category of "positions which might thereafter be created, or existing positions not elsewhere provided for." For Group IV, salary increases had to be approved by the mayor. For the other groups, annual increments were automatic. Evidence was produced to show that the wording for Group IV was enacted because of prior litigation regarding clerical employees; but the majority of the Appellate Division did not agree that the wording was intended to cover clerical employees only, to the exclusion of others.

Three judges concurred in the *per curiam* decision of the court: Judges Harold A. Stevens, Aron Steuer, and Owen McGivern. Judge Samuel W. Eager wrote a dissenting opinion, in which he was joined by Judge Louis J. Capozzoli. They would have held that the Board of Higher Education is a "separate and distinct body corporate" expressly vested with exclusive authority in the establishing of positions to carry out its purposes, and the fixing of the salaries therefor.

Moreover, "the Board of Higher Education may not be deemed to be an agency of the City within the meaning of Section 123 of the New York City Charter. It is a public agency created by the State Legislature; 'its administration of the city colleges is a State function and the Board itself is a State agency'. . . . The right of the Board of Higher Education to work freely within the budgetary appropriations for its purposes is not limited by general provisions in the local charter."

In this view, the judgment of the majority in this case was an infringement upon the autonomous powers of the Board.[7] This is an important issue. The dissenting judges cited New York decisions to support this position, especially *Board of Higher Education* v. *Carter*, 14 N.Y. 2d 138, 250 N.Y.S. 2d 33, 199 N.E. 2d 141 (1962), in which the Court of Appeals, highest tribunal in the State of New York, enunciated it.

### Appointment of Members of the Governing Board by the Governor and the Senate; Succession

On January 5, 1971, Governor Farrar of South Dakota was succeeded by the incoming Governor Richard F. Kneip. Meantime the outgoing Governor Farrar on January 2 notified the secretary of state

---

7. *Application of Arthur H. Kahn* v. *Eugene M. Becker, Director of the Budget of the City of New York*, 27 A.D. 2d 436, 280 N.Y.S. 2d 412 (1967).

that he had appointed Schmidt and Varilek to succeed Burke and Witt, whose terms were about to expire, as members of the statewide Board of Regents, which governs all the state institutions of higher education. The terms of office were six years, or until their successors shall have qualified, subject to confirmation by the state senate.

Then on January 11 the new Governor Kneip notified the secretary of state that he was withdrawing the "recommended" appointments of Schmidt and Varilek. When the legislature began its session on January 19, the secretary of state transmitted to the senate the January 2 letters of former Governor Farrar, but not the January 11 letters of the incumbent Governor Kneip. Consequently the state supreme court held, in an original action in *quo warranto*, that the old members, Burke and Witt, were entitled to the seats until their successors had qualified, because although Schmidt and Varilek had been inducted and seated by the Board, they had in fact not been properly appointed.

The first issue to be decided was that the governorship is a continuing office, irrespective of the person who occupies it, and a succeeding governor has the same power over an appointment as the predecessor governor would have had if he had continued in office. Therefore the letters of withdrawal were effective and the secretary of state was derelict in not transmitting them to the senate. The second question was whether a governor has power to withdraw an "appointment" or "nomination" of this type at any time up to the time it is confirmed by the senate. The court decided this in the affirmative, though noting that there is a divergency of judicial opinion in different states and citing both favorable and adverse decisions. The result was that Burke and Witt, having presented themselves at meetings of the Board to continue their service as members, and having been rejected by the Board, were nevertheless entitled to continue to function as members until successors were properly appointed and qualified.[8] Presiding Judge Biegelmeier wrote the opinion, and Judges Hanson and Woolman concurred. Judge Winans entered a dissenting opinion.

After stating his theory that the governor had no right to withdraw appointments once made, and citing precedents to support it, he took occasion to point out that in the stipulation of facts in this case it appeared that on the same day Governor Kneip wrote the letters withdrawing the proposed appointments of Schmidt and Varilek, he

---

8. *Burke and Witt* v. *Schmidt and Varilek,* (S.D.), 191 N.W. 2d 281 (1971).

conferred with Burke and Witt and told them he wanted them to serve at least one year until the "master plan" then being considered had been drafted, but he could not assure them as to how much longer he might want them to serve; and he directed each of them to leave with him a signed and undated letter of resignation, which they did. This exposed the whole maneuver as a ploy to keep control of the Board in the governor's hands—an example of the appetite for totally centralized power that currently afflicts many governors in many states.

### Election of Members of the Governing Board: Applicability of the "One Man, One Vote" Principle

The "one man, one vote" decision of the United States Supreme Court is to the effect that an individual's right to vote for state legislators is unconstitutionally impaired when its weight is diluted in a substantial fashion when compared with votes of citizens living in other parts of the state.[9]

Does this rule apply also in the election of the members of the Board of Regents of the University of the State of New York, who are elected by the legislature in joint session? No, despite the fact that in the joint session each member has one vote of equal weight with all others, though there were only 57 senators as compared with 150 assemblymen, so that according to the census of 1960 the average senator represented 2.62 times as many people as the average assemblyman.

Litigation was instituted by a defeated candidate for a place on the Board of Regents who contended that he would have been elected if the vote of each senator had been weighted as 2.62 votes as compared with one vote of each assemblyman; and that this weighting was mandated by the "one man, one vote" rule of the Supreme Court. He sought judgment declaring null and void the action of officers of the legislature and the Board of Regents certifying the election of his successful opponent, and directing them to declare and certify that he (plaintiff) had been duly elected to the Board of Regents.

Justice Lawrence H. Cooke of the Albany County supreme court dismissed the petition, on the ground that it failed to state a cause of

---

9. *Reynolds* v. *Sims*, 377 U.S. 533, 84 S. Ct. 1362, 12 L. Ed. 2d 506 (1964).

action. "The principle of 'one man, one vote' has no relevancy here." There was no provision of law permitting or requiring the application of a weighted voting system to such a joint session of the legislature. The Board of Regents is not a general elective body; local voters can not vote for any member thereof; and it is not a general legislative body. It performs essentially executive, administrative, or ministerial functions.[10]

Section 207 of the *Education Law* provides in part: "Subject and in conformity to the constitution and laws of this state, the regents shall exercise legislative functions concerning the educational system of the state, determine its educational policies, and, except as to the judicial functions of the commissioner of education, establish rules for carrying into effect the laws and policies of the state relating to education, and the functions, powers, duties and trusts conferred or charged upon the university and the education department." (In New York official parlance, the University of the State of New York, headed by the Board of Regents, embraces the entire statewide system of education at all levels; and the commissioner of education, appointed by the Regents, is a chief state school officer of broad authority.)

Illinois enacted in 1965 a public junior college act specifying anew the manner in which such a district could be created and the mode by which its governing board should be elected, along with many other prescriptions regarding the organization and operation of such districts. An attack on the constitutionality of this act took the form of an action in *quo warranto* by the state's attorney of Kankakee County, asking for ouster of the members of the Board of Junior College District No. 520.

Thirteen grounds were alleged as bases for the contention that the act of 1965 was unconstitutional. Many of these involved in one way or another interpretations of earlier school statutes and constitutional provisions in Illinois, and required a lengthy didactic opinion of the court. The Kankakee County circuit court held the act constitutional, and dismissed the complaint, whereupon the state's attorney appealed to the supreme court of Illinois, where the judgment of dismissal was affirmed. The opinion was by Justice Byron Orvil House.

Here we deal with only two of the points raised, because they

---

10. *MacKenzie v. Travia and Board of Regents*, (N.Y. Misc.), 286 N.Y.S. 2d 965 (1968).

relate to the "one man, one vote" principle of *Reynolds* v. *Sims*, as applied in a Texas case involving the mode of election of members of a board of county commissioners, such board having general governmental powers over the entire geographic area served by the county;[11] and a case arising in Virginia involving a similar problem.[12]

The objections to the Illinois act were that it stipulated that where more than 15 per cent or less than 30 per cent of the taxable property is located in unincorporated territory, then one member of the seven-member board must be a resident of unincorporated territory; and where 30 per cent or more of the taxable property is so located, then at least two members must reside in unincorporated territory. Only the specified *residence* is required; all members are elected by the voters of the whole district voting at large. This, decided the Illinois supreme court, creates no clash with the principle of one man, one vote.

The Commissioners' Court of Midland County, Texas, had five members, one being the county judge elected by the county at large and voting only in case of a tie. The other four were chosen from districts whose population respectively approximated 67,906; 852; 414; and 828. The city of Midland, forming one district, had 95 per cent of the county's population. Declaring that this scheme of election was a denial of equal protection of the law, the United States Supreme Court said: ". . . the Constitution permits no substantial variation from equal population in drawing districts for units of local government having general governmental powers over the entire geographic area served by the body." It added, however, that ". . . the one man, one vote principle does not require that a uniform straitjacket bind citizens in devising mechanisms of local government suitable for local needs and efficient in solving local problems," citing its own decision in the Virginia case.

In Virginia the county of Princess Anne had been consolidated with the city of Virginia Beach, to form a city government composed of seven boroughs, of which three were primarily urban, three primarily rural, and one predominantly a tourist resort. Their respective 1960 populations were: 29,048; 23,731; 13,900; 7,211; 2,504; 733; and 8,091. Of the 11-member city council, 4 were elected at large without regard

11. *Avery* v. *Midland County, Texas*, 390 U.S. 474, 88 S. Ct. 1114, 20 L. Ed. 2d 45 (1968).

12. *Dusch* v. *Davis*, 387 U.S. 112, 87 S. Ct. 1554, 18 L. Ed. 2d 656 (1967).

to residence, and 7 were also elected at large, but each one of these 7 was required to reside in a different borough.

The Supreme Court of the United States said, "The seven-four plan makes no distinction on the basis of race, creed, or economic status or location. Each of the 11 councilmen is elected by a vote of all the electors in the city . . . he is the city's, not the borough's councilman. . . . The constitutional test under the Equal Protection Clause is whether there is an 'invidious' discrimination. . . . The seven-four plan seems to reflect a détente between urban and rural communities that may be important in resolving the complex problems of the modern megalopolis in relation to the city, the suburbia, and the rural countryside."

Thus the Illinois supreme court had good precedent for its decision that the Illinois junior college act was not rendered unconstitutional by its requirement that in specified circumstances some of the board members must be residents of unincorporated territory, though all were elected at large by the district as a whole.[13]

Only a few weeks earlier than the Illinois decision, the supreme court of Oregon, construing a somewhat ambiguously worded statute, decided that in a public junior college district which had been divided into several "zones," with one of the seven members of its Board of Directors to be elected from among the *residents* of each zone, the elections must be held *separately* by the voters of each zone and not at large by the voters of the whole district.

The court relied rather heavily on administrative history, showing that from 1962 to 1964 the State Board of Education had interpreted the statute as requiring that the Directors be elected by zone; but that thereafter the elections in zoned districts were generally at large, though one such district had continued uninterruptedly to elect its directors by zones. Thus the court was able to say there had been no really uniform administrative practice in favor of elections at large; and it issued a peremptory writ of mandamus commanding the State Board to arrange for elections by zone in the "area education district" (junior college district) comprising the metropolitan area of the city of Portland and portions of surrounding counties.[14]

To the objection that the zones might eventually become im-

---

13. *People of the State of Illinois* v. *Francis*, (Ill.), 239 N.E. 2d 129 (1968).
14. *School District No. 1, Multnomah County* v. *Oregon State Board of Education*, (Ore.), 441 P. 2d 243 (1968).

balanced as to population, and thus defeat the rule of "one man, one vote" in the district, the court responded that it would be the task of the legislature to reapportion the zones or provide machinery for re-apportionment.

### U.S. Supreme Court Held "One Man, One Vote" Must Be
### Applied in Junior College District of
### Metropolitan Kansas City

Again in 1970 the U.S. Supreme Court spoke on the application of "one man, one vote" in a large composite junior college district. Residents and taxpayers of the Kansas City School District, one of eight school districts constituting the Junior College District of Metropolitan Kansas City, claimed their right to vote for trustees of the district was unconstitutionally diluted because their separate district contained approximately 60 per cent of the total apportionment basis of the entire composite junior college district, but the state statutory formula resulted in the election of only 50 per cent of the trustees from their district.

Missouri courts, including the state supreme court, dismissed the suit, holding that "one man, one vote" was inapplicable to the junior college district. This judgment was reversed by the U.S. Supreme Court. In the opinion of the high tribunal, by Mr. Justice Hugo L. Black, as summarized in the *Headnote*, it was held that "Whenever a state or local government by popular election selects persons to perform public functions, the Equal Protection Clause (of the Fourteenth Amendment) requires that each qualified voter have an equal opportunity to participate in the election, and when members of an elected body are chosen from separate districts, each district must be established on a basis that as far as practicable will insure that equal numbers of voters can vote for proportionally equal numbers of officials."[15] Mr. Justice John M. Harlan wrote a lengthy dissent, in which Mr. Chief Justice Warren Burger joined. The Chief Justice also made a short addendum, protesting that the decision laid down no guidelines for the states and local subdivisions.

---

15. *Hadley* v. *Junior College District of Kansas City*, 397 U.S. 50, 90 S. Ct. 791, 25 L. Ed. 2d 45 (1970); reversing (Mo.), 432 S.W. 2d 328 (1968).

# APPENDIX

## Updating of THE DEVELOPING
## LAW OF THE STUDENT
## AND THE COLLEGE

Many owners and users of *The Colleges and the Courts: The
Developing Law of the Student and the College* (published in 1972 by
The Interstate Printers & Publishers, Inc., of Danville, Illinois) will
also possess copies of this present companion volume, *The Colleges and
the Courts: Faculty and Staff Before the Bench*, published in 1973.
The lapse of about one year, together with continued activity in the
courts relative to the rights and obligations of students, has made it

possible and desirable to place here this appendix consisting of brief treatment of recent cases carrying forward the story of the 1972 volume to include approximately that calendar year.

## 1. Obligation of Divorced Parents to Pay College Expenses

The trend of half a century toward holding divorced or separated parents responsible for college education of their children, at least up to age 21, may be affected if the states proceed to enact statutes making age 18 the age of majority for all purposes.

Meantime, in an unusual Pennsylvania case, a physician, who was separated from his wife, was ordered by the court of common pleas in 1968 to pay the wife $100 a week for her own support and $5,000 for one year's support of their 23-year-old son in medical school at West Virginia University; and subsequently ordered to pay $4,000 for the son for another year; but this second order was eventually set aside by the multiple-judge Superior Court in an opinion by Judge G. Harold Watkins, who thought that under the Pennsylvania support law there was no obligation to support and pay medical school expenses of a 24-year-old son who had married and established his residence with his wife in another state, even though the court did not doubt that in this case the parent was financially able to do so without undue financial hardship to himself. A majority of the Superior Court agreed, but Judge Theodore Spalding dissented in an opinion in which he was joined by Judge J. Sydney Hoffman. They would have affirmed the order of the lower court on the ground that the father, having failed to appeal the order of 1968 within the time specified for filing an appeal, had waived the legal question of whether a parent is legally obligated to support "an adult son in medical school or in any other graduate school."

—*Colantoni* v. *Colantoni*, (Pa. Super.), 281 A. 2d 662 (1971).

## 2. Admission as a Student

The press of October 26, 1972, reported that the University of Colorado had been ordered by the U.S. District Court, and had complied with the order, to admit as a student one Jesus Urbrieta, a Chicano applicant who was denied readmission because criminal charges might conceivably be filed against him. In June 1971, while a student at the university, he had been charged with assault with a deadly weapon. The charge had been "dismissed without prejudice," which means the trial court left the door open for a second filing, if his accusers so chose. This did not cast such a shadow on Urbrieta's status as to justify denying him readmission to the university.

—*University of Colorado* v. *Urbrieta*, (U.S.D.C., Colo.), citation not reported (1972).

### 3. Progress in Racial Desegregation

At North Carolina Central University, a predominantly black state institution, *The Echo*, the university-subsidized student newspaper, allegedly carried on a program of "harassment, discourtesy, and indicia of unwelcome" directed at white students and prospective students. The president of the university, Albert N. Whiting, correctly perceived that this was a violation of the law of the land requiring North Carolina and other states to proceed with "an affirmative duty to dismantle racially identifiable dual systems of higher education," and also that it was a violation of the mandate against discrimination on the basis of race or color. Accordingly he ordered all university financial support of *The Echo* cut off in November 1971. Knowing that this action would be in contravention of the First Amendment freedom of the press (under authority of the several recent federal decisions discussed at pages 197-212 in *The Developing Law of the Student and the College*) if the university subsidized or sponsored any other student newspaper, he also announced that the university, having terminated its support of *The Echo*, would not sponsor any student newspaper.

The position of President Whiting, when he was made defendant in a petition for injunction was sustained in all respects by Chief U.S. District Judge Eugene A. Gordon.

—*Joyner* v. *Whiting*, (U.S.D.C., N.C.), 341 F. Supp. 1244 (April 7, 1972).

## 4. Exclusion for Academic Reasons; Conferring of Degrees

Courts have usually declined to interfere when a university faculty refuses admission to a student solely because of his low academic standing; but the supreme court of Montana held in 1971 that refusal to admit a graduate of the University of Chicago to the University of Montana Law School because he had received a grade of "D" in a required pre-legal course in accounting was an abuse of discretion on the part of the faculty, and ordered him admitted.

—*State ex rel. Bartlett* v. *Pantzer*, (Mont.), 489 P. 2d 375 (1971).

A Nigerian student spent five years in the New York State Veterinary College (administered by Cornell University), but was denied a degree in June 1966, by a vote of 39 to 1 of the veterinary faculty, and rejected for readmission because his grades had always been low (he had repeated the third year because of failure), and for his senior year, especially for the final semester, his "grade point average" was distinctly below that of the next lowest man in the class of 54, and generally below that of the lowest man permitted to graduate in any class of the past 10 years.

He asked the trial court to compel the university to award him the degree of Doctor of Veterinary Medicine, and a judgment for $95,000 in damages for reduced earnings, alleging that his treatment by the veterinary faculty was malicious, arbitrary, and capricious. In an accompanying statement he charged that he had been discriminated against because he was black; that one of the professors on a crucial committee had falsely called him a Communist; and that the dean had been told that he engaged in interracial dating.

In the view of the Madison County supreme court, "beyond the mere allegation, there was no showing that denial of plaintiffs degree was in any way discriminatory." Regular procedures for reviewing the record of each student existed, and were applied to his case fairly, as well as to all other members of his class. Accordingly, Justice Howard A. Zeller summarily dismissed the complaint. Aside from any quibbling about "grade points" and percentages, a published rule of the veterinary college placed recommendations for degrees entirely in the discretion of the veterinary faculty.

—*Balogun* v. *Cornell University*, 70 Misc. 2d 474, 333 N.Y.S. 2d 838 (1971).

## 5. Tuition Fees and Other Charges to Students

*A student, who has paid tuition fees in advance for a semester and then breached his contract of enrollment a few days before classes begin, can not recover any part of the fees paid, holds New York Appellate Division.* A trial court ordered a refund of $910 to an applicant for admission to the dental school. The student had prepaid both a $200 installment and the $910 balance of his tuition fees for one semester, and then resigned his place six days prior to the beginning of classes, having decided to attend another school. This court decision was later reversed by a unanimous judgment of the Appellate Division.

On April 4, 1969, the original order was reversed by Justices Groat, Margett, and Rinaldi in the Appellate Term of the Second and Eleventh Judicial Districts: "In our opinion, the contract was entire and indivisible. Irrespective of whether plaintiff's enrollment was subject to the conditions contained in the Bulletin, it clearly appears that plaintiff breached the contract without cause and, consequently, is not entitled to recover tuition paid in advance. It is well settled that a party may not recover any payments made under a contract which he has breached." (Citing several New York cases and *Williston on Contracts*, Opinion at 59 Misc. 2d 789 (1969).)

The judgment of reversal was affirmed without opinion by the Appellate Division (Justices Brennan, Hopkins, Benjamin, Munder, and Martuscello) and reported in the *New York Law Journal* February 4, 1970. The order of 1968, now reversed and vacated, is reported and discussed at page 46 in *The Developing Law of the Student and the College*.

—*Drucker* v. *New York University*, 57 Misc. 2d 937 (1968).

## 6. Differential Fees for Out-of-State Students

The supreme court of Arizona sustained the policy of the Regents of the three state universities in requiring a student to maintain "legal residence" in the state for at least one year prior to becoming eligible for classification as an in-state student. The court conceded that both physical presence and *evidences of intent* are elements to be considered when a reclassification is at issue.

—*Arizona Board of Regents* v. *Harper*, (Ariz.), 495 P. 2d 453 (April 6, 1972).

The state supreme court held that a university rule requiring that a student must have been domiciled in North Carolina for a period of six months while not in attendance at an institution of higher education, prior to becoming eligible for classification as an in-state student, was reasonable and did not violate the equal protection clause of the Fourteenth Amendment. Justice Higgins recorded a cogent dissent, believing that the rule creating an irrebuttable presumption of nonresidence as long as a student is in continuous attendance is a violation of the equal protection clause.

—*Glusman* v. *Trustees of the University of North Carolina*, (N.C.), 190 S.E. 2d 213 (July 31, 1972).

A similar bone of contention was at issue in a case involving two complaining students at the University of Connecticut. A three-judge federal court recently decided in favor of the students. The U.S. Supreme Court has agreed to review this case and decide the constitutional issues. Compare with the cases in number 8, "Various Facets of Student Life," in the section on student voting, in this appendix; and with the cases discussed at pages 57-65 and 88-90 in *The Developing Law of the Student and the College*.

### 7. Aspects of Student Financial Aids

*Act of Congress intended to deny federal student aid to students convicted of "crime of a serious nature" was declared unconstitutional because of vagueness and lack of precision.* In January 1973, it was reported that a three-judge U.S. District Court in Illinois had declared unconstitutional for vagueness the provision in the federal Higher Education Act of 1965 intended to deny for two years any further federal student aid to "an individual . . . convicted of . . . any crime . . . which involved the use of

. . . force, disruption, or the seizure of property under control of any institution of higher education . . . if such crime was of a serious nature," and so on.

A female graduate student at the Chicago Circle campus of the University of Illinois was arrested and convicted of "criminal trespass" for participation in a peaceful sit-in demonstration in the ROTC building in the spring of 1970. Thereafter, the university cancelled her eligibility for future federally sponsored student loans.

Said the court: "Crime 'of a serious nature' does not have a generally understood meaning, is not a phrase commonly used in law or elsewhere, and is too susceptible of subjective interpretation to fairly advise in advance what in fact a student is forbidden to do. A student has a right to fair warning under the Fourteenth Amendment, and the failure to give this warning violates the First Amendment." The court was careful to say: "Nothing here said or decided is intended to imply that Congress may not properly condition or withdraw federal aid to students under appropriately precise standards."

—*University of Illinois* v. *A female graduate student*, citation not reported (1972).

*Illinois' restriction of Aid to Families with Dependent Children benefits for students aged 18 through 20 to those in high school or technical school was invalidated by the U.S. Supreme Court.* The Social Security Act, Section 406 (a) (2) (B), as amended, extends the benefits of the act to "needy dependent children aged 18 to 20 attending school, college or university." This applies to children in families receiving Aid to Families with Dependent Children (AFDC). An Illinois statute restricted this benefit to children in the specified age-group attending high school, vocational school, or within one year of receiving a degree in a college, and excluded those of the same age-group attending junior college or any college or university if not within one year of receiving a degree.

The rationale of the statute was that attendance at a vocational school is likely to contribute directly and quickly to employability and earning-power; but that attendance at a junior college or any college where the prospect is that more than a year of further attendance will be necessary to lead to a degree has little immediate effect on earning-power. Obviously this takes no account of the general social value of education, or of the principle of equal educational opportunity.

On December 20, 1971, the U.S. Supreme Court declared the Illinois statute unconstitutional and void, in an opinion by Mr. Justice William J. Brennan: "We hold that the Illinois statute and regulation are invalid under the Supremacy Clause, and do not reach the Equal Protection issue."

Nevertheless, Mr. Justice Brennan wrote in a footnote: "A classification which channels one class of people, poor people, into a particular class of low-paying, low-status jobs would plainly raise substantial questions under the Equal Protection Clause."

The decision resulted from two companion cases: (1) Omega Townsend, daughter of a disabled mother, enrolled in a junior college in the fall of 1966, whereupon AFDC benefits for Omega were soon cut off, resulting in a reduction of $47.94 per month in family income. (2) Jerome Alexander, 18-year-old son in an AFDC family, enrolled in a junior college in September 1968, and his AFDC benefit payments were terminated November 1 of that year, resulting in a loss of $23.52 per month in family income.

—*Townsend* v. *Swank*, 404 U.S. 282, 92 S.Ct. 502, 30 L.Ed. 2d 448 (December 20, 1971), reversing 314 F. Supp. 1082 (1970).

*Graduate fellowships provided for by New York Legislature, by act of 1969 which was repealed in 1971, were thereby lawfully cancelled because no contract rights were involved.* A plaintiff had applied for one of the Herbert H. Lehman graduate fellowships provided for in Chapter 1154 of the *New York Laws* of 1969, and in March 1971 had been notified that his application had been granted, whereupon he communicated his acceptance of the fellowship. One month later, Chapter 1154 (1969) was repealed by Chapter 121 of the *Laws* of 1971, and he was immediately notified that his fellowship was cancelled. Alleging that the enactment of Chapter 121 was an unconstitutional impairment of the obligation of a contract, he sued the state for breach of contract, unsuccessfully.

Judge Milton Alpert, for the state court of claims, held that the granting of fellowships is not contractual in nature. The grant was in anticipation of the next academic year, and since prior to that period the legislature had repealed the authorizing statute and made no appropriation for the purpose, there was no recourse. One session of a legislature can not bind its successors, except by contract.

—*Ewing* v. *State of New York*, (N.Y. Court of Claims), 331 N.Y.S. 2d 287 (April 18, 1972).

## 8. Various Facets of Student Life

*Compulsory chapel attendance at U.S. armed forces academies was declared unconstitutional by U.S. Supreme Court.* In mid-December 1972, the U.S. Supreme Court, in a unanimous summary action, declined to hear an appeal from a recent decision of the U.S. Court of Appeals for the District of Columbia that compulsory chapel attendance by cadets at the U.S. armed forces academies is in contravention of the prohibition of an establishment of religion enunciated in the First Amendment. Thus reversed is *Anderson* v. *Laird*, (U.S.D.C., D.C.), 336 F. Supp. 1081 (1970), discussed at page 84 in *The Developing Law of the Student and the College.*

*The New York Appellate Division holds that any First Amendment obligation of governments and their agencies to abstain from attacking religion, as set forth in a trial court decision of 1969, is outweighed by the obligation not to censor the student press. Panarella* v. *Birenbaum,* 60 Misc. 2d 95, 302 N.Y.S. 2d 427 (1969), discussed at page 85 in *The Developing Law of the Student and the College,* was reversed in *Panarella* v. *Birenbaum,* (N.Y. App. Div.), 327 N.Y.S. 2d 755 (1971). For details see in this appendix under Number 16, "Freedom of the Student Press."

*Student voting: the trend appears to be toward prohibiting election registrars from requiring discriminatory evidence of residence from student registrants, that are not required of other registrants.* In voting precincts wherein an institution of higher education is located, local elderly residents and real estate interests sometimes bitterly resist the idea of student voting, especially since the adoption of the Twenty-sixth Amendment (July 1, 1972), which safeguards the suffrage for persons aged 18 or more. State or local authorities have sometimes demanded special proof of residence from student registrants, not required of other registrants. A very good argument can be made that this kind of discrimination violates the equal protection clause of the Fourteenth Amendment. This was the decision of a U.S. District Court in Kentucky, which granted an injunction against the practice of denying students at the University of Kentucky the opportunity to register for voting unless they successfully completed answers to a series of questions designed to overcome the ancient presumption that their homes were those of their parents.

U.S. District Judge Mac Swinford held that no special or additional criteria for proof of residence may be imposed upon students because they are students. Each applicant for registration should be asked the same questions, regardless of occupation, and nothing can be presumed or implied from the fact that an applicant is a student.

—*Bright* v. *Baesler*, (U.S.D.C., Ky.), 336 F. Supp. 527 (December 30, 1971).

In a somewhat similar case in Ohio the decision of another U.S. District Court was to the same effect.

—*Anderson* v. *Brown*, (U.S.D.C., Ohio), 332 F. Supp. 1195 (1971).

The Michigan supreme court has also recently held that the state statute providing that "no elector shall be deemed to have gained or lost a residency (for voting) . . . while a student at any institution of learning" is, in the context of related Michigan statutes, unconstitutional and void as violative of both the equal protection clause and the due process clause of the Fourteenth Amendment.

—*Wilkins* v. *Bentley*, (Mich.), 189 N.W. 2d 423 (1971).

Compare with the cases on residence for tuition fee-paying purposes, under number 6, "Differential Fees for Out-of-State Students" in this Appendix.

## 9. College Dormitory Residents

U.S. Chief District Judge Benjamin C. Dawkins granted a preliminary injunction against enforcement of a rule of Southeastern Louisiana University *as currently applied and implemented*, on the ground that, though ostensibly requiring students under the age of 23 to live in college-owned dormitories, the university allowed students under that age to reside in off-campus houses operated by recently-organized fraternity groups, while denying plaintiffs the privilege of living in the 90-bed Cardinal Newman Club directly across the street from the campus.

"The fraternity-Cardinal Newman Hall classification is clearly unreasonable and must be held to amount to systematic invidious discrimination which is prohibited by the Equal Protection Clause of the Fourteenth Amendment." Judge Dawkins carefully limited his decree to the unique facts of this case and reserved judgment on all other constitutional questions involved, pending anticipated further proceedings in his court. He is the judge who wrote the opinion for the special three-judge federal court which upheld housing rules at Louisiana Polytechnic University in 1970, and was summarily affirmed by the U.S. Supreme Court on April 6, 1971.

—*Cooper* v. *Nix*, (U.S.D.C., La.), 343 F. Supp. 1101 (May 29, 1972).

It has been reported in the press that when 14 students sought to overturn the rule of Indiana State University at Terre Haute that required them to live in college-operated housing, the U.S. District Court denied their plea and held that the rule was not unconstitutional as unduly restricting the right of privacy. The court reminded the students that they knew of the housing rules before enrolling, and were given adequate opportunity for a hearing and appeal on their applications for individual exceptions to the housing policy.

## 10. Unreasonable Searches and Seizures

After the unjustified slaying of four students at Kent State University on May 4, 1970, the Portage County Common Pleas Court ordered all students to leave the campus and to return to their homes, on or before noon of the next day, May 5. The same order also restrained all persons from "entering onto the geographical confines of Kent State University without the express authority of the Ohio National Guard." The order was modified on May 7 to substitute "Kent State University Security Office" for "Ohio National Guard." On May 8, the campus security officer (chief of police), acting in concert with one Captain Chester Hayth of the Ohio State Highway Patrol and with H. W. Kane, Prosecuting Attorney of Portage County, ordered the campus security force to search all dormitory rooms, without search warrants, for items which might indicate violations of Ohio law, to identify all such items with tags showing in which rooms they were found, and to confiscate them. The search was completed on May 16.

On May 18, the university announced room check-out times for the students, at which times they were allowed to pick up personal belongings from their rooms and surrender their room-keys and meal tickets. Later, during July, they received refunds reaching back to May 4.

U.S. District Judge William K. Thomas, faced with a petition for declaratory and equitable relief against possible repetitions of the allegedly unreasonable and unconstitutional searches and seizures, held that the individual students' contracts for room-rental were not terminated until the check-out times, and their contractual rights as tenants and occupants of their rooms continued up to those times, even though they were temporarily ousted from their possession and occupancy.

This being true, the mass search of all rooms, for the obvious purpose of seizing items intended to be used as evidence in subsequent criminal prosecutions, was a bald violation of the Fourth Amendment, following the precedent of *Piazzola* v. *Watkins*, (U.S.C.A., 5 Cir., 1971) and other similar federal decisions. (Discussed at pages 112-113 in *The Developing Law of the Student and the College*.)

Said Judge Thomas: "In view of the clear criminal investigatory purpose of the room-by-room search, with evidence of possible violations of state criminal laws being discovered, I conclude that the Fourth Amendment required individual and particularized search warrants, based on probable cause, to be obtained from a magistrate to authorize such a search by the campus security officers."

Having thus decided the issues, the court denied any further declaratory or equitable relief as inappropriate in the circumstances, with one exception: jurisdiction was retained for the sole purpose of issuing, if necessary, orders under which individuals could recover non-contraband personal property from the security office of the university.

—*Morgan* v. *Hayth*, (U.S.D.C., Northern District of Ohio, Eastern Division, Civil Action No. C 70-691, June 2, 1972).

## 11. Confidentiality of Student Records

(No important changes noted since 1971)

## 12. Torts Against Students

(No important changes noted since 1971)

## 13. Freedom of Speech and Assembly

*The public interest in orderly operation of the university outweighs student's wish to conduct a non-credit course contrary to regulations.* A student at Florida State University in Tallahassee attempted, on his own initiative, to teach a non-credit course entitled, "How to Make a Revolution in the U.S.A.," in disregard of university regulations. For this breach of discipline he was suspended after having been given the notice and hearing required by due process.

The suspension was sustained by the U.S. District Court, apparently believing that in this instance the First Amendment rights of free speech and assembly had been overstepped. In other words, to whatever extent these rights were involved, in this instance they were outweighed by the compelling interest of the state and the university in maintaining its orderly operation.

—*Center for Participant Education* v. *Marshall*, (U.S.D.C., Fla.), 337 F. Supp. 126 (1972).

*Administrative modification of university schedule in emergency does not deprive students of First Amendment freedoms.* A reverse twist in viewing the constitutional rights of freedom of speech and assembly as appertaining to college and university students was exemplified in a suit by certain students of the University of Wisconsin at Madison, claiming that a temporary cessation of regularly scheduled classes ordered by the president for the purpose of lessening the imminent danger of personal clashes and destruction of property on the campus, *ipso facto* deprived them of a right to attend classes as scheduled. The constitutional rights of speech and assembly, said they, "are interwoven into the normal operations of the university," and any suspension of its "normal operations" deprives them of these rights. Not so, decided U.S. District Judge Myron L. Gordon. No constitutional question was involved. The university administration had merely exercised the discretion vested in it by state law, to administer the affairs of the university in the best interest of all persons involved.

This judgment was affirmed by the Seventh Circuit U.S. Court of Appeals in an opinion by Chief Circuit Judge Luther M. Swygert, joined by Senior Circuit Judge F. Ryan Duffy. The grievance of the plaintiffs, if any valid claim existed, was primarily a matter of contract, thought the court, and could not be escalated into a constitutional issue. There was a dissent by Senior District Judge William J. Campbell, sitting by designation.

—*Asher* v. *Harrington*, (U.S.C.A., Wis.), 461 F. 2d 890 (1972).

*An art exhibit is a form of expression protected by the First Amendment; but the protection is not absolute.* There is no question that an exhibit of art is a form of expression protected by the First Amendment; but the issue of when such an exhibit oversteps the boundaries of the protected area can be a difficult one.

A student at one of the California State Colleges placed an exhibition of his master's degree art project on the campus, with the approval of the college administration. The exhibit consisted of nude sculptures, some of which depicted erotic acts. The chancellor of the 19-campus system of state universities and colleges (until recently known as the state colleges), overruled the local college administration and ordered the exhibit removed. The California court of appeal ruled that the chancellor's order was not an abuse of discretion, and upheld it.

—*Appelgate* v. *Dumke*, (Cal. App.), 101 Cal. Rptr. 645 (1972).

Compare this case with *Close* v. *Lederle*, (U.S.C.A., Mass.), 424 F. 2d 988 (1970), reversing (U.S.D.C., Mass.), 303 F. Supp. 1109 (1969).

### 14. The "Speaker Ban" Furor

(No important changes noted since 1971)

### 15. Student Organizations

The decision in *Healy* v. *James*, affirmed by Second Circuit Court of Appeals, 40 *U.S. Law Week* 2071 (August 3, 1971), sustained the refusal of the president of Central Connecticut State College to allow recognition as a registered campus organization of a local student group calling itself a local chapter of Students for a Democratic Society but disavowing any subservience to the national organization of the same name. This decision was reversed by the unanimous U.S. Supreme Court in 405 U.S. 1037, 33 L.Ed. 2d 266 (1972); reversing 445 F. 2d 1122 (1971), and 319 F. Supp. (1970).

In the opinion, Mr. Justice Lewis Franklin Powell said: "The precedents of this Court leave no room for the view that, because of the acknowledged need for order, First Amendment protections should apply with less force on college campuses than in the community at large.

"The college classroom with its surrounding environs is peculiarly the 'market place of ideas' and we break no new constitutional ground in reaffirming this nation's dedication to safeguarding academic freedom.

"The organization's ability to participate in the intellectual give and take of campus debate, and to pursue its stated purposes, is limited by denial of access to the customary media for communication for communicating with the administration, faculty members and other students. Such impediments can not be viewed as insubstantial."

Mr. Justice William O. Douglas, concurring, said that the case "indicates the sickness of our academic world, measured by First

Amendment standards" of free speech, expression, and association. (The lower federal court decisions, now reversed, are discussed at page 182 of *The Developing Law of the Student and the College.*)

—*Healy* v. *James*, (U.S.D.C., Conn.), 311 F. Supp. 1275 and 319 F. Supp. 113 (1970). Reversed in 405 U.S. 1037, 33 L. Ed. 2d 266 (1972).

At the University of Southern Mississippi, a faculty-student committee voted to deny recognition to a campus chapter of the Mississippi Civil Liberties Union, and the decision was confirmed by the president of the university. Eventually this determination was sustained by the U.S. District Court; but in the Fifth Circuit U.S. Court of Appeals the judgment was reversed (No. 71-1801 5 Cir. 71, reversing No. 2455 U.S.D.C. SD Miss. 71), and the university was ordered to approve the application for recognition as a student organization. (Compare with *American Civil Liberties Union of Virginia, Inc.* v. *Redford College*, (U.S.D.C., Va.), 315 F. Supp. 893 discussed at page 183 in *The Developing Law of the Student and the College.*)

Apparently an opposite result has been reached in a case arising at Florida State University, where a U.S. District Court denied any redress to an organization known as the Young Socialist Alliance that was recently refused recognition by order of the president of the university. An adverse directive against recognition of this organization had been issued to all the state universities in Florida by the chairman of the Florida Board of Regents. Its fate, if and when appealed to higher federal courts, is not now known.

—*Merkey* v. *Board of Regents of State of Florida*, (U.S.D.C., Fla.), 344 F. Supp. 1296 F. Supp. 1296 (1972).

### 16. Freedom of the Student Press

In April 1971, Palo Alto police entered the offices of *The Stanford Daily*, carrying a search warrant granted by a municipal judge. They hoped to find and seize photographs of student demonstrators who may have participated in recent campus assemblies at Stanford University. When the editors of the *Daily* alleged that this search was unconstitutional under both the First Amendment (free press) and the Fourth Amendment (unreasonable searches and seizures), U.S. District Judge Robert F. Peckham sustained their contentions in full, according to press reports.

*The Stanford Daily*, once controlled and subsidized by the Associated Students of Stanford University, is said now to be in process of reorganization to become an independent nonprofit corporation. Compare with *Joyner* v. *Whiting*, involving *The Echo* of North Carolina Central University, cited earlier in the appendix under number 3, "Progress in Racial Desegregation."

In 1969, Justice Vito J. Titone of the supreme court of Richmond County (Staten Island) ordered the Staten Island Community College and Richmond College (each a component of The City University of New York, governed by the Board of Higher Education of the City of New York, and tax-supported by the city and the state) to prevent their respective student newspapers from publishing anti-religious articles. One had recently printed a vitriolic attack on Catholicism, and the other a blasphemous vilification of Jesus Christ. Each paper was funded in part by mandatory student fees, received office space and telephones on campus, and was held out as an agency of its college. The First and Fourteenth Amendments, said Justice Titone, require a stance of neutrality on the part of government toward religion.

Said he: "The students, or anyone else, are perfectly free to hold views against religions, to voice those views and to publish them. They may not, however, use public facilities to do so." (Quoted on page 85 of *The Developing Law of the Student and the College*.)

On November 29, 1971, the Appellate Division reversed this judgment and dismissed the proceedings: "These newspapers have been established as a forum for the free expression of the ideas and opinions of the students who attend these institutions of higher learning. It has repeatedly been held that, once having established such a forum, the authorities may not then place limitations upon its use which infringe upon the rights of the students to free expression as protected by the First Amendment, unless it can be shown that the restrictions are necessary to avoid material and substantial interference with the requirements of appropriate discipline in the operation of the school. . . . There is no showing herein, nor is it contended that publication of the matter sought to be suppressed constitutes a threat to the orderly functioning of these institutions. We must hold that the imposition of these restrictions upon the operation of campus newspapers is unconstitutional, as an infringement of the right of free expression of the students attending these colleges."

—*Panarella* v. *Birenbaum*, (N.Y. App. Div.), 327 N.Y.S. 2d 755 (1971). Reversing 60 Misc. 2d 95, 302 N.Y.S. 2d 427 (1969).

## 17. "Due Process" in Disciplinary Proceedings

The principle that university discipline is one thing and criminal law is another, and that the two are not to be confused, was convincingly re-stated by a California court of appeal in *Anderson* v. *Regents of University of California*: "By judicial mandate to impose upon the academic community in student discipline, the intricate, time-consuming, and sophisticated procedures, rules and safeguards of criminal law would frustrate the teaching process and render the institutional control impotent."

And again: "Procedures for dismissing college students are not analogous to criminal proceedings and could not be so without at the same time being both impractical and detrimental to the educational atmosphere and functions of a university. . . . If under all the circumstances the student was given a fair hearing and opportunity to meet any charges brought against him, the courts will not interfere."

—*Anderson* v. *Regents of University of California*, (Cal. App.), 99 Cal. Rptr. 531 (January 10, 1972).

Another illustration that disciplinary procedures are not generally held to as high standards of due process as criminal proceedings is afforded by a U.S. District Court decision that a student at the University of South Carolina who, with others, having refused to leave the student union building when ordered to do so on pain of suspension, was given proper notice and a hearing on the accusation of interfering with the normal operation of the university, and was suspended. The procedure was held to be acceptable despite the fact that some members of the Special Hearing Committee which recommended the suspension were also members of the Board of Trustees which heard the appeal from it and confirmed it.

—*Herman* v. *University of South Carolina*, (U.S.D.C., S.C.), 341 F. Supp. 226 (1971).

This judgment was affirmed by the Fourth Circuit U.S. Court of Appeals, holding that the University's procedures in this case satisfied the requirements of due process in disciplinary cases, but expressing some concern about the possibility of violating the safeguard of equal protection of the law if, in such a case, the plaintiff was suspended indefinitely while other students who had participated equally in the disorder were quickly reinstated.

—*Herman* v. *University of South Carolina*, (U.S.C.A., S.C.), 457 F. 2d 902 (1972).

The Fourteenth Amendment guarantee of due process of law stands as a safeguard against arbitrary actions by state governments or their agencies and instrumentalities, including local civil units and public universities and schools. Traditionally, private nonprofit universities or colleges have not been regarded as state agencies. It would follow that the Fourteenth Amendment restraints on state agencies would not apply to private institutions (as demonstrated in several decisions cited and discussed on pages 242-246 of *The Developing Law of the Student and the College*).

A different view was expressed by Justice Bertram Harnett of the Nassau County supreme court, when he ordered the reinstatement of a student at Hofstra University who had been hastily expelled for a disciplinary infraction involving window-breaking in a university building.

Said Justice Harnett: "Society's administration has become so complex that private organizations are in a position of performing governmental functions and may be subject to the constitutional requirements of using fair and equal procedures. . . . Hofstra has the major state governmental presence of the New York Dormitory Authority. . . . Over half of the total book value of Hofstra University consists of assets not only constructed but owned by the Dormitory Authority. . . . A private university like Hofstra

is an oligarchal form tending to be self-perpetuating. Its fundamental legal responsibilities are to the public. Its existence and
favored position can be justified only as a public stewardship. . . .
Hofstra is discharging a public function for the State, as part of
a State policy of mobilizing higher education resources."

Defects in the process of expelling this student included campus
police requiring him to make a written confession, only two days'
time in which to prepare his defense before a disciplinary committee of three faculty members, and expulsion on the third day
after being accused. He was not allowed to exercise an option to be
heard before a Student Judiciary Board, as provided in the Hofstra
rules. The university imposed upon him and his family a money
fine (restitution) of more than $1,000 without submitting proof of
damage and upon the testimony of only one claimed eyewitness.
This, said the court, was "precipitous"; it pointed out that a more
appropriate course would have been to suspend him temporarily
pending complete determination of the circumstances, including
his mental condition. Moreover, there was evidence that the university "materially delayed" the scheduling of a review hearing.
All in all, the university's behavior in this case was arbitrary and
an abuse of discretion.

—*Ryan* v. *Hofstra University*, (Supreme court of Nassau County),
324 N.Y.S. 2d 964 (October 14, 1971).


## 18. How Specific Must Disciplinary Rules Be?

(No important changes noted)


## 19. State Statutes as Applied to Campus Disruptions

Hastily enacted, unnecessary, redundant, and patently unconstitutional state legislative acts, owing their origin to the nightmare
period of hysteria about campus disorders, continue to be invalidated by state and federal courts. An example is an enactment of
the Indiana legislature of 1971: "It shall be a misdemeanor for any
person to refuse to leave the premises of any institution established
for the purpose of the education of students enrolled therein when
so requested, regardless of the reason, by the duly constituted officials of any such institution." In 1972, the Indiana supreme court

declared this statute void on its face, due to unconstitutional vagueness and overbreadth and plain violation of the First and Fourteenth Amendments.

The opinion for the unanimous court was by Justice Roger O. DeBruler: "A college truly thrives only when it fosters open debate and principled dissent to the conventional wisdom of the day."

"This statute is clearly unconstitutionally overbroad. It empowers the official to order any person off the premises because he does not approve of his looks, his opinions, his behavior, no matter how peaceful, or for no 'reason at all.'"

—*Alleged Trespasser* v. *College campus*, (Ind.), citation unreported (1972).

In mid-December 1972, the press reported that the Illinois supreme court had sustained a state statute providing criminal penalties for persons convicted of interfering with the operation of a state university. A charge against Valeria A. Witzkowski, who allegedly failed to leave the Illini Union Building at the University of Illinois after being informed by a university security guard that her presence was interfering with the operation of the university, had been dismissed by the Champaign County district court on the ground that the statute was void for vagueness; but the state supreme court reversed the judgment and remanded the case for trial.

—*Witzkowski* v. *University of Illinois*, (Ill.), citation unreported (1972).

A student, suspended for participating in a fight with members of a visiting basketball team immediately following a heated game, advanced the untenable argument that the rules mandated for state university campuses by section 6450 of the Education Law were intended to apply only to large demonstrations and disruptions, and not to small local brawls, and that the campus authorities were without power to adopt other and supplementary rules of discipline.

—*Hanger* v. *State University of New York at Binghamton*, (N.Y. App. Div.), 333 N.Y.S. 2d 571 (June 29, 1972).

## 20. *Executive, Judicial, and Grand Jury Overkill*

In early December 1972, the U.S. Supreme Court dismissed the appeal of Arthur Krause of Pittsburgh from a judgment of the Ohio supreme court holding the state immune from liability in damages for the wrongful death of Allison Krause, his daughter, who was one of the four students unjustifiably slain by national guardsmen on the campus of Kent State University early in May 1970. The state's defense was the doctrine of governmental immunity, or the mediaeval dogma that "The King can do no wrong."

*—Appeal of Arthur Krause.*

On June 2, 1972, the U.S. District Court for the Northern District of Ohio, Eastern Division, held that a mass search of hundreds of dormitory rooms at Kent State University, by state police, campus police, and the county prosecuting attorney, all without warrants from any magistrate and for the purpose of seizing evidence for use in subsequent criminal prosecutions, was in violation of the Fourth Amendment guarantee against unreasonable searches and seizures. See in this appendix, under number 10, "Unreasonable Searches and Seizures."

## 21. *Selective Service in the Armed Forces*

(A volume could be written on the selective service judicial history, but this is not the place for it.)

## CASES MENTIONED IN APPENDIX

### *U.S. Supreme Court*

## By state of origin, with decisions of inferior federal courts marked "US"

# BIBLIOGRAPHY

## BOOKS AND PAMPHLETS

1. Alexander, Kern, and Erwin S. Solomon. *College and University Law.* Charlottesville, Virginia: The Michie Company, 1972. 776 pp.
2. Blackburn, Robert T. *Tenure: Aspects of Job Security on the Changing Campus.* Atlanta: Southern Regional Education Board, Research Monograph No. 19, July 1972. 60 pp.
3. Bolmeier, Edward C. *Teachers' Legal Rights, Restraints and Liabilities.* Cincinnati: The W. H. Anderson Company, 1971. 149 pp.
4. Boyd, William B., William T. Bulger, and others. *Agreement, 1971-74, Between Central Michigan University and Central Michigan University Faculty Association.* Mt. Pleasant, Michigan, 1971. 40 pp.
5. Brubacher, John S. *The Courts and Higher Education.* San Francisco: Jossey-Bass, Inc., 1971. 150 pp.
6. Brubacher, John S. *The Law and Higher Education: A Casebook.* Teaneck, New Jersey: Fairleigh Dickinson University Press, 1971. Two vols. 700 pp.
7. Chambers, M. M. *The Colleges and the Courts: The Developing Law of the Student and the College.* Danville, Illinois: The Interstate Printers & Publishers, Inc., 1972. 316 pp.
8. Chambers, M. M. *The Colleges and the Courts, 1962-66.* Danville, Illinois: The Interstate Printers & Publishers, Inc., 1967. 326 pp.
9. Chanin, Robert H. *Protecting Teacher Rights: A Summary of Constitutional Developments.* Washington: National Education Association, 1970. 41 pp.

237

10. McCarney, Bernard J. (Ed.). *Perspectives on University Collective Negotiations.* Normal, Illinois: Illinois State University Foundation, 1971. 122 pp.

11. Rose, Arnold M. *Libel and Academic Freedom: A Lawsuit Against Political Extremists.* Minneapolis: University of Minnesota Press, 1968. 287 pp.

12. Shulman, Carol H. *Collective Bargaining on Campus.* Washington: American Association for Higher Education, 1972. 45 pp.

13. Tax Foundation, Inc. *Unions and Government Employment.* New York: Tax Foundation, Inc., 1972. 45 pp.

14. Tice, Terrence N., and Grace W. Holmes (Eds.). *Faculty Power: Collective Bargaining on Campus.* Ann Arbor: Institute of Continuing Legal Education, 1972. 368 pp.

15. U.S. Department of Labor. Workplace Standards Administration. Wage and Hour Division. *Institutions of Higher Education Under the Fair Labor Standards Act.* Washington: WH Publication No. 1317, March 1971. 12 pp. litho.

16. *Wisconsin Law Review 1971*, No. 1, pp. 1-295. *Collective Negotiations in Higher Education: A Symposium.* Madison: University of Wisconsin Law School, 1971. 295 pp.

## ARTICLES

17. Asper, Lewis D. "The Long and Unhappy History of Loyalty Testing in Maryland." *American Journal of Legal History* 13: 97-109 (April 1969).

18. Astin, Helen S., and Alan E. Bayer. "Sex Discrimination in Academe." *Educational Record* 53: 101-118 (Spring 1972).

19. Brown, Ralph S., Jr., "Collective Bargaining in Higher Education." *67 Michigan Law Review* 1067 (1969).

20. Brown, Ronald C. "Professors and Unions: The Faculty Senate; An Effective Alternative to Collective Bargaining in Higher Education." *William and Mary Law Review* (1970): 302-308.

21. Buford, Rivers, Jr., "Constitutional Rights and Non-renewal of Faculty Contracts." Pp. 47-51 in *Higher Education: The Law and Individual Rights and Responsibilities.* Athens: University of Georgia Institute of Higher Education, 1971.

22. Costello, James J. "Faculty Relations." Ch. 3 (pp. 1-41 through 1-50)

in *Handbook of University Administration: Academic,* edited by Asa S. Knowles. New York: McGraw-Hill, 1970. (Not consecutively paginated, but approx. 1,200 pp. in each of two vols.)

23. "Developments in the Law of Academic Freedom." 81 *Harvard Law Review* 1050.

24. Farber, M. A. "Professors' Union Movement a Growing Presence in U.S. Campus Power." *Times (London) Higher Education Supplement,* November 26, 1971.

25. Ferguson, Tracy H. "Collective Bargaining in Universities and Colleges." 19 *Labor Law Journal* 778 (December 1968).

26. Fields, Cheryl M. "Women Seeking Campus Rights Hit Many Snags." *Today's Education-N.E.A. Journal* (January 1972), 75-78.

27. Finkin, Matthew W. "Collective Bargaining and University Government." *Wisconsin Law Review* (1971): 125-149.

28. Freedman, Haskell C. "The Non-tenured Teacher and the Civil Rights Act of 1871." Pp. 72-81 in *Critical Issues in School Law.* Topeka: National Organization on Legal Problems of Education, 1970. 199 pp.

29. Halverson, Jerry F. "The Analysis of a Strike." Pp. 1-14 in *Critical Issues in School Law.* Topeka: National Organization on Legal Problems of Education, 1970. 199 pp.

30. Howlett, Robert G. "Legality of Strikes in the Coming Decade." A Special Report of *Educator's Negotiating Service,* October 15, 1971. 6 pp.

31. Jacobson, Sol. "Faculty Collective Bargaining at the City University of New York." *School and Society* (October 1971): 346-349.

32. "Job Protection in the Federal Courts for Probationary Teachers in Public Colleges and Universities." 3 *University of West Los Angeles Law Review* 135 (1971).

33. Keck, Donald J. "Faculty Governance and the 'New Managerial Class.'" *Today's Education-N.E.A. Journal* (March 1972), 73-76.

34. Kugler, Israel. "Collective Bargaining for the Faculty." *Liberal Education* 56: 78-85 (March 1970).

35. Kugler, Israel. "The Union Speaks for Itself." *Educational Record* 49: 414-418 (Fall 1968).

36. Le Francois, Richard H. "Bargaining in Higher Education: A Maze of State Legislation." *National Society of Professors Forum* (November-December 1970), 14-16.

37. Lemmer, William P. "Arbitration: Use, Value, and Precautions in

Institutional Labor Contracts." *The College Counsel* 5:209-244 (1970).

38. Lieberman, Myron. "The Future of Collective Negotiations." *The Phi Delta Kappan* (December 1971): 214-216.

39. Lieberman, Myron. "Professors, Unite!" *Harper's Magazine* 243:61-71 (October 1971).

40. Livingston, Frederick R., and Andrea S. Christensen. "State and Federal Regulation of Collective Negotiations in Higher Education." *Wisconsin Law Review* (1971): 91-111.

41. McHugh, William F. "Collective Bargaining with Professionals in Higher Education: Problems in Unit Determinations." *Wisconsin Law Review* (1971): 55-90.

42. McHugh, William F. "The National Labor Relations Board Finishes Sophomore Year." (A 17-page typescript copyrighted by its author, and to appear in a future issue of *The College Counsel*).

43. McHugh, William F. "National Labor Relations Board Goes To College." *College and University Business* (July 1970), 44.

44. McHugh, William F. "Recent Developments in Collective Bargaining in Higher Education." *The College Counsel* 5 (1970): 159-208.

45. Moscow, Michael H. "The Scope of Collective Bargaining in Higher Education." *Wisconsin Law Review* (1971): 33-54.

46. Proulx, Pierre-Paul. "Collective Negotiations in Higher Education— Canada." *Wisconsin Law Review* (1971): 177-186.

47. Sands, C. Dallas. "The Role of Collective Bargaining in Higher Education." *Wisconsin Law Review* (1971): 152-176.

48. Sigworth, Heather. "The Legal Status of Anti-nepotism Regulations." *American Association of University Professors Bulletin* (Spring 1972), 31-34.

49. Stetson, Damon. "Study Panel Recommends That Public Employees Have Limited Right to Strike." *New York Times,* November 1, 1971.

50. Tyler, Gus. "The Faculty Joins the Proletariat." *Change Magazine* (Winter 1971-72), 40-45.

51. Van Alstyne, William W. "The Constitutional Rights of Teachers and Professors." *Duke Law Journal* (1970): 841-854.

52. Van Alstyne, William W. "The Demise of the Right-Privilege Distinction in Constitutional Law." 81 *Harvard Law Review* 1430 (1968).

53. Woollett, Donald H. "The Status and Trends of Collective Negotiations for Faculty in Higher Education." *Wisconsin Law Review* (1971): 2-32.

# TABLE OF CASES

## UNITED STATES SUPREME COURT

# FEDERAL COURTS AND STATE COURTS

(Cases in federal courts are entered under the name of the state in which they originated. They are preceded by the letters "US.")

# INDEX

## A

Academic freedom, 32, 34, 36, 55, 66, 125-127, 130-133, 139-141, 148-150, 159, 163-167

Academic promotions, 80-81, 119-120

Adelphi University, 156, 175

Administrative officers, 174, 200-203

Ainsworth, Robert A., U.S. Circuit Judge, 47, 88, 110, 164

Alabama State University, 17-20, 112

Alaska, University of, 31

Aldrich, Bailey, U.S. Circuit Judge, 129, 131, 157

American Association of University Professors, 12, 50, 153, 180-181

American Council on Education, 121

American Federation of Teachers, 38, 180

Anderson, Robert P., U.S. Circuit Judge, 92

Andreen, Kenneth, California judge, 83

Appointment, letter of, 8

Appointment of governing board members, 204-205

Arkansas A & M College, 132-133

Arkansas, University of, 193

Assembly, freedom of, 135-139

Association, freedom of, 161-172

Association of New Jersey State College Faculties, 179, 181

Association of Pennsylvania College and University Professors, 181

Atlantic Community College, 186

*Atlantic Monthly*, 128

## B

Auburn University, 83, 111

Austin, Richard B., U.S. District Judge, 168, 198

Baltimore County Board of Education, 86

Bargaining unit, what is appropriate, 173-175

Barksdale, Alfred E., U.S. District Judge, 34

Bell, Griffin B., U.S. Circuit Judge, 14, 152

Bell, J. Spencer, U.S. Circuit Judge, 34, 35, 107, 110

Black, Mr. Justice Hugo L., 127, 159, 165, 210

Blackmun, Mr. Justice Harry A., 16, 59, 158

Bloustein, Francis J., New York judge, 87, 199

Blumenfeld, M. Joseph, U.S. District Judge, 118

Board of Higher Education of the City of New York, 85, 115, 199, 203-204

Board of Junior College District 508 (Cook County, Illinois), 176

Board of Regents of the University of the State of New York, 156, 207

Bolivar County, Mississippi, 14-16

Books and articles, causing storm when used in classroom, 34, 128-131

Boreman, Herbert S., U.S. Circuit Judge, 35, 107, 110

253